CONFLICT UNENDING

CONFLICT UNENDING

India-Pakistan Tensions since 1947

SUMIT GANGULY

Columbia University Press
New York

**Woodrow Wilson
Center Press**
Washington, D.C.

Editorial offices
Woodrow Wilson Center Press
1 Woodrow Wilson Plaza
1300 Pennsylvania Avenue N.W.
Washington, D.C. 20004-3027
www.wilsoncenter.org

Order from
Columbia University Press
New York   Chichester, West Sussex

136 South Broadway
Irvington, N.Y. 10533 USA
(800) 944-8648 or (914) 591-9111
www.columbia.edu/cu/cup

∞

Printed in the United States of America on acid-free paper.

10 9 8 7 6 5 4 3 2 1

Library of Congress Cataloging-in-Publication data applied for.

To Traci

Contents

Appendices

Preface

This work does not purport to be a complete history of Indo-Pakistani relations since the emergence of the two countries as independent states following the collapse of the British Indian empire in 1947. That is a task for diplomatic historians, one that I am ill equipped to pursue. Instead, my principal goal as a political scientist and an analyst of regional security is to explain why the two states have remained locked in a seemingly endless spiral of hostility and conflict since their creation.

This work is firmly rooted in the canons of positivist social science. I attempt to show on the basis of standard and novel historical scholarship how certain structural features of both polities, embodied in their nationalist agendas, predisposed them toward conflict over the disputed territory of Jammu and Kashmir. Briefly stated, the Indian nationalist leadership chose to hold on to this Muslim-majority state to demonstrate that all minorities could thrive under the aegis of a plural and secular polity. Pakistani nationalists argued with equal force that they could not part with Kashmir because Pakistan had been created as the homeland for the Muslims of South Asia. I also attempt to explain why tension, hostility, and violence have persisted long after the pristine ideological visions of the two states had dissipated.

My explanation is two-fold. At one level, I contend that certain structural features of the Pakistani polity prevented a rational calculation of the costs and benefits of warring with India. At another level, I show that India, as any other state that adheres to Westphalian norms, has been singularly unwilling to concede territory for fear of state disintegration. In the final section of this book I discuss the pathways followed by the two states toward the overt acquisition of nuclear weapons and then proceed to assess their implications for war and peace in the region.

Acknowledgments

I wish to express a deep debt to a number of individuals and organizations without whose assistance this manuscript would not have been written. My wife, editor, and in-house critic, Traci, must necessarily head this list. Any felicity of expression that can be found in these pages is the result of her labours; all shortcomings are mine. The entire manuscript has also benefited from the valuable comments and criticisms of Kanti Bajpai, Stephen P. Cohen, David Edelstein, Jack Gill, Dennis Kux, Jack Snyder, Ashley Tellis, and Harrison Wagner. I am indebted to Sunila Kale, John Mearsheimer, T. V. Paul, Yvette Rosser, and Scott Sagan for suggestions pertaining to particular aspects of this book. Gregory Brown, my research assistant, provided able assistance in the final stages of the preparation of this manuscript.

The hospitality and collegiality of the Center for International Security and Cooperation (CISAC) at Stanford University, where I spent the 1999–2000 academic year as a visiting fellow, gave me the chance to research and write a significant portion of this book. The Carnegie Corporation of New York and its programme officer David Speedie provided me with a timely grant to augment my CISAC fellowship. Joseph Brinley, my heroic editor at the Woodrow Wilson Center Press, has borne my many complaints over the past several years with good grace and has gently prodded me to meet deadlines. In another corner of the world, my editors at Oxford University Press in New Delhi have encouraged and supported this work.

Sumit Ganguly

Introduction:
A Relationship of Unremitting
Hostility?

Since their emergence as independent states from the detritus of the British Indian empire, India and Pakistan have gone to war four times: in 1947–48, almost immediately after Independence, they fought a long and intense battle over the formerly independent state of Jammu and Kashmir; in 1965 they fought another war over the same piece of land; in 1971 the two engaged during the civil war that severed East Pakistan into the nascent state of Bangladesh; and in 1999 they fought once more in the mountains of Kashmir. In addition to these actual wars, twice during the past fifty years the two countries have endured crises that brought them close to war.[1]

At the start of the new millennium, despite several efforts at reconciliation, the two sides remain locked in an embrace of seemingly unending conflict. Few other conflicts in the post–World War II era, with the possible exception of the Arab-Israeli dispute, have proved as intractable. Both India and Pakistan have expended considerable blood and treasure fighting each other since their independence. In choosing antagonism, each has incurred significant opportunity costs and forgone the chance to increase domestic investment in order to fund a substantial defence and, for Pakistan, an occasional offence against its neighbour.

An analysis of this conflict is significant for a number of compelling reasons. It is crucial for scholars and policymakers concerned, because of the spread and possible use of nuclear weapons, to understand the dynamics of conflict in this region. On at least one occasion, the former US President, Bill Clinton, referred to South Asia as 'the most dangerous place on earth.'[2] Clinton made this statement just before embarking on his trip to Bangladesh, India, and Pakistan in 2000. His remark underscored US concerns about the imminence of nuclear war in the region in the aftermath of the Indian and Pakistani nuclear tests of May 1998. While some regional security specialists share his concerns, others remain more sanguine about the prospects of war in the region. Nevertheless, the situation in the subcontinent remains fraught with tension.

Much of the theoretical literature on the causes of war has a profound Eurocentric bias.[3] Thus, a study of the Indo-Pakistani conflict is also important because it offers a useful opportunity to test hypotheses about the causes of war in a non-European context. Simultaneously, a theoretically-grounded study of the Indo-Pakistani wars would also fill an important lacuna in the existing literature.[4]

Searching for Explanations

What explains this seemingly unending stream of conflict between the two states? There is no dearth of explanations for it, at both scholarly and popular levels. Some have suggested that the conflict has a primordial basis and is rooted in the divergent and essentially antithetical world views of Islam and Hinduism.[5] According to this argument, these two religious visions informed the respective state-building enterprises in South Asia and, thereby, set the two states on a collision course. India, as a predominantly Hindu state, could not develop a cooperative relationship with Pakistan, the putative homeland of the Muslims of South Asia, and vice versa.

But this argument, though superficially attractive, explains little. There is little question that India at the time of Independence and Partition was, and today remains, a predominantly Hindu polity. However, and most certainly at the time of Independence, the majority of the leaders of the Indian nationalist movement were firmly committed to the creation of a secular polity with appropriate guarantees for religious minorities. The dominant strain of Indian nationalism was based not on primordial notions of ethnic identity but on the premise of civic nationalism.[6] Consequently, the putatively 'Hindu' features of the Indian polity could not naturally or inevitably have come into conflict with the South Asian Islamic 'homeland' of Pakistan.

Furthermore, the very concept of India as a 'Hindu' polity is dubious at best, and chimerical at worst. Hinduism is an inherently plural faith and is riven by local, regional, and historical peculiarities.[7] Anthropologists have long noted that the Sanskritic 'great tradition' of Hinduism has little influence over the lives of significant numbers of Hindus across India, who propitiate local deities and uphold 'little traditions' of their own.[8] Despite the polemical arguments of Pakistani apologists and Hindu zealots, no unified, monolithic Hinduism exists. It is therefore, hard to imagine a genuinely 'Hindu' polity in South Asia.[9]

Nor was South Asian Islam monolithic. A variety of doctrinal, regional, and cultural differences have long characterized Islam in the subcontinent. Apart from the two major sects of Islam, Shia and Sunni, the subcontinent was also home to a variety of other sects and movements. Among others, in the state of Jammu and Kashmir, the principal battleground between India and Pakistan, a mystical and syncretic sect of Islam, Sufism, took root as early as the fourteenth century AD.[10]

The principal architect of the movement for a separate state of Pakistan, Mohammed Ali Jinnah, through his skilled and dextrous rhetoric, forged a mythical construct by which the Muslims of South Asia constituted a distinctive, primordial nation. As a result, according to Jinnah, they deserved a separate state: only an independent, Muslim-majority state could provide effective guarantees for their rights and privileges.[11] Yet, despite Jinnah's success in creating the state of Pakistan, millions of Muslims stayed on in India as loyal citizens long after Independence and Partition, thereby undercutting assertions that Muslims needed a separate homeland. Long after its Independence and even after its break-up in 1971, a variety of sectarian and regional conflicts continue to cleave Pakistan, giving lie to the myth of primordial Muslim solidarity.[12]

Other scholars have argued that Hindu-Muslim conflict is rooted in British colonial practices in the subcontinent: specifically, they assert that colonial constructions of religious identity precipitated communal conflict in India.[13] In fairness, the proponents of this argument do not explicitly argue that Indo-Pakistani conflict is a direct consequence of the construction of ethnic categories under British colonialism. Nevertheless, it is possible to extend their argument to the inter-state realm. Since one of the key legacies of British colonialism was the forging of implacably hostile identities, the two states that emerged from the collapse of the British Indian empire would be predisposed to conflict.

This argument is flawed in historical terms and has disturbing normative implications. It is historically untenable because Hindu-Muslim conflict long preceded the arrival of the British in India. Various

Muslim monarchs showed scant regard for their Hindu subjects, destroyed Hindu religious edifices, and sought to repress their Hindu population. At a normative level, the argument is deeply unsettling because it suggests that the British Raj could manipulate, at will, the various Hindu and Muslim communities in India. Left to themselves, the argument suggests, these communities would not have engaged in any form of hostile or internecine behavior. In effect, then, to use a quintessentially post-modern expression, Hindus and Muslims lacked sufficient 'agency' to act in mutually destructive ways. For good or ill, a dispassionate examination of historical records suggests otherwise.[14]

A third argument can be inferred from a body of literature that seeks to explain the rise of militarism in Pakistan. One of the principal proponents of this line of thought has asserted that the forging of the US-Pakistan military relationship in the early 1950s contributed to military dominance in Pakistan and the militarization of Pakistani society. Since the military in Pakistan has played a critical role in fomenting Indo-Pakistani discord (as will be shown throughout this book), one can therefore hold the United States responsible for fueling the Indo-Pakistani conflict.[15]

Sufficient historical evidence, to the contrary, disproves this thesis. For one thing, the first Indo-Pakistani war took place long before the emergence of the US-Pakistan military nexus. Also, following the Chinese attack on India's northern frontiers in 1962, the United States provided military assistance to India over Pakistan's strenuous objections.[16] Finally, following the outbreak of the second Indo-Pakistani war, the United States cut off all military assistance to both India and Pakistan; if the United States had been intent on hurting India and fomenting Indo-Pakistani discord, it would have made India the sole target of the arms embargo.

An Alternative Explanation

As this brief survey reveals, all of the explanations proffered to date have important shortcomings: none can account for the post-independence history of conflict between India and Pakistan. What factors, then, explain the four Indo-Pakistani wars in particular and the tension-ridden relationship in general? The alternative explanation that will be laid out in this book attributes the conflict to three distinct components.

The first element underlying the Indo-Pakistani friction is the fundamentally divergent ideological commitments of the dominant nationalist elites in the Indian and the Pakistani anti-colonial movements. This issue is closely tied to the second factor, the irredentist/anti-irredentist relationship between the two states.

At one level, Pakistan was created as a homeland for the Muslims of South Asia; as Jinnah saw it, the people of South Asia were already divided into two nations, one Hindu and the other Muslim. But beyond that vision, it is not entirely clear whether Jinnah had an explicit conception of the state that he wanted to create. Some evidence can be gleaned from his first speech to the Constituent Assembly of Pakistan, in which he sought to relegate the religious affiliation of Pakistan's citizens to the private sphere.[17] His successors, however, failed to implement his vision of a religiously neutral but Muslim-majority state. For the purposes of state construction his successors saw Pakistan's identity as an Islamic state, although not a theocracy. The precise connotations of what it meant to be a Muslim state, however, remain the subject of contestation within Pakistan.[18]

The basis and the evolution of India's state-building enterprise was relatively more straightforward. As argued earlier, the predominant strain of the Indian nationalist movement was secular. In addition, as mentioned earlier, the post-independent India's constitutional dispensation helped create a secular state that challenged Jinnah's 'two-nation' hypothesis. Any success of India's secular polity would crush the very foundation on which Jinnah built his state. In effect, the underlying basis of the Indo-Pakistani conflict is really an argument about the fundamentals of state-construction. A secular state based on civic nationalism is antithetical to those who believe in primordial conceptions of identity as a viable basis for state-building.[19]

The second factor underlying the origins of Indo-Pakistani conflict is Pakistan's irredentist claim to Kashmir.[20] As the putative homeland for the Muslims of the subcontinent, Pakistan sought to incorporate the Muslim-majority state of Jammu and Kashmir into its domain. Pakistani leaders forcefully stated that they sought Kashmir's merger into Pakistan to ensure the latter's 'completeness.'[21] India, committed to a vision of civic nationalism, sought to thwart this goal to demonstrate that all communities, regardless of their religious orientation, could thrive under India's secular dispensation.[22]

The force of this irredentist/anti-irredentist relationship started to decline in the aftermath of the 1971 Indo-Pakistani war. Once it had been demonstrated that Pakistan could not hold together its two wings on the basis of religion alone, Indian and foreign critics could correctly argue that Pakistan's claim to Kashmir on the basis of religious confraternity was in fact chimerical.[23]

By the same token, however, India's normative claim to Kashmir began to decline, as well, starting in the mid-1980s. During the latter part of that decade, despite the absence of any significant constitutional changes, India's secularism went into a precipitous decline.[24] In attempts to deal with more assertive minorities and simultaneously mollify the misgivings of segments of the Hindu majority, India's politicians frequently departed from their professed commitments to secular practices.[25] For example, during particular electoral campaigns in the early 1980s, especially in the sensitive state of Jammu and Kashmir, Prime Minister Indira Gandhi made veiled communal references in campaign speeches. Her son and successor, Rajiv Gandhi, on the other hand, in an attempt to court the Muslim vote, overturned a Indian Supreme Court judgement which had granted alimony to an indigent Muslim woman. These actions contributed to a steady erosion of the secular features of the Indian state.

Consequently, for Pakistan after 1971 and India after the mid 1980s, their pristine commitments to particular visions of state construction had dramatically declined. Thereafter, the two sides sought to hold on to Kashmir out of the imperatives of statecraft and little else.[26] India feared that relinquishing its claim to Kashmir would set off an internal domino effect, in which other disaffected minorities would demand to secede from the Indian union. For its part, Pakistan, the abject loser in the 1971 war, remained unadjusted to its diminished status in the subcontinent. In effect, the two states had come to accept Westphalian and Weberian concepts of statehood, which, among other matters, prohibit states from willingly ceding territory that they deem to be their own.[27]

These two factors explain the overall state of hostility between India and Pakistan, but they do not by themselves explain the outbreak of the four Indo-Pakistani wars. The factors adduced above have been constant over extended periods of time. Constants, however, cannot explain discrete events. Consequently, these two factors must be seen as *predisposing* conditions for conflict. The immediate precipitants of war in the region, on the other hand, were all *opportunistic* events: in each case, one or both parties saw significant opportunities at critical historical junctures to damage the other's fundamental claims either to the territory of Kashmir or to the larger project of state construction. These opportunistic events will be detailed in the chapters to follow.

The opportunistic precipitants were augmented by *false optimism*, which in the Indo-Pakistani conflict falls into three categories:[28] the misreading of an opponent's (a) relative military strength, (b) relative will, and (c) allies, and their respective number, power, and will. Such false optimism arises from chauvinist nationalism, as explained by Steven Van Evera:

Chauvinist nationalism is a prime source of false optimism about the balance of will. Nationalist propaganda often inflates the bravery of one's own people and denigrates the opponents' toughness and character. . . . Such propaganda is bound to foster illusions about one's own fortitude and that of others.

Nationalist mythology exaggerates the righteousness of the national cause, leading groups to misread the balance of legitimacy between their own and their adversary's claims. The balance of legitimacy, in turn, helps shape the balance of will. Those in the wrong can concede more easily because their concessions set smaller precedents, casting doubt only on their will to defend illegitimate claims; those in the right find concessions harder to make because they set a broader precedent, casting doubt on their will to defend many interests, both illegitimate and legitimate. Thus, a misreading of the balance of legitimacy will likely lead to a misreading of the balance of will. Those who conclude that 'our side is right' will deduce that 'our adversaries know we are right, they are testing us to see if we know it too, and they will back down if we stand firm.' Adversaries will back down because 'once they learn we know we are right, they will realize that we have more will than they do and that we can outlast them; so they will fold if we stand firm.' These chains of misperception rest on a false chauvinist-nationalist definition of the situation.[29]

This book will show that, on a number of occasions, but especially in 1947–48, 1965, and 1999, Pakistani decision-makers grossly underestimated Indian military prowess and likely Indian responses to military challenges. It will argue that the sources of such false estimation were rooted in the structure, organization, and ideology of the Pakistani state. The anti-Indian and chauvinistic ideology of the authoritarian Pakistani state repeatedly contributed to a flawed assessment of India's military capabilities and will. Such chauvinist propaganda was able to thrive within the Pakistani state because of the arrested development of democratic institutions and prolonged periods of authoritarian military rule. Alternative assessments of Indian motivations and capabilities were rarely aired in Pakistani political discourse. Images of Indian perfidy and duplicity pervaded Pakistani official publications and educational materials.[30] The popular press, which failed to develop norms of dispassionate reportage and analysis, contributed to chauvinist accounts of Indian malfeasances and Pakistan's grievances.[31]

Such jingoism was, of course, not limited to Pakistan. Within India, as well, powerful chauvinist elements sought to demonize Pakistan. But because of India's well-embedded democratic institutions and practices, alternative views and assessments of Pakistan could be and were aired within its decision-making elite and its attentive public.[32]

The erosion of certain normative commitments within the Indian state in the 1990s, especially that to secularism and political liberalism, may in the coming years lead Indian decision-makers to make similarly flawed assessments of their own capabilities and prowess. Such propensities could contribute to military tensions and possibly prompt another war in the subcontinent.

The Background to the Dispute

As mentioned above, at the time of Independence and Partition in 1947, two divergent conceptions of state-building animated the Indian and Pakistani nationalist movements. The Indian nationalist movement, under the aegis of the Indian National Congress (INC), despite organizational and ideological tensions, agreed on the need for a secular and democratic post-independence India. The extraordinary cultural, regional, and ethnic heterogeneity of India rendered other possible political arrangements considerably less desirable. This vision fundamentally challenged Jinnah's 'two-nation' hypothesis, which necessitated the creation of a Muslim homeland amid the remnants of the British Indian empire in South Asia.

It is beyond the scope of this study to trace the sources of these two divergent ideologies of state-building in any detail. This enterprise has been ably performed elsewhere.[33] Instead this analysis will identify key intellectual lineages, elite political choices, and historical turning points to trace the evolution of the two competing ideologies.

It is widely accepted in historical literature that the nationalist movement embodied in the Indian National Congress drew on ideas prevalent in nineteenth-century British liberalism and sought to implant those beliefs in the Indian context.[34] The INC at the time of its inception in 1885 was a quintessentially upper-middle-class, predominantly Hindu, Anglicized organization committed to constitutional and incremental growth of self-government in India. Under the leadership of Mohandas Gandhi in the 1920s, however, the organization was transformed into a mass-based political party seeking to represent all segments of Indian society. Under his tutelage the INC encompassed individuals and even groups of varying political persuasions: it comprised committed socialists as well as supporters of free enterprise and adherents of other forms of socio-economic and political organization. In effect, it functioned as a parliament within an emergent democracy.[35]

While Gandhi played a vital role in democratizing the INC, Jawaharlal Nehru, who would become India's first prime minister, was responsible for instilling a secular tenor in its political orientation.[36] Despite this commitment to a secular ideology, in practice, the INC often had to make compromises at local levels in order to maintain electoral strength.[37] Not surprisingly, this failure to fully realize the commitment to secularism at the grass roots contributed to fears among India's Muslim communities of a Hindu domination of the INC and, therefore, of the emergent India, which grew rapidly as the end of British rule approached.

These concerns among the Muslim elite about their position in a future Hindu-dominated India, combined with the legacy of British colonial imperatives, led to the emergence of Pakistani nationalism. At one level, the idea emerged in an embryonic form from the impassioned writings of a prominent Muslim intellectual of the nineteenth century, Sir Sayyid Ahmad Khan. He contended that the creation of British-inspired representative institutions would place India's Muslims at a permanent disadvantage vis-à-vis the Hindu communities because of the numerical preponderance of the latter. To avoid this eventuality, he argued, separate electorates should be created for Muslims and a system of proportional representation should be instituted:

Let us suppose first of all that we have universal suffrage as in America and that everybody, chamars [i.e., persons of low caste] and all, have votes. And first suppose that all Mahomedan electors vote for a Mahomedan member and all the Hindu electors for a Hindu member. . . . It is certain that the Hindu member will have four times as many [votes] because their population will have four times as many. . . . [A]nd how can the Mahomedan guard his interests? It would be like a game of dice in which one man had four dice and the other only one.[38]

The imperatives of British colonial rule aided the development of Muslim separatism in India.[39] As British historian Peter Hardy writes,

[Pre-independence British viceroy] Lord Mayo had recognized before his assassination that Muslims formed a distinctively dangerous class of Her Majesty's subjects in India, which would be politic to conciliate. His papers on education indeed suggest that for him they were indeed Her Majesty's Catholic subjects in India, requiring for political reasons recognition of their peculiar cultural traditions.[40]

British colonial authorities saw considerable merit in Sir Sayyid's proposal because it enabled them to bifurcate the incipient Indian nationalist movement. To this end, as part of the Minto-Morley constitutional reforms of 1909, they substantially granted his demands for the creation of separate electorates. This development, whether it was intended or not, consolidated the Muslim community. By placing Muslims in a distinct political and communal category, the reforms limited the prospects of a unified Indian nationalism. The forging of this seemingly monolithic community, subsequently, enabled leaders such as Jinnah to press for the creation of a separate state on the basis of religious affiliation.

To this end, the Pakistani nationalist leadership, the Muslim League, pursued a markedly different strategy to rid India of British rule. Until about 1946, Jinnah and the League adhered to constitutional politics, eschewing agitational strategies. Unlike the Congress, the League did not embrace mass contact politics and did not organize membership drives at the grass roots level. Nor did they resort to campaigns of mass-based civil disobedience. Instead, until the late 1940s the League's leadership negotiated with the British in legal and constitutional contexts.

Not only were its methods different, the Muslim League's organizational structure and ideology also differed considerably from those of the INC. Whereas the INC increasingly became a representative body and allowed a considerable degree of internal debate, the Muslim League remained woven around the personality of Jinnah and its principal support base remained confined to the Muslim landed gentry of the United Provinces (which after independence would become the Indian state of Uttar Pradesh) in northern India.[41]

Conclusion

The Congress and the League had markedly divergent organizational strategies and also espoused different ideological goals. The organizational and ideological bases of the two parties were diametrically opposed and thereby embodied competing visions of nationalism and state-building. Consequently, the two emergent states were already locked into a potential collision course after the demise of the British Indian empire.

Notes

1. I refer to the Kargil conflict of 1999 as a war because it involved at least 1,000 battle deaths. This is the standard that is adhered to in the field of strategic studies based upon the pioneering quantitative work of J. David Singer and Melvin Small and their Correlates of War (COW) project. See J. David Singer and Melvin Small, *The Wages of War, 1816–1965, A Statistical Handbook* (New York: John Wiley and Sons, 1972).

2. Former President William Jefferson Clinton, as quoted in Barry Bearak, 'The Mystery of Chittisinghpora,' *The New York Times Magazine*, December 31, 2000, pp. 26–55.

3. See for example, Quincy Wright, *A Study of War* (Chicago: University of Chicago Press, 1964); A.F.K. Organski and Jacek Kugler, *The War Ledger* (Chicago: University of Chicago Press, 1984); Bruce Bueno de Mesquita, *The War Trap* (New Haven: Yale University Press, 1981); Jack S. Levy, *War in the Modern Great Power System, 1495–1975* (Lexington: University of Kentucky Press, 1983); Geoffrey Blainey, *The Causes of War* (New York: The Free Press, 1988).

4. Much of the existing literature on the subject is at worst polemical and at best descriptive. Most of them are single-case studies. For polemical accounts see D.R. Mankekar, *Pakistan Cut to Size* (New Delhi: India Book Company, 1972). For solid, descriptive accounts see Russell Brines, *The Indo-Pakistani Conflict* (New York: Pall Mall, 1968); Robert Jackson, *South Asian Crisis* (New York: Praeger, 1975).

5. See, for example, S. M. Burke, *Mainsprings of Indian and Pakistani Foreign Policies* (Minneapolis: University of Minnesota Press, 1974). This primordial view of the Indo-Pakistani conflict is discussed in Stephen P. Cohen, 'The Strategic Imagery of Elites,' in James Roherty, ed., *Defense Policy Formation* (Columbia: University of South Carolina Press, 1976). Cohen calls this primordial hatreds thesis the 'communal conflict with armor' model.

6. See Jawaharlal Nehru's brilliant construction of India's national identity in *The Discovery of India* (Calcutta: Signet Press, 1946).

7. Gavin Flood, *An Introduction to Hinduism* (Cambridge: Cambridge University Press, 1996).

8. The fundamentally plural features of Hinduism are dealt with in Marshall Singer, 'Beyond Tradition and Modernity in Madras,' *Comparative Studies in History and Society*, Volume 13, Number 2, 1971, pp. 160–196. For a searching critique of the myth of Muslim unity see the chapter titled 'Making a Separate Nation,' in Mushirul Hasan, *Legacy of a Divided Nation: India's Muslims since Independence* (New Delhi: Oxford University Press, 1997).

9. A particularly trenchant and sensitive analysis of this issue can be found in the chapter titled 'The Myth of Muslim Unity: Colonial and National Narratives,' in Hasan, *Legacy of a Divided Nation*.

10. See Vernon Hewitt, *Reclaiming the Past: The Search for Political and*

Cultural Unity in Contemporary Jammu and Kashmir (London: Portland Books 1995); also see Navnita Chadha Behera, *State, Identity and Violence: Jammu, Kashmir and Ladakh* (New Delhi: Manohar, 2000).

11. Anthony Smith, *The Ethnic Origins of Nations* (Oxford: Blackwell, 1994), provides a sophisticated version of the primordialist argument about ethnicity.

12. See Samina Ahmed, 'Pakistan,' in Michael Brown and Sumit Ganguly, eds, *Government Policies and Ethnic Relations in Asia and the Pacific* (Cambridge: MIT Press, 1997).

13. For two perspectives on this thesis see Nicholas B. Dirks, *Colonialism and Culture* (Ann Arbor: University of Michigan Press, 1992), and Gyan Prakash, *The Construction of Communalism in Colonial North India* (New Delhi: Oxford University Press, 1990).

14. John F. Richards, *The Mughal Empire* (Cambridge: Cambridge University Press, 1993).

15. For one formulation of this argument see Ayesha Jalal, *The State of Martial Rule: The Origins of Pakistan's Political Economy of Defence* (Cambridge: Cambridge University Press, 1990). For a more explicit statement of American attempts to militarily bolster Pakistan and thereby undermine India's position in the subcontinent and beyond see Baldev Raj Nayar, *American Geopolitics and India* (New Delhi: Vikas, 1976). For an alternative explanation of the rise of militarism in Pakistan see Allen McGrath, *The Destruction of Pakistan's Democracy* (Karachi: Oxford University Press, 1996).

16. Dennis Kux, *Estranged Democracies* (Washington, D.C.: National Defense University Press, 1994).

17. Stanley Wolpert, *Jinnah of Pakistan* (New York: Oxford University Press, 1984).

18. For two useful discussions see McGrath, *The Destruction of Pakistan's Democracy*, and John L. Esposito and John O. Voll, *Islam and Democracy* (Oxford: Oxford University Press, 1996).

19. The implied counterfactual calls for some discussion. Would a Hindu ethnic state not have been at odds with Pakistan? It is possible to argue that a Hindu nationalist state may have been more willing to part with Kashmir, a predominantly Muslim region, as the regime would have had little interest in demonstrating its secular credentials. Other *casus belli* with Pakistan may have persisted. For the use of counterfactual analyses in the study of international politics see Philip E. Tetlock and Aaron Belkin, eds, *Counterfactual Thought Experiments in World Politics: Logical, Methodological and Psychological Perspectives* (Princeton: Princeton University Press, 1996).

20. For a discussion of irredentist nationalism see Michael Hechter, *Containing Nationalism* (New York: Oxford University Press, 1999).

21. See Zulfiquar Ali Bhutto, *The Myth of Independence* (Lahore: Oxford University Press, 1969).

22. On India's status as a secular state see Donald Eugene Smith, *India as*

a Secular State (Princeton: Princeton University Press, 1963). For the ongoing debate about secularism in India see Rajeev Bhargava, ed., *Secularism and Its Critics* (New Delhi: Oxford University Press, 1999).

23. On this point see Pran Chopra, *India's Second Liberation* (New Delhi: Vikas Publishing House, 1973); also see Richard L. Merritt, 'The Fragile Unity of Pakistan,' in James Rosenau, ed., *Linkage Politics: Essays on the Convergence of National and International Systems* (New York: The Free Press, 1969).

24. Subrata Kumar Mitra, 'Desecularizing the State: Religion and Politics in India after Independence,' *Comparative Studies in Society and History*, Volume 33, Number 4, October 1991.

25. For a discussion of the rise of Hindu nationalism see Peter van der Veer, *Religious Nationalism* (New Delhi: Oxford University Press, 1996).

26. For a discussion of the conditions under which states may redefine their national boundaries and maintain legitimacy see Ian Lustick, *Disputed States, Unsettled Lands: Britain and Ireland, France and Algeria, and Israel and West Bank–Gaza* (Ithaca: Cornell University Press, 1993).

27. For a discussion of these ideas see Hedley Bull and Adam Watson, eds, *The Expansion of International Society* (Oxford: Clarendon Press, 1984); and Stephen D. Krasner, *Sovereignty: Organized Hypocrisy* (Princeton: Princeton University Press, 1999).

28. The concept of false optimism is derived from Stephen Van Evera, *Causes of War: Power and the Roots of Conflict* (Ithaca: Cornell University Press, 1999).

29. Van Evera, *Causes of War*, p. 27.

30. Some of these problems of historical scholarship are discussed in Pervez Amirali Hoodbhoy and Abdul Hameed Nayyar, 'Rewriting the History of Pakistan,' in Asghar Khan, ed., *Islam, Politics and the State: The Pakistan Experience* (London: Zed Books, 1985).

31. The dangers of such scapegoating are discussed in Jack Snyder, *From Voting to Violence* (New York: W.W. Norton and Company, 2000).

32. The term 'attentive public' is derived from Gabriel Almond, *The American People and Foreign Policy* (New York: Praeger, 1960).

33. The literature on this subject is voluminous. See, for example, Hafeez Malik, *Moslem Nationalism in India and Pakistan* (Washington, D.C.: Public Affairs Press, 1963); also see Bipan Chandra, Mridula Mukherjee, Aditya Mukherjee, K.N. Panikkar, and Sucheta Mahajan, *India's Struggle for Independence* (New Delhi: Viking, 1988).

34. Eric Stokes, *The English Utilitarians and India* (Oxford: Clarendon Press, 1959).

35. The Indian political scientist Rajni Kothari has referred to this phenomenon as 'the Congress system'—that is, an organization whose members had internalized the norm of democratic debate and thereby were well-suited to foster democratic political institutions in the post-independence era. See Rajni Kothari, *Politics in India* (New Delhi: Orient Longman, 1970).

36. This point is dealt with admirably in Jawaharlal Nehru, *Toward Freedom: The Autobiography of Jawaharlal Nehru* (1941; reprint Boston: Beacon, 1958).

37. John Gallagher et al., *Locality, Province and Nation* (Cambridge: Cambridge University Press, 1973).

38. Khan, as quoted in Peter Hardy, *The Muslims of British India* (Cambridge: Cambridge University Press, 1972), p. 130.

39. For a particularly trenchant analysis of British justifications of colonial rule see Charles Metcalfe, *Ideologies of the Raj* (Cambridge: Cambridge University Press, 1994).

40. Hardy, *The Muslims of British India*, p. 116.

41. See Mary Doreen Wainwright and C. H. Phillips, eds, *The Partition of India: Policies and Perspectives* (London: Allen and Unwin, 1975).

Chapter One

The First Kashmir War

By the late 1940s the limits of Indian unity had been reached. The INC and the Muslim League could not arrive at a viable compromise to achieve a unified India.[1] As the time of independence neared, Lord Mountbatten, the last viceroy, passed an edict about the division of the British Indian empire. The states of British India, which were ruled directly from Whitehall, would be divided on the basis of demographics: predominantly Muslim states and areas would go to Pakistan; predominantly Hindu areas would go to India. The INC and the Muslim League, though not entirely satisfied with this arrangement, accepted this dispensation.

A similar dispensation awaited the 'princely states' of the region, which were nominally independent but recognized the 'paramountcy' of the British Crown. With the end of British rule, paramountcy would lapse. The rulers of the princely states were now expected to choose one of the two nascent states, India or Pakistan, basing their decisions on considerations of geographic location and demographic features.[2]

The state of Kashmir posed a particular problem. It had a Hindu monarch, Maharaja Hari Singh, and a Muslim-majority population, and its borders abutted both the future India and the future Pakistan.[3] Jinnah had actively campaigned in Kashmir for its accession to Pakistan. Indeed, sections of the Muslim intelligentsia and clergy in the Kashmir Valley supported the Muslim League. For example, one of the key Muslim religious leaders in the state, Mirwaiz Yusuf Shah, harboured distinctly pro-Pakistan leanings. Another Muslim leader, Ghulam Abbas, who founded a local political party, the Muslim Conference, also favoured Kashmir's accession to Pakistan.[4]

Yet support for accession to Pakistan was hardly uniform in Kashmir.

The Hindus of Jammu and the Buddhists of Ladakh were loath to join a state premised on Muslim rule. More important, however, the vast majority of the Muslim inhabitants of the state were also unwilling to cast their lot with Pakistan. This lack of enthusiasm for Pakistan stemmed from compelling material considerations. Given the social composition of the Pakistani political leadership and the centrality of landed gentry in the Muslim League's support base, the prospects of land reform in Pakistan were dim. On the other hand, such a prospect loomed large within India. Thus the bulk of the Kashmiri Muslim population, mostly poor peasantry, saw a brighter economic future in India.[5]

Their beliefs found refuge in the personality and political programme of a Kashmiri Muslim leader, Sheikh Mohammed Abdullah, the founder of a mass-based political party, the All Jammu and Kashmir Muslim Conference. In the late 1930s, Abdullah came under the influence of Nehru, under whose tutelage Abdullah expanded the scope of his party to include all three major communities in the state—Buddhists, Hindus, and Muslims. He also changed the name of the party to the Jammu and Kashmir National Conference to reflect its inclusiveness. Two of Abdullah's positions commanded widespread support among the impoverished Muslim peasantry of Kashmir: he was committed to a process of land reform and redistributive justice, and he was a staunch opponent of the maharaja's rule—Abdullah had served time in prison for his anti-monarchy activities.

The Road to Accession and War

Even after Partition and Independence came about for India and Pakistan, Maharaja Hari Singh refused to accede to either one. He did sign a 'standstill agreement' with Pakistan, which enabled the two states to carry on certain basic commercial transactions. (He did not enter into a similar agreement with India as he was less dependent on the nascent Indian state for commercial and other transactions.) In the months immediately after Partition, he came under pressure from both India and Pakistan to accede. He nevertheless prevaricated on the question of accession. Meanwhile, during the first week of October 1947 a tribal rebellion broke out in Poonch, in the southwestern reaches of Kashmir.[6] Sections of the Pakistani Army quickly moved to aid the rebels with arms, transport, and men.[7] The maharaja's state forces soon proved to be incapable of stemming the onslaught. Within two weeks the insurgents and their Pakistani military supporters had reached the outskirts of Srinagar, the capital of Jammu and Kashmir. The maharaja, by now panicked, appealed to India for military assistance to prevent further encroachment by the intruders. It is worth noting that Hari Singh made no appeal to Pakistan to desist from aiding the insurgents.

Nehru, by then India's prime minister, agreed to provide assistance only if two preconditions were met: the maharaja would have to accede to India, and this act would have to receive the imprimatur of Sheikh Abdullah. Nehru's caution was warranted. Under the terms of the British transfer of power, the maharaja possessed the *legal* right to accede to India, but Nehru was also concerned about the *legitimacy* of the accession. In the absence of a referendum, which the urgent circumstances did not allow, the only viable means of ascertaining the wishes of the majority of Kashmiris was to turn to their political leader. On October 26, once the maharaja had signed the Instrument of Accession and Abdullah granted his approval, Nehru instructed Indian troops to be airlifted into Kashmir.[8] The Indian troops managed to stop the onslaught, but the raiders had already managed to capture about a third of the territory of the now-former princely state.[9]

War Ensues

During the fall and early winter of 1947, pitched battles continued in Kashmir between the Indian and Pakistani armies, with both sides suffering significant losses. Not surprisingly, Indian and Pakistani accounts of the evolution of the conflict differ.[10] The following narrative is an attempt to reconstruct the major military developments as they unfolded between October 24, 1947, and January 1, 1949, the date on which the war ended with a United Nations–sponsored cease-fire.

The principal Indian military unit that was sent to Kashmir was the 161st Infantry Brigade.[11] This brigade succeeded in arresting the advance of the Pakistani-backed forces, which included Hazara and Afridi tribesmen from the Northern Areas of Kashmir state, paramilitary forces such as the Muslim League National Guards, and regular Pakistani Army personnel disguised as tribesmen. The desertion of significant numbers of the maharaja's state forces, who were entrusted with the defence of the Domel-Abbotabad Road, an arterial highway, facilitated the raiders' march toward Srinagar, the ultimate prize. Having squashed the weak resistance, the invaders launched a three-pronged attack on a communications center located in Uri from Muzaffarabad, Domel, and Poonch. This time, a vastly outnumbered unit of the state forces managed to tie them down for two days. After capturing Uri, the Pakistan-backed forces seized Mahura and damaged the power grid that supplied electricity to Srinagar. By October 24, Srinagar was without power.[12] In the next several days, the invaders managed to get within a few miles of the Srinagar airfield.

Only around November 7 did the Indian army manage to launch a decisive counter-attack using armoured cars and some infantry. This clear-cut offensive caught the Pakistan-backed forces by surprise and enabled the Indians to secure the Srinagar airfield. The Indians managed to press the Pakistani forces further and soon succeeded in capturing Baramula. Within four days of this advance, on November 13, the Indian forces entered Mahura. They quickly repaired the power station there and restored electricity to Srinagar.

In December 1947, logistical difficulties dealt the Indian forces an important military setback. The principal problem that the Indian forces encountered was a lack of supplies and of adequate high-altitude warfare equipment. Worse still, many of the troops who had been airlifted to these high altitudes were from the plains and had had little or no training in coping with extremely cold temperatures.[13]

Taking advantage of the Indian lapse, the 'Azad Kashmir' (literally, 'free Kashmir') forces compelled the Indians to retreat. In the spring of 1948, the Indians launched a counter-offensive that led to more direct Pakistani involvement in the war. In a battle near the city of Poonch, the Pakistani army used mountain guns to support the Azad Kashmir forces. Later in the year, regular Pakistani army units entered the fray as the Indian army made important territorial gains. The Pakistanis concentrated a parachute brigade, two field artillery regiments, and a medium artillery battery west of the city of Jammu. This placement of troops and artillery enabled the Pakistanis to threaten the tenuous logistical lines between Amritsar (in the Indian state of Punjab) and Jammu, Pathankot, and Poonch in the state of Kashmir.

As the fighting continued, the Indian political leadership came to the ineluctable conclusion that the war would drag on indefinitely unless Pakistani support for and involvement with the insurgents ended. To achieve this, India would have had to dramatically expand the scope of the conflict. It had neither the military resources nor the political will to pursue such a strategy.[14] Furthermore, no evidence exists to support the Pakistani assertion that India had significant territorial ambitions in the portions of Kashmir that had been occupied by pro-Pakistani troops. Indeed, quite early in the peace-negotiation process, Nehru suggested a partition of the state along the cease-fire line.

The Indian lack of interest in reclaiming the remainder of the original princely state stemmed from pragmatic political considerations. Most important, Sheikh Abdullah's writ was confined primarily to the Kashmir Valley. Beyond the Valley, in such Muslim areas as Mirpur, Poonch, Muzaffarabad, Gilgit, and Baltistan, he had little standing. In Mirpur and parts of Poonch, his old rival and pro-Pakistani agitator Mohammed Yusuf Shah wielded considerable influence over the Muslim population. India's national leadership knew how difficult it would be to win the support of the Muslims in those areas. Accordingly, the Indian army was not encouraged to push much beyond the territory that it had come to control.[15] On the advice of Governor-General Lord Mountbatten, India referred the Kashmir question to the United Nations (UN) Security Council on January 1, 1948, where a new battlefield opened up.[16]

Explaining the 1947–48 War: False Optimism

Given the disarray of Pakistan's social, organizational, political, and military structures in the wake of Partition, it is hard to understand how any responsible Pakistani decision-maker could have believed that a war with India over Kashmir would result in Pakistani victory.[17] More to the point, any dispassionate assessment of the relative capabilities of the two states should have made it clear to Pakistan's political-military leadership that India's military strength was substantially greater. To begin with, under the terms of the transfer of power, all movable military infrastructure had been divided on a 30:70 ratio between Pakistan and India. Many of the units of the old colonial British Indian army were divided along these lines, and as a consequence the Pakistani army was desperately short of officers. A number of formations were considerably short of their sanctioned strength. The existing units were also tied down in 'aid to the civil' responsibilities due to the extraordinary refugee burden emanating from the process of Partition.[18] To compound matters, the vast majority of the former British Indian army's military bases, ordnance factories, and training camps were located within the states that became part of India. Finally, thanks to the intransigence of India's deputy prime minister, Sardar Vallabhbhai Patel, the transfer of movable assets was progressing quite slowly, leaving Pakistan in a militarily vulnerable position.[19]

Despite these crippling military disadvantages, Pakistan decided to provoke a war with India. Why? The sentiments of the Pakistani decision-makers are well captured in Maj.-Gen. Akbar Khan's account of the war:

In the remotest of our villages, the humblest of our people possess a self-confidence and ready willingness to march forward into India—a spirit the equivalent of which cannot be found on the other side. It may take many generations to create such a spirit [in India]. . . . In India, in the absence of homogeneity, a penetration in any direction can result in separation of differing units geographically as well as morally because there is no basic unity among the Shudras, Brahmins, Sikhs, Hindus and Muslims who will follow their own different interests. At present, and for a long time to come, India is in the same position as she was centuries ago, exposed to disintegration in emergencies.[20]

Negotiations at the United Nations

India had referred the Kashmir issue to the Security Council by invoking Articles 34 and 35 of the UN charter, which deal with situations that pose threats to international peace and security. The essence of the Indian complaint was that Pakistani nationals as well as local tribesmen had attacked the state of Jammu and Kashmir. Accordingly, the government of India enjoined the Security Council to condemn Pakistan's complicity in the act of aggression. It also asked the Security Council to take the necessary steps to inhibit Pakistan from continuing with its actions in Kashmir. The Pakistani regime countered the Indian accusations and denied that it had provided any official assistance to the tribals. More to the point, it deftly shifted the onus onto India by arguing that India was responsible for carrying out a genocidal policy toward its Muslim population in the wake of Partition. Finally, the Pakistani representative questioned the terms of Kashmir's accession to India.

In response to these two diametrically opposed complaints, the Security Council passed a resolution on January 20, 1948, which led to the creation of a three-member commission to investigate the situation in the state and to undertake efforts to mediate the dispute. However, the gap between the Indian and Pakistani positions was so wide that this resolution accomplished little beyond the formation of the UN commission. A second resolution was passed on April 21, 1948, which spelled out the ambit of the likely UN efforts to resolve the problem. In addition to increasing the number of the commission members to five, this resolution called on the government of Pakistan to secure the withdrawal of the tribesmen and Pakistani nationals from Kashmir. Simultaneously, it asked the government of India to start withdrawing Indian forces from the region while maintaining the minimum force level necessary to maintain law and order. The Security Council resolution also proposed the creation of a coalition cabinet of the state of Jammu and Kashmir that would represent the entire political spectrum of the state's population. Finally, it mandated that a free and fair plebiscite be held to determine the wishes of the Kashmiris about accession to either India or Pakistan. Joseph Korbel, a prominent Czechoslovakian diplomat and a member of the commission, has written that

[t]he resolution of April 21 was of cardinal importance. It outlined the Security Council's stand on the Kashmir conflict, recommended the method of its solution, and became the principal term of reference for various United Nations representatives who ever since have been trying to bring about a peaceful and final settlement of the problem.[21]

Armed with this mandate the commission members visited the two subcontinental capitals in the late summer of 1948. The commissioners received their initial shock in Karachi when the Pakistani minister of foreign affairs, Sir Mohammed Zafrullah Khan, in an opening statement indicated that three Pakistani brigades had been involved in the hostilities since May of 1948. Sir Zafrullah defended this decision to send in regular Pakistani army formations on the grounds of self-defence: India, he argued, had territorial designs on Pakistan as well as Pakistan-controlled Kashmir. This revelation was greeted with some dismay on the part of the commission, quite understandably, since it constituted a material change in the situation.

The commission's task did not prove to be any easier in New Delhi. Indian decision-makers were already upset with the Security Council's failure to explicitly brand Pakistan as the aggressor state. Indian leaders consistently insisted that little progress could be made toward the resolution of the Kashmir question unless Pakistan's aggression was recognized and condemned.

Following the consultations in Karachi and New Delhi, the commission prepared a second resolution, which was unanimously passed by the Security Council on August 13, 1948. This resolution had three components. The first part called on the governments of India and Pakistan to agree on a cease-fire within forty days of their joint acceptance of the terms of the resolution, after which the commission would appoint military observers to supervise each side's adherence to the cease-fire. Second, Pakistan was asked to withdraw its troops from

Kashmir; the tribesmen and Pakistani nationals were also requested to leave Kashmir. The territory that was evacuated by the Pakistani troops would be administered by local authorities under the tutelage of the UN commission. The resolution also enjoined India to withdraw its forces *following* the departure of the Pakistani troops, nationals, and tribesmen. Third and finally, the two sides were asked to reaffirm their commitment to a plebiscite to settle the dispute.

Both sides sought extensive clarifications of the key provisions of the resolution, as each feared that components would adversely affect their interests. The commission tried to assuage the misgivings of both parties about the terms and scope of the resolution. In an effort to supplement it and clarify its terms, the commission drafted yet another resolution, which was passed unanimously on January 5, 1949. This resolution reaffirmed the need for a free and fair plebiscite in Kashmir and also called for the appointment of an international plebiscite administrator.

The troop withdrawal and the plebiscite, of course, failed to transpire. The Indian side focused on the withdrawal of the Pakistani troops and the Azad Kashmir irregulars from Kashmir, while Pakistan insisted on the holding of the plebiscite. Both positions were self-serving and contributed to a deadlock.[22]

In an attempt to break the initial logjam, the commission appointed a single mediator, Gen. A.G.L. McNaughton of Canada, who at the time held the presidency of the Security Council. McNaughton quickly came up with a series of proposals that focused on demilitarization of the region. The Indian leadership, however, objected to these proposals on the grounds that they would not lead to the disbanding of the Azad Kashmir forces. Nevertheless, the Indians did not reject the McNaughton proposals out of hand.

The task of implementing the McNaughton proposals fell on the Australian jurist Sir Owen Dixon. He came up with a number of proposals, including the provision of a set of regional plebiscites. None of them, however, found favour with both parties. In the end, Sir Owen left the field having made little or no progress toward a resolution of the dispute.

The Security Council once again returned to this vexing issue in February 1951, passing yet another resolution that called for international arbitration to settle the dispute in the event that the demilitarization of the state did not take place within three months of the passage of the resolution. Pakistan accepted this resolution but India rejected it on the grounds that it could ill afford to consign the fate of some four million of its citizens to the vagaries of an international arbitrator. Nevertheless, the Security Council appointed an American academic, Dr Frank Graham, as the new UN representative for Kashmir. Graham had established his credentials as a skilled negotiator because of his earlier role in mediating the Indonesia-Netherlands dispute. By the time Graham arrived in the subcontinent, two separate war scares, as well as developments within Kashmir, had further vitiated the atmosphere.

Developments in Jammu and Kashmir

In 1950 and again in 1951, for example, India and Pakistan had again teetered on the brink of war.[23] In 1950, communal riots were raging in the Indian border states of West Bengal and Tripura and in the eastern wing of Pakistan. These riots drove several hundred thousand Hindu refugees from East Pakistan into West Bengal and about the same number of Muslim refugees from Bengal and Tripura into East Pakistan. Fearing an outbreak of full-scale hostilities because the flight of refugees had stirred communal passions, Prime Minister Liaquat Ali Khan of Pakistan and Nehru agreed to meet in New Delhi. On April 8, 1950, they issued a declaration, subsequently referred to as the Nehru-Liaquat pact, which, among other matters, guaranteed protections to minority populations in both states. Despite this solemn declaration, however, the plight of the Hindu minority in Pakistan did not substantially improve and refugee flow continued, especially from East Pakistan into Bengal. In an attempt to nudge Pakistan on the refugee and Kashmir questions, India massed troops along its border with West Pakistan, setting off alarms in Karachi about the danger of an impending conflict.

The second crisis, in 1951, emerged from Pakistani allegations of Indian troop concentrations along the Indo-Pakistani border in the state of Jammu and Kashmir. This crisis dissipated after an exchange of acrimonious letters between Nehru and Liaquat in which each side accused the other of having precipitated the crisis.

In addition to these two war scares, certain political developments within the India-controlled portion of Kashmir had also strained Indo-Pakistani relations. In October 1950, the General Council of the Jammu and Kashmir National Conference had passed a resolution demanding elections for a constituent assembly that would then determine the contours of Kashmir's relationship with India. To no one's particular surprise, Sir Zafrullah Khan, on behalf of the Government of Pakistan, vigorously protested this decision, but Sheikh Abdullah and his colleagues in the National Conference remained unmoved. The elections were held in September and October of 1951 and the National Conference won handsomely, albeit amid charges of widespread electoral fraud.[24] A Constituent Assembly was duly convened on October 31, 1951. In November 1951, it passed the Jammu and Kashmir Constitution Act, 1951, which effectively stripped the maharaja of all his powers and made him subordinate to the assembly. Simultaneously, this act also sought to carve out a distinctive status for Kashmir within India's overall constitutional dispensation. It limited India's jurisdiction in Kashmir to three areas: defence, foreign affairs, and communications. This legislation, in turn, was ratified under the terms of the Delhi Accord reached in New Delhi on July 24, 1952. Sadly, the Delhi Accord proved to be of extremely limited duration. In 1953, Abdullah was summarily removed from the chief ministership of Jammu and Kashmir and placed under house arrest on the grounds that he was toying with a declaration of independence. The Delhi Accord, for all practical purposes, lapsed.

A Turn to Bilateral Negotiations

At the United Nations, Graham's efforts had amounted to little. Nevertheless, some hopes for a bilateral settlement had arisen after a new prime minister in Pakistan, Mohammed Ali Bogra, had been placed in office in a constitutional coup with the ouster of Khwaja Nazimuddin in 1953. Not long after his election, Bogra met Nehru at a conference of the prime ministers of the members of the British Commonwealth in London. This meeting led to a second meeting in New Delhi against a backdrop of increasing disquiet in Indian-controlled Kashmir. Sheikh Abdullah's arrest and incarceration on the grounds of sedition had precipitated these disturbances. Despite conditions in Kashmir, the Nehru-Bogra meeting of August 20, 1953, proved fruitful. The two sides agreed that the Kashmir dispute would be resolved without resort to the use of force, that a plebiscite would be held to ascertain the wishes of the Kashmiris, and that a new plebiscite administrator should be appointed for that purpose. They also reached an informal agreement that the initial UN-appointed plebiscite administrator, Adm. Chester W. Nimitz of the United States, would have to be replaced by an individual of comparable stature from a small Asian country. India had taken the lead in pushing for Nimitz's removal because it had perceived a pro-Pakistani bias on the part of the United States in the Security Council debates. However, when word of this informal agreement became public, an outcry ensued against the Indian position throughout influential sections of the Pakistani press. Nehru and Bogra, to their mutual credit, nonetheless managed to limit the damage and placed the negotiations back on track.[25]

Their success, however, was short-lived. In late February 1954, the Eisenhower administration announced its intention to provide military assistance to Pakistan. Later that year on April 2, 1954, the United States signed a military pact with Pakistan and Turkey. A separate agreement, necessary to address congressional legalities, was reached with Pakistan on May 19, 1954. Under the terms of this agreement, the United States promised to provide Pakistan with substantial military equipment as well as training for the Pakistani armed forces. US president Dwight Eisenhower, in an attempt to assuage India's deep misgivings about this pact, wrote to Nehru promising that US military hardware to Pakistan would not be used against India.[26] Simultaneously, he offered to sell similar weaponry to India. Eisenhower's attempts to address Nehru's worst fears, however, proved utterly unsuccessful. Worse still, the emergent US-Pakistan military nexus made Nehru acutely hostile toward the plebiscite.[27]

More to the point, India's non-aligned status and Pakistan's courting of the West led to the politicization of the Kashmir question. From the Indian perspective, the major powers, particularly the United Kingdom and the United States, adopted a decidedly pro-Pakistani stance in the Security Council proceedings. The conclusion of the executive agreement between the United States and Pakistan in 1954 produced a fundamental shift in the Indian position on the UN's role in Kashmir. In the aftermath of the pact, Nehru categorically rejected the use of a plebiscite to settle the Kashmir dispute.

Despite rejecting a plebiscite in Kashmir, Nehru offered Bogra a 'no-war pact.' Bogra quickly rebuffed Nehru's offer on the grounds that such a pact would mean little unless it was coupled with an agreement on some mechanism to settle the Kashmir dispute.[28] Given these widely divergent positions, the 'no-war pact' failed to materialize.

Bilateral talks did resume in 1955, but Iskander Mirza, the new governor-general of Pakistan, took a tough and unyielding stance on the Kashmir dispute. Matters worsened in 1956 when Nehru suggested that he would be willing to see the state partitioned along the cease-fire line. This suggestion was met with a furious reaction within Pakistan and signaled an end to the bilateral discussions.

Back to the United Nations

In 1957, Pakistan's foreign minister, Feroze Khan Noon, reintroduced the Kashmir question in the Security Council. Two factors explain this decision to shift back to a multilateral forum. First, the bilateral discussions had generated little but frustration for the Pakistanis. Second, India's pro-Egyptian posture during the Suez crisis in 1956 and its decidedly equivocal stand on the Soviet invasion of Hungary had irritated a number of the Western powers, especially the United Kingdom. Cognizant of this disenchantment with India, the Pakistani government admitted its motivations:

The Pakistani Government felt encouraged in its expectations by the attitude of the Western powers toward India in consequence of India's policies during the crises relating to Suez and Hungary in October-November 1956.[29]

Pakistani leaders' calculations about Western support for their position on Kashmir were hardly ill-founded. A new resolution directed the president of the Security Council, Gunnar Jarring of Sweden, to seek a demilitarization of Kashmir and make provisions for a UN force to be stationed there. The Soviets, who had earlier endorsed India's position on the dispute, vetoed the resolution. Despite the Soviet veto, Jarring persisted in his efforts to bring the two parties closer. Jarring's eventual report to the Security Council made a veiled allusion to the adverse consequences of the American arming of Pakistan. Not surprisingly, Pakistan responded harshly to Jarring's report. In its aftermath, the Security Council asked Graham to return to the subcontinent. Graham visited India and Pakistan again in January 1958 and presented his recommendations to the Security Council in March. Little in his proposals was especially new, except that he called for a conference of the two prime ministers to discuss the modalities of a plebiscite. Predictably, Pakistan accepted the proposals and India rejected them. In a now-familiar vein, the Indians argued that Graham's call for a prime ministers' conference placed the two sides on an equal footing and overlooked India's position that it was the aggrieved party. Graham's recommendations came to nought.

Two other events in the region also vitiated the prospects of further negotiations. First, Sheikh Abdullah, who had been released after his initial arrest of 1953, was once again incarcerated in May 1958. His second arrest led to a spate of demonstrations in Jammu and Kashmir. From the Indian standpoint, given these disturbed circumstances, the moment was hardly conducive for the conduct of negotiations with Pakistan.

Second, on October 27, 1958, Gen. Ayub Khan (who would later self-style himself 'field marshal') overthrew the regime of Iskander Mirza and re-imposed martial law. Nehru was wary of negotiating with a regime brought to power by a military coup. Fundamentally distrustful of the military, Nehru stated the following in an address:

Where power is concentrated in an individual, and that individual is a military person, the normal checks which occur in a government or a society are absent. . . . But one thing is clear, that nowhere in the wide world today is there such a naked military dictatorship as in Pakistan. There is no veil about it. Inherent in such a system are always certain risks and dangers.[30]

The Security Council, in its 104th meeting on the subject, sought to pass one more resolution on Kashmir. This effort, too, failed when the Soviet delegate promptly vetoed it. For all practical purposes, the Security Council's role in the dispute drew to a close.

Consequences and Conclusions

The failure of these multilateral efforts had significant consequences for regional politics. The politicization of the Kashmir question at the United Nations undermined India's faith in multilateral diplomacy. The unanticipated adverse outcome, wherein the victim and the aggressor were placed on the same plane, drove India's leadership away from multilateral initiatives to resolve the Kashmir problem.

Indian intransigence, however, did not deter Pakistan from its quest for Kashmir. For the Pakistani leadership, the absorption of all of Kashmir into its realm remained a normative and strategic goal. At a normative level, Pakistan's claim to Kashmir remained irredentist: Pakistan's identity as the homeland of the Muslims of South Asia made it a moral imperative to include Kashmir in its domain.[31] But it was also a strategic imperative: Pakistan could be better defended if the entire state of Jammu and Kashmir were within its ambit. Committed to the pursuit of these ends, the leadership remained fundamentally unreconciled to the status quo and sought to exploit any opportunities to bring diplomatic and military pressures on India to cede ground on the Kashmir question. Pakistan's inability to make India budge on this question in the multilateral and diplomatic arena led its leaders several more times to formulate military strategies to wrest Kashmir from India. In this quest, they frequently exhibited false optimism, exaggerated the support of potential allies, and bolstered their self-image on the basis of dubious and flawed inferences.

India remained equally determined to hold on to Kashmir to demonstrate its commitment to secularism.[32] It ignored Pakistan's demands and steadily tightened its grip on the state. These two antithetical strategies placed the two states on a collision course toward another war in 1965.

Notes

1. The literature on this subject is quite substantial. See, for example, Penderel Moon, *Divide and Quit: An Eyewitness Account of the Partition of India* (Delhi: Oxford University Press, 1998); R.J. Moore, *Escape from Empire: The Attlee Government and the Indian Problem* (Oxford: Clarendon Press, 1983); Anita Inder Singh, *The Origins of the Partition of India, 1936–1947* (Delhi: Oxford University Press, 1987).

2. For an eyewitness account of these complex negotiations see Alan Campbell-Johnson, *Mission with Mountbatten* (New York: Dutton, 1953).

3. It should be noted that a British author has alleged that Sir Cyril Radcliffe, the head of the Radcliffe Commission, which had been assigned the task of drawing the post-independence boundaries of India and Pakistan, at Lord Mountbatten's instance, granted the Gurudaspur district of the Punjab to India. The transfer of this small tract of land gave India a contiguous border with the district of Jammu. See Alastair Lamb, *Kashmir, 1947: The Birth of a Tragedy* (Hertingfordbury: Roxford Books, 1992). The Scotch verdict 'not proven' applies to Lamb's allegation.

4. Sumit Ganguly, *The Crisis in Kashmir: Portents of War, Hopes of Peace* (Cambridge: Cambridge University Press; and Washington, D.C.: Woodrow Wilson Center Press, 1999).

5. Interview with senior Indian Administrative Service officer with extensive experience in Kashmir, November 1999. On this point also see Ian Copland, 'The Abdullah Factor: Kashmiri Muslims and the Crisis of 1947,' in D.A. Low, ed., *The Political Inheritance of Pakistan* (New York: St. Martin's Press, 1991).

6. While most Pakistani writers suggest that the rebellion stemmed from the obvious unjustness of the maharaja's rule, some Indian commentators question the spontaneity of the rebellion. See for example, Prem Shanker Jha, *Kashmir, 1947: Rival Versions of History* (New Delhi: Oxford University Press, 1996).

7. For evidence of Pakistan's complicity see Maj.-Gen. Akbar Khan, *Raiders in Kashmir* (Karachi: Pak Publishers, 1970), and H. V. Hodson, *The Great Divide: Britain, India and Pakistan* (Karachi: Oxford University Press, 1997).

8. In recent years a controversy has arisen about the timing of Kashmir's accession to India and the airlift of Indian troops. Most of the allegations of Indian malfeasance stem from Alastair Lamb, *Kashmir: A Disputed Legacy,*

1846–1990 (Karachi: Oxford University Press, 1992). For a rejoinder to Lamb, see Jha, *Kashmir, 1947.* For a dispassionate account of the circumstances surrounding the accession of Jammu and Kashmir to India, see Pauline Dawson, *The Peacekeepers of Kashmir: The UN Military Observers Group in India and Pakistan* (London: Hurst and Company, 1994), pp. 221–22.

9. For a 'worm's-eye view' of the Indian operations in Kashmir, see Lt. Col. (Ret.) Maurice Cohen, *Thunder Over Kashmir* (Hyderabad: Orient Longman, 1955).

10. More information is available from the Indian side; the relevant works are cited in the subsequent notes. One of the few available Pakistani accounts is Khan, *Raiders in Kashmir.*

11. For a detailed and comprehensive account from the Indian military's standpoint see Maj.-Gen. (Ret.) Lionel Protip Sen, *Slender Was the Thread* (New Delhi: Orient Longman, 1988).

12. Much of the evidence of this section has been derived from Lt.-Gen. (Ret.) S. K. Sinha, *Operation Rescue* (New Delhi: Vision Books, 1987).

13. On this point, see Sen, *Slender was the Thread*, 1988, pp. 159–161.

14. Raju G.C. Thomas, *Indian Defense Policy* (Princeton: Princeton University Press, 1986).

15. Interview with K. Subrahmanyam, New Delhi, December 1992.

16. For a more detailed account of the history of the UN discussions over Kashmir, see Joseph Korbel, *Danger in Kashmir* (Princeton: Princeton University Press, 1954).

17. Ayesha Jalal, *The State of Martial Rule: The Origins of Pakistan's Political Economy of Defence* (Cambridge: Cambridge University Press, 1990), describes Pakistan's military and organizational weaknesses in the immediate aftermath of Partition.

18. The onus that these refugees placed on the Pakistani (as well as the Indian) leadership is discussed in Hodson, *The Great Divide*, pp. 403–418.

19. For a discussion of the politics of the division of military assets see A. Martin Wainwright, *Inheritance of Empire: Britain, India, and the Balance of Power in Asia, 1938–1955* (Westport: Praeger, 1994), especially pp. 71–81. Also see Stephen P. Cohen, *The Pakistan Army* (Berkeley: University of California Press, 1984), p. 7, and, for a Pakistani perspective, Pervaiz Iqbal Cheema, *Pakistan's Defence Policy, 1947–58* (New York: St. Martin's Press, 1990), pp. 29–30.

20. Khan, *Raiders in Kashmir*, p. 191.

21. Korbel, *Danger in Kashmir*, p. 113.

22. Only the key turning points and epochs in the tortured history of the failure of multilateral negotiations are discussed here. For more detail, see P.L. Lakhanpal, *Essential Documents and Notes on Kashmir Dispute* (Delhi: International Books, 1965).

23. For a fairly dispassionate account of the two crises, see Pervaiz Iqbal Cheema, *Pakistan's Defence Policy, 1947–58* (New York: St. Martin's Press, 1990), pp. 102–103. For an Indian perspective on these crises see Jyoti Bhusan

Das Gupta, *India-Pakistan Relations, 1947–1955* (Amsterdam: Djambatan, 1960); for a Pakistani perspective see S.M. Burke and Lawrence Ziring, *Pakistan's Foreign Policy: An Historical Analysis* (Karachi: Oxford University Press, 1990).

24. For a discussion of Abdullah's propensity for electoral malfeasances, see Jyoti Bhusan Das Gupta, *Jammu and Kashmir* (The Hague: Martinus Nijhoff, 1968), p. 209.

25. For a detailed American assessment of the substance and the significance of the Nehru-Bogra talks see A.Z. Gardiner, 'Dispatch from the Embassy of Pakistan to the Department of State,' June 29, 1956, in John P. Glennon, Robert J. McMahon, and Stanley Shaloff, eds, *Foreign Relations of the United States [FRUS], 1955–1957, South Asia,* Volume 8 (Washington, D.C.: US Government Printing Office, 1987), pp. 86–90. In a remarkably prescient fashion Gardiner's telegram concluded with the following: 'The Embassy hopes that the Department [of State] will treat this case on its merits: a dispute in which the inhabitants of Kashmir are primarily concerned, and one where justice demands that their wishes be consulted under conditions where the fair and free expression of the public will can be had. Failing such a solution, the prestige of the United States and the United Nations is bound to suffer irreparably. *Kashmir, like Palestine, will remain a deadly cancer'* (emphasis added).

26. 'Memorandum of a Conversation, Department of State, Washington, D.C.,' December 19, 1956, *FRUS, 1955–1957, South Asia,* Volume 8, pp. 100–101. For an especially thorough account of the trilateral relationship between India, Pakistan, and the United States during this period see Robert J. McMahon, *The Cold War on the Periphery: The United States, India and Pakistan* (New York: Columbia University Press, 1994).

27. On the hardening of Nehru's attitudes toward the plebiscite, see Escott Reid, *Envoy to Nehru* (Delhi: Oxford University Press, 1981); Reid was Canada's High Commissioner to India during this period.

28. Sumit Ganguly, *The Origins of War in South Asia: The Indo-Pakistani Conflicts Since 1947* (Boulder: Westview Press, 1994), pp. 58–59.

29. Government of Pakistan, *White Paper on the Jammu and Kashmir Dispute* (Islamabad: Ministry of Foreign Affairs, 1977).

30. Jawaharlal Nehru, *India's Foreign Policy* (New Delhi: Government of India, Publications Division, 1961), p. 494.

31. For a discussion of the concept of an ethnic homeland, see Anthony D. Smith, *The Ethnic Origins of Nations* (Oxford: Blackwell, 1986).

32. For a discussion of the theory and practice of secularism in India, see Donald Eugene Smith, *India as a Secular State* (Princeton: Princeton University Press, 1963).

Chapter Two

The Second Kashmir War

The second Indo-Pakistani war, also fought over Kashmir, underscored the logic of *windows of opportunity*. Pakistan chose to attack India because it perceived that various other options for winning the territory had been exhausted. Multilateral and bilateral negotiations with India had yielded little. The great powers were starting to tire of the Indo-Pakistani dispute. Kashmir was being steadily integrated into India (thereby denuding Pakistan's irredentist claim) as New Delhi legislatively began to dispense with a number of constitutional provisions that had safeguarded Kashmir's special status within the union. Before long, the Pakistanis feared, Kashmir would assume the status of any other state within India.

Furthermore, after a disastrous defeat at the hands of the Chinese People's Liberation Army (PLA) in October-November 1962 along its Himalayan frontiers, India had embarked on a major attempt to revamp its military infrastructure. Pakistan's strategists looked into the future: India's growing military prowess would soon foreclose the possibilities of meaningful military action. From the Pakistani standpoint the window of opportunity was rapidly closing. A 'now or never' mentality gripped the decision-makers in Rawalpindi, where the Pakistani army had its headquarters. They reasoned that Pakistan had to act promptly if it wished to stop the seemingly inexorable process of Kashmir's integration into India.

A State of Denial

As the mid-1960s approached, Pakistan's leaders remained fundamentally unreconciled to the disputed status of Kashmir.[1] In their view,

Pakistan, as the homeland of the Muslims of South Asia, remained 'incomplete' without Kashmir. This predominantly Muslim territory, especially because it abutted their Muslim homeland, had to merge with Pakistan to complete Pakistan's distinctive identity. As Zulfiquar Ali Bhutto, the then foreign minister of Pakistan, wrote after the war:

> If a Muslim majority can remain a part of India, then the *raison d'etre* of Pakistan collapses. These are the reasons why India, to continue her domination of Jammu and Kashmir, defies international opinion and violates her pledges. For the same reasons, Pakistan must unremittingly continue her struggle for the right of self-determination of this subject people. *Pakistan is incomplete without Jammu and Kashmir both territorially and ideologically* [emphasis added]. It would be fatal if, in sheer exhaustion or out of intimidation, Pakistan were to abandon the struggle, and a bad compromise would be tantamount to abandonment; which might, in turn, lead to the collapse of Pakistan.[2]

Pakistani officials, however, were not so forthright: they couched their claim to Kashmir in terms of India's denial of the right of 'self-determination' for the Kashmiris.[3]

The strength of Pakistan's commitment to acquire all of Kashmir had not waned despite several setbacks at both multilateral and bilateral levels. The multilateral negotiations at the United Nations had made no tangible progress. As noted in Chapter 1, after India's initial referral of the issue to the UN, the Kashmir issue had become deeply politicized and India evinced little interest in the implementation of the Security Council resolutions.[4] By the early 1960s, it was amply clear to most foreign observers that the UN would be unable to forge any agreement between the two antagonists.

Bilateral Talks

Though the question of Kashmir remained deadlocked in the UN, the United States and the United Kingdom managed to prod India and Pakistan into talks. In December 1962, an Anglo-American mission led by Duncan Sandys, the British minister of defence, and Averell Harriman, a former governor of New York State, went to South Asia in an attempt to persuade the adversaries to open bilateral negotiations. The team was composed of James Grant, the US deputy assistant secretary of state for the Near East and South Asia; Roger Hilsman, then director of the US State Department's Bureau of Intelligence and Research; Paul Nitze, the US assistant secretary of defense for international affairs; Gen. Paul Adams, the commander of the US Strike

Command; and Carl Kaysen, a member of the US National Security Council staff. The team first went to New Delhi and then to Islamabad. At this time, the United States attached considerable significance to its military bases in Pakistan, which were critical for electronic eavesdropping on the Soviet missile programme. Thus, there was great unwillingness within the Pentagon to lean on Pakistan for fear of the loss of US bases. Simultaneously, there was deep distrust of India within the Pentagon particularly because of India's closeness to the Soviet Union. The American ambassador to India, John Kenneth Galbraith, and his successor, Chester Bowles, disagreed with the Pentagon's assessment, but to little avail.[5]

Thus the team's strategy was to persuade Prime Minister Nehru to engage Pakistan on the Kashmir question. Their leverage was not insubstantial: India was dependent on American and British military assistance, and Nehru was under fire domestically because of the disastrous loss in the border war with China.[6] He could ill afford to rebuff these pressures, and so reluctantly agreed to enter into talks.

The first round of talks was held in Rawalpindi, Pakistan, between December 26 and 29, 1962. The head of the Indian delegation was Sardar Swaran Singh, the minister of railways; his Pakistani counterpart was Zulfiquar Ali Bhutto, the minister for industries, national resources, and works. In this initial round, the two sides largely reiterated their well-known positions. The Pakistanis insisted on a plebiscite to determine the wishes of the Kashmiris. In response, the Indians argued that, as a secular state, they were unwilling to countenance any arrangement for self-determination that was based on religious identity.

A separate but related development on the eve of the talks significantly affected their course.[7] On December 26, the Pakistanis announced that they had reached an agreement with the People's Republic of China to cede some 2,050 square miles of territory of Pakistan-controlled Kashmir to China. This territorial concession would permit China to build a road linking its Xinjiang province with Tibet, the locus of the Khampa rebellion in the late 1950s. Understandably, India protested this Sino-Pakistani agreement but did not scuttle the negotiations. In the end, the talks simply set the stage for the next round. In the interim, the two sides agreed to refrain from engaging in 'adverse propaganda.'

The second round took place in New Delhi between January 16 and 19, 1963. This round, despite a shaky start, was more productive. At the outset both sides did little more than reiterate their familiar positions. The Indian delegation put forward a proposal to partition

Kashmir, suggested the disengagement of military forces, and proffered a 'no-war' pact. In the end the two sides settled for a joint communiqué that, among other matters, announced their agreement to explore a settlement of the Kashmir dispute without prejudicing the basic position of either side. They also agreed to delimit an international boundary in Jammu and Kashmir, to seek the disengagement of both Indian and Pakistani forces in and around Kashmir as part of a settlement, and to pursue other measures to promote bilateral cooperation.[8]

The third round of talks was held between February 8 and 10, 1963, in Karachi. At this session the discussions focused on the issue of border delimitation in Kashmir. Bhutto, who had now assumed the foreign ministry portfolio, made territorial claims to the Kashmir and Chenab valleys and to parts of Jammu. To no one's surprise, this proposal made little headway with the Indian delegation.

The fourth round of negotiations took place between March 12 and 15, 1963, in Calcutta. This round proved to be of little or no value. The Indians were in a hostile frame of mind because of the formalization of Pakistan's border agreement with China on March 2, 1963. They publicly protested that the border agreement violated the terms of the 1948 and 1949 UN resolutions that had forbidden both sides from changing the status quo in Kashmir. The Pakistanis rejected the charge and turned it back on the Indians, contending that the Indian alteration of the constitutional dispensation of Kashmir since the dismissal of Sheikh Abdullah in 1953 had also constituted a change in the status quo.[9]

The lack of appreciable progress at the Calcutta round caused alarm in Washington, D.C., and in London. The administration of US president John F. Kennedy was especially anxious about the dim prospects of Indo-Pakistani rapprochement in light of the larger threat that Chinese communism posed to South Asia and beyond. US policymakers explicitly, albeit privately, made clear that they had little intrinsic interest in settling the Indo-Pakistani dispute but that they were acutely concerned that continued Indo-Pakistani hostility would undermine other American Cold War objectives, most notably the curbing of Chinese adventurism in Asia. In an attempt to prod the two sides to make some meaningful progress, just prior to the fifth round, between April 21 and 25, 1963, the United States and the United Kingdom submitted a memorandum to India. This document urged the two sides to consider the following propositions in their discussions: that neither India nor Pakistan could completely renounce its respective claims to the Kashmir Valley; that both India and Pakistan would need 'assured access to and from the Vale for defence of their positions to the north and east'; that India had an interest in defending Ladakh; and that Pakistan had concerns about the development of water-storage facilities on the Chenab River. In pursuit of these ends, the proposal urged the two parties to define arrangements for sovereignty and the maintenance of law and order, to allow political freedom and some measure of self-rule for the inhabitants of the Valley, to permit the free movement of the Valley's population to other parts of Kashmir, India, and Pakistan, and to encourage the rapid development of tourism in the Kashmir area.[10]

The Pakistanis liked this proposal and pushed it in the fifth round. India, however, felt that the proposal did not adequately address its concerns about the defensibility of Ladakh. It also objected that the development of water-storage facilities on the Chenab would entail re-negotiating the Indus Waters Treaty of 1960.

Despite Anglo-American pressure, the Indians refused to budge significantly on the division of the Valley. Nevertheless, the two sides agreed to meet for a sixth round from May 14 to 16 in New Delhi. This last set of talks ended in a complete deadlock and neither side showed any interest in further bilateral negotiations. The failure of both multilateral and bilateral negotiations had a profound impact on Pakistani political calculations about the future of Kashmir.

Integrating Kashmir: The View from Rawalpindi

In the aftermath of the failure of the bilateral negotiations the Pakistanis had additional cause for distress. From 1963 onward, India had been stripping Kashmir of many of the constitutional provisions that had granted the state an autonomous position within the Indian federal structure. On December 21, 1964, under an ordinance issued by Sarvapalli Radhakrishnan, the then president of India, Articles 356 and 357 of the Indian Constitution were extended to Jammu and Kashmir, thereby eroding its special federal status. These two provisions would enable the Indian central government in New Delhi to promulgate so-called president's rule in the state during times of crisis. When president's rule was in force, the Indian parliament was empowered to make laws in the state and the central government became responsible for day-to-day administration. Even more distressing to the Pakistanis was the decision of the Kashmir Legislative Assembly on March 30, 1965, to dispense with the title of *sadr-i-riyasat* (head of state) for the state's ceremonial head, calling him instead simply 'governor' of the state. The implication of this semantic change was immense: the position of 'governor' would be subject to appointment by the president of India, not the Kashmir Legislative Assembly. In a further blow to Kashmir's autonomy, the formerly 'prime' minister of the state would henceforth be known as the 'chief' minister, as elsewhere in India.

As Kashmir was increasingly melded into the Indian polity through such measures, Pakistani leaders correctly saw that their irredentist claim on the state was slipping away. President Mohammed Ayub Khan expressed the prevailing Pakistani sentiments:

We reasoned with the United States . . . but we got no response. We could not even convince them that so long as relations between India and Pakistan remained what they were, there could be no stability or peace on the subcontinent. I think the British were more conscious of the need for bringing about an agreement between India and Pakistan, but they had little leverage in terms of economic and military influence. It was the United States alone that had the requisite influence but declined to exercise it.[11]

Ayub's misgivings about India's efforts to integrate Kashmir into the Indian union were also clearly reflected in his public statements. For example, in a nationwide broadcast in January 1964, he stated,

The arming of India has emboldened her to announce plans to integrate the state of Jammu and Kashmir. We have said repeatedly that we object in the strongest possible terms to this high-handed violation of solemn international pledges. The arms build-up in India will make no difference to our stand on the Jammu and Kashmir question. We are determined to secure to the people of Jammu and Kashmir their rightful freedom to choose which country they wish to join. . . . I can only express the hope that world opinion, and the saner elements in India, will assert themselves and make the Indian Government come to a reasonable and honourable settlement with us. If not, the arming of India and her aggressive action in proposing to integrate Jammu and Kashmir will continue to pose a serious threat to our security.[12]

To Ayub's dismay, however, Indian decision-makers paid little heed to his publicly stated concerns. This was hardly surprising: since their humiliating defeat two years earlier at the hands of the Chinese, the Indians' attention had been focused almost solely on the defence of India's northern borders.

The Impact of the Sino-Indian War on Indo-Pakistani Relations

The Sino-Indian border war of 1962 had been nothing short of a complete rout of the Indian armed forces. Questions still persist about

India's failure to use its superior air power to dislodge and harry the Chinese troops along the Himalayan frontier during the war.[13] This failure to use air power and, more importantly, the Indians' utter military unpreparedness cost them dearly: India lost several thousand troops and some 14,000 square miles of territory.

In the aftermath of this conflict, India embarked on a dramatic and much-needed programme of military modernization. Specifically, it sought to create a 45-squadron air force equipped with supersonic aircraft and a million-man army with ten new mountain divisions equipped and trained for high-altitude warfare. Simultaneously, it also drew up plans for the modernization of the Indian navy. These new commitments for men and equipment were reflected in the sharp growth of the Indian defence budget: the budgetary outlays for defence rose from 2.1 per cent of the gross national product (GNP) in 1961–62 to 3.0 per cent of the GNP in 1962–63 and 4.5 per cent of the GNP in 1964–65.[14]

Pakistani decision-makers were quite cognizant of India's significantly larger forces and industrial capacity. By 1965, India had 870,000 men under arms in sixteen divisions. Two of these infantry divisions were deployed in Kashmir and eight of them were positioned along the western and eastern borders with Pakistan. The other six were deployed along the Sino-Indian border. Pakistan, by contrast, had a total of seven divisions confronting India in West Pakistan and one division in East Pakistan. India had two armoured divisions, composed of Sherman and Centurion tanks. Pakistan had one armoured division of American-built M47/48 Patton tanks, as well as a few regiments of M-4 Sherman medium tanks and M-24 Chaffee light tanks. India had more than 700 aircraft, mostly French Mystere IVs, British Canberras and Hunters, and Indian-made Gnats, compared to Pakistan's total of 280 aircraft that included 168 F-86 Sabres and 12 F-104A Starfighters.[15] (The naval capabilities of each side, while in India's favour, played little or no role in shaping the onset or outcome of the 1965 war.)

This build-up caused considerable consternation among key members of Pakistan's decision-making elite. Echoing the sentiments of President Ayub, Air Marshal Asghar Khan, the chief of the Pakistani air force, stated:

The build-up of the Indian Armed Forces had been causing great concern to all thinking people in the Pakistan Armed Forces. Under the guise of preparations against China they succeeded in securing substantial military aid from the United States and were building up a million-strong army, almost doubling the Air Force, [and] increasing tank production capacities. . . . Pakistan was faced with a very dangerous situation. If we did not face up to it and prepare ourselves immediately, the time would come when, having built up her Armed Forces sufficiently, India would be in a position to achieve her political objectives without recourse to war.[16]

In late 1964, the military correspondent of the respected Pakistani English-language newspaper *Dawn* questioned the premise that India's defence modernization was largely directed toward countering the threat from the People's Republic of China.[17] He laid out his arguments in a four-part article titled 'Survival or Extinction?' In it he stated:

Pakistan is India's main target, and it is for the physical annihilation of Pakistan by overwhelming military force that India is frantically arming herself—a process in which Pakistan's so-called friends and allies are helping India.[18]

The Indian Military Strategy

To forestall a possible Pakistani attack on Kashmir, key Indian decision-makers had evolved a fairly sophisticated strategy, an amalgam of defence and deterrence through punishment and retaliation.[19] Indian war plans called for carrying out a holding action in Kashmir while the main segment of the Indian army would make a determined and rapid thrust further south, toward Rawalpindi or Karachi, to prevent a concentration of Pakistani forces in the principal operational theatre of western Punjab. India's forces were configured and its assets deployed in accordance with this strategy, whose key aims were to inflict a decisive defeat on the Pakistani army as quickly as possible, occupy the border city of Lahore in the Punjab, and then coerce the Pakistani regime to seek peace.

A series of statements by high-level Indian civilian officials had explicitly communicated India's deterrent and defensive postures. The Indian political-military leadership, over a span of a decade, had made explicit statements about India's willingness and ability to use its military capabilities in the event of a Pakistani attack on Kashmir. For example, as early as 1952, Prime Minister Nehru in a New Year's address had stated categorically that if Pakistan 'by mistake invades Kashmir, we will not only meet them in Kashmir, but it will be a full scale war between India and Pakistan.'[20] Much later, in April 1965, in response to a Pakistani military probe into Indian territory, Prime Minister Lal Bahadur Shastri stated:

If Pakistan continues to discard reason and persists in its aggressive activities our army will defend the country and will decide its own strategy and the employment of its manpower and equipment in a manner that it deems best.[21]

The foregoing analysis shows that India had not only mustered the requisite forces to deter and defend against a Pakistani attack on Kashmir but had also configured and deployed the forces in a credible fashion and had communicated its resolve to the Pakistani leadership. The Pakistani leadership were cognizant of India's capabilities, force deployments, and willingness to use its military assets. On May 1, 1965, for example, President Ayub responded to Shastri's just-quoted statement with the following remarks:

India has threatened us with further aggression in the battleground of her choice. Does she realize that this will mean a general and total war between India and Pakistan with all its unpredictable consequences? How can such a reckless and provocative statement be made by highly responsible persons? If such a situation is forced on us, nobody can expect us not to meet the challenge.[22]

The Pakistanis had a significant geographical advantage in Kashmir: Pakistan was physically much closer to the region, and thus it would have much shorter supply lines. The Indian military had, therefore, forged a military doctrine to counter this vulnerability. In the most important element of this strategy, Indian leaders had decided that they would not discriminate between Azad Kashmir forces and members of the regular Pakistani army. Two factors had led them to make this decision. The first was the Pakistani geographical advantage just mentioned. The other stemmed from Indian doubts about the loyalty and reliability of portions of the Kashmiri Muslim population of the Valley to the Indian state. India's military doctrine was designed to dramatically raise the costs to Pakistan of a Pakistani invasion and thereby deter any hostile action.[23]

In pursuit of these goals the Indian army was deployed in the following fashion: three infantry divisions were assigned to the defence of the Kashmir Valley, Jammu, and the Poonch-Mindhar-Rajouri area across the northwestern salient. An additional infantry battalion was stationed in Leh, the capital of Ladakh. Apart from these forward troop deployments, a counter-strike force composed of two infantry divisions was based in Punjab at Ambala, Amritsar, Gurudaspur, Jullunder, and Khasali. The only armoured division was stationed in Jhansi, south of New Delhi, and was at least seventy-two hours away by train from its operational take-off point in eastern Punjab.[24]

The Pakistani Military Strategy

The Pakistanis developed a plan, code-named 'Operation Gibraltar,' to infiltrate the Valley and foment a rebellion there. The political initiative behind the operation came directly from Foreign Minister Zulfiquar Ali Bhutto and Foreign Secretary Aziz Ahmed. Maj.-Gen. Akhtar Husain Malik, the commander of the Twelfth Division of the Pakistani army, was placed in charge of the operation.

The initial phase of the plan involved infiltrating some five thousand armed men, who would capitalize on the disturbed conditions in the state to start a mass uprising against Indian rule. (Kashmiri discontent with Indian rule had been aroused by the changes being made to Kashmir's special federal status, by the theft of a relic from the Hazratbal shrine in Srinagar, and by the incarceration of Sheikh Abdullah and his lieutenant, Mirza Afzal Beg, in spring 1965.) As a senior Pakistani general closely connected with the operation wrote later:

Broadly, the plan envisaged, on a short-term basis, sabotage of military targets, disruption of communications, etc., and, as a long-term measure, distribution of arms to the people of [India-]occupied Kashmir and infiltration of a guerilla movement there eventually.[25]

In the next phase, regular Pakistani army troops would move to seize significant positions in Kashmir, especially in the Valley, in a series of quick, decisive thrusts. Assuming that the first two stages went as planned, the Pakistanis would accomplish all this before the Indian army had a chance to mobilize against them, and the Pakistani leadership could present the supposedly rebellious situation as a *fait accompli* to the international community and call for assistance to the Kashmiris. This plan, the Pakistani decision-makers hoped, would enable them finally to settle the Kashmir dispute on terms favourable to Pakistan.

Explaining the Onset of War

Why was the Pakistani politico-military leadership not deterred from attacking Kashmir? They were well aware that India had substantial military capabilities, had deployed them in a fashion to tackle a Pakistani incursion, and had, repeatedly, expressed a willingness to use them as deemed necessary. The Pakistani decision to resort to war against India under these circumstances, therefore, is an important puzzle.

A particular conjunction of factors explains Pakistan behaviour. First, the Pakistanis believed that the Indian forces were not prepared to defend against an attack. This assumption was based on the Indian response to a military provocation by Pakistan earlier that year (a provocation specifically designed to test Indian mettle). In early 1965, the Pakistanis had conducted a 'limited probe' along a disputed area, the Rann of Kutch, near the western Indian state of Gujarat.[26] The Rann is largely trackless waste and had a poorly demarcated border. In January 1965, several border skirmishes took place in the Rann. Hostilities escalated through the next several months, with both sides bringing in regular forces and the Pakistanis using their newly acquired Patton tanks. The Rann of Kutch conflict was brought to a close in May 1965 with British mediation at a conference of the prime ministers of members of the British Commonwealth; India agreed to refer the matter to an international arbitration commission.

Much to the delight of Pakistani hawks, the Indian response to the probe was not particularly vigorous. Two factors account for the lackadaisical Indian response: the political leadership did not consider the Rann to be of much material or symbolic value, and Indian military strategists realized that the terrain favoured the Pakistanis. The higher echelons of the Indian military were loath to tie down their forces in what they deemed to be an operation that would entail significant costs for little practical gain. According to Asghar Khan, both the military and the civilians in the higher echelons of decision-making were not impressed with the Indian army's performance in the Rann of Kutch. The Indian unwillingness to respond with alacrity and military strength coupled with their readiness to seek third-party intervention led the Pakistani leadership to make a fundamentally flawed inference: that the Indians lacked stomach for battle and were still reeling from the psychological shock of the disastrous 1962 Sino-Indian border war.[27]

The second factor influencing the Pakistani decision to proceed with Operation Gibraltar was the belief among the Pakistani elite that there was widespread popular support for Pakistan within the Kashmir Valley. They came to this conclusion after a series of restive events in Kashmir. In December 1963, widespread and violent anti-Indian sentiment had erupted in the Kashmir Valley in the wake of the theft of the *moe-e-moeqqdas*, a relic sacred to Kashmiri Muslims and believed to be a hair of the Prophet Mohammed. Fortunately for the Indian state, its intelligence operatives managed to locate the relic, had it authenticated by local clerics, and returned it to the Hazratbal shrine, from which it had been stolen.[28] Subsequent events have shown that the agitation grew out of the resentment of the people of Jammu and Kashmir at their subjugation by India and the Indian designs to integrate the state and curtail its special status.[29] Key Pakistani leaders, however, mistakenly construed the anti-Indian tenor of the demonstration as evidence of considerable pro-Pakistani sentiment in the Valley. As Air Marshal Khan would later write:

It was *assumed* [emphasis added] that widespread support existed within occupied Kashmir to make such a guerilla campaign a success. It was considered unlikely that, as a consequence of this action, India would be inclined to attempt a military offensive against Azad Kashmir territory. Lastly, the possibility of India crossing the international frontier in the East and West Pakistan was ruled out.[30]

Worse still, they reinforced these beliefs about Indian military pusil-lanimity and the existence of extensive local Kashmiri support with pernicious and racist notions of the inherent 'martial' qualities of Muslim soldiers vis-à-vis their putatively 'non-martial' Hindu coun-terparts.[31]

The third major factor swaying Pakistani leaders to carry out their plan was their recognition that their armed forces' ability to fight a protracted war against India was limited. As detailed above, India's forces were superior in numbers, equipment, and funding. The military leadership in Pakistan knew full well that their forces would not last long against the Indians. The Pakistani leadership also believed that in the years ahead India's military prowess would increase so significantly that the window of opportunity for taking action in Kashmir would rapidly close. In their view, they could ill afford to accept the proposition that the growth of Indian military capabilities was directed solely against China. In the future, as Foreign Minister Bhutto underscored, India would be able to maintain the status quo in Kashmir simply by virtue of its overwhelming conventional superiority. Unless Pakistan forged a strategy to seize Kashmir soon, they believed, the opportunity to do anything would be irretrievably lost. Of course, the failure of both multilateral and bilateral negotiations with India had only bolstered Bhutto's resolve and commitment to military action.

Finally, President Ayub Khan and Foreign Minister Bhutto concluded after an eight-day trip to China in March 1965 that the Chinese would assist Pakistan in the event of a war with India. This inference was based on Marshal Ch'en Yi's intemperate public remarks about India during a Pakistani state visit. At no point, however, did Ch'en Yi specifically hold out the promise of Chinese military assistance to Pakistan should another war with India ensue.[32] But the Pakistanis, already leaning toward a military action, heard only what they had hoped to hear. (When war did break out, the Chinese did little or nothing to assist the Pakistanis.)

The Onset of War

Emboldened by these four factors, and after having convinced themselves of the distinct possibility of military success in a short, sharp incursion, the Pakistanis embarked on Operation Gibraltar. The forces required for this operation were assembled in the Pakistani hill resort town of Murree on May 26, 1965. The groups were composed of eight to ten 'forces,' each comprising six units of five companies. Approximately 110 men were assigned to each company. Each company was composed of regular personnel of the so-called Azad Kashmir army, which was in fact part of the Pakistani army, and of *mujahid* and *razakar* irregulars.[33]

The infiltration started across the 470-mile-long cease-fire line (CFL) in Kashmir around August 5, 1965. The insurgents were dressed as local inhabitants and carried mostly small arms, grenades, plastic explosives, and radio equipment. Lt-Gen. Harbaksh Singh, the commanding officer of India's western front during the war, nicely summarizes the entry and activities of the intruders in Indian-controlled Kashmir:

The intruders set about their task with a missionary zeal, confident of spontaneous cooperation from the masses whom they had come to 'liberate'. . . . The period of the infiltration campaign was characterized by intense, hectic activity throughout the [Jammu and Kashmir] theatre with special emphasis in the Valley. The raiders and [our] own forces marched and counter-marched all over the inhospitable terrain in a vast grim game of hide and seek. Several times during the day the opponents met, clashed and reeled apart in a series of bloody actions, weaving a confused pattern hard to unravel.[34]

The intruders' grand hope of linking up with the disaffected population of Kashmir and quickly fomenting a rebellion, however, failed to materialize. Worse still, native Kashmiris quickly alerted the local authorities about the infiltration that was taking place along the CFL. The Indian authorities moved with dispatch to seal the border and started vigorously to hunt down those infiltrators who had already penetrated the Valley.

Despite this loss of tactical surprise, the Pakistani political-military leadership persisted with the initial plan. On August 14, a significant infiltration took place in Jammu near the 'Azad Kashmir' town of Bhimbar. According to Indian sources, Pakistan used its regular forces in this operation. On August 15, the Indian forces retaliated by crossing the CFL. The Pakistanis counter-attacked shortly thereafter, moving closer to the CFL and shelling the Indian troop deployments at Tithwal, Uri, and Poonch. This counter-attack prompted a powerful Indian thrust on August 24 into 'Azad Kashmir.' These Indian gains led the Pakistanis to mount 'Operation Grand Slam' on August 31–September 1 in southern Kashmir.[35] Seventy tanks followed by two infantry brigades spearheaded the Pakistani incursion. The Indian forces were caught quite unprepared for the Pakistani onslaught and suffered significant casualties. The sheer strength of the Pakistani movement led the Indian army to call in air support. Within an hour and a half the Indian air force had struck at the advancing Pakistani forces. The next day the Pakistanis called in their own air force to support their ground operations. From this point onward, both sides relied on air support in the conduct of ground operations.

On September 5, the Pakistani forces captured the village of Jaurian, some fourteen miles inside Indian-controlled territory. From here they would be able to proceed directly to the town of Akhnur, the capture of which would enable them to seal off the state of Jammu and Kashmir from the rest of India. Having decided that the terrain was unsuitable for defence, Indian strategists had already made plans for relieving a potential Pakistani thrust in this vulnerable area. Accordingly, when the Pakistanis attacked Akhnur, the Indian forces escalated horizontally: on September 6, the Indian army launched a powerful attack directed toward the western Punjabi city of Lahore. Simultaneously, the Indian forces launched another powerful attack toward the town of Sialkot, a major railway and road centre in Punjab. These two attacks produced the desired result: the Pakistanis were forced to withdraw from Akhnur. The Indians were reasonably successful in their drive toward Lahore and captured a number of villages along the way. However, an actual assault on the city of Lahore was thwarted by the Ichogil irrigation canal on the city's outskirts. Anticipating an attack on Lahore, Pakistani authorities had turned the canal into a veritable moat by blowing up as many as seventy bridges across it.

In order to draw the Indian forces away from Lahore, the Pakistani army launched a counter-offensive at Khem Karan in Punjab. The Pakistani First Armoured Division, which had an active strength of 125–150 tanks, led the attack. The Indian army, through aerial reconnaissance, had obtained advance warning of this impending attack.[36] Indian authorities called in the Second Armoured Brigade that was composed of Centurion tanks. Quickly emplaced on high ground in a horseshoe pattern, these tanks laid in wait for the Pakistani Patton tank column to enter firing range. Despite their superior firepower, the US-manufactured Pattons proved to be of little use when trapped in an ambush and subjected to punishing fire from three sides. Worse still, these gasoline-powered Pattons quickly caught fire.

Meanwhile, another major tank battle emerged in the Sialkot sector. This battle turned out to be the major engagement of the war and involved a combined number of 400 to 600 tanks. The outcome of this battle was inconclusive: the Indian army failed to take the city of Sialkot. However, there is some ambiguity about the Indian objectives regarding the capture of Sialkot. Some analysts argue that the Indians were actually interested in capturing Sialkot with the intention of trading it for other, Pakistani-held areas. They also hold that this objective was thwarted by an untimely cease-fire. Others contend that the Indians were interested only in putting pressure on Sialkot to induce the Pakistanis to withdraw elsewhere, especially in Kashmir.

The 1965 war brought very limited action to East Pakistan. Military engagements there were limited because India had no plans to seize territory in the east and was interested in encouraging the incipient and growing disenchantment with West Pakistani domination of the country's eastern wing. Simultaneously, the Pakistani political-military leadership had long since decided that 'the defence of the east lay in the west.' This proposition eventually would prove to be quite costly for the West Pakistani politico-military elite as the Bengali population of East Pakistan would reach the inexorable conclusion that their security depended upon India's sufferance.

By mid-September, the war was reaching a stalemate. The UN Security Council unanimously passed a resolution on September 20 calling for an end to the hostilities. The Indian government accepted the cease-fire resolution on September 21, and the Pakistanis did so on September 22. The Indian decision to accept a cease-fire was made on political and not military grounds. India was facing considerable pressure from the UN in general, and the United States and the United Kingdom in particular, to stop the fighting. (Immediately after the outbreak of the war both these major powers had imposed military embargoes on India and Pakistan.) Faced with these pressures, Prime Minister Shastri decided to rein in the Indian military despite the opposition of his defence minister, Y.B. Chavan. Gen. J.N. Chaudhuri, the Indian chief of army staff, also opposed the decision to limit the scope of and then terminate the war. In his view, the army had been given sufficient time to inflict attrition on Pakistan but not enough to embark on a more punishing offensive.[37]

The Pakistani setbacks at Khem Karan and Sialkot demoralized Ayub Khan and he lost his will to prosecute the war further. Efforts on the part of the Pakistani military brass to persuade him to continue the war proved impotent. Worse still, the Chinese promise of assistance failed to materialize; all the Chinese did was issue a two-part ultimatum on September 17 in which they threatened 'grave consequences' unless India dismantled certain fortifications it had supposedly erected in Sikkim and near Tibet. Although there is no evidence that the fortifications had been erected in the first place, on September 20 the Chinese announced that they had been dismantled. The Chinese decision to let the ultimatum lapse without any aggressive action was no doubt a face-saving gesture: shortly after the issuance of the ultimatum, the Soviet Union and the United States had issued stern warnings to the Chinese.

The second part of the Chinese ultimatum, demanding the immediate return of 800 sheep and 60 yaks, provided an occasion for much merriment in New Delhi after the war. Following the declaration of the cease-fire, some citizens of New Delhi gathered 800 sheep and paraded them before the Chinese embassy. The sheep bore placards around their necks with such slogans as 'We are here, no need to start a war,' and 'Eat us but save the world.'

Negotiations at Tashkent

The United States, which had made concerted if somewhat partisan attempts to resolve the dispute over Kashmir, evinced no interest in a post-war settlement. According to one American State Department official long connected with South Asia, key officials in Washington, D.C. wished 'a pox on both your houses.' Furthermore, the Johnson administration's increasing concern about the expanding war effort in Vietnam diminished its ardour for brokering peace between the two subcontinental rivals. The American unwillingness to devote further resources to the resolution of the Indo-Pakistani dispute enabled the Soviets to step into the breach after having remained mostly neutral during the conflict. Soviet premier Alexei Kosygin, in an attempt to expand Soviet influence in South Asia and limit Chinese influence in Pakistan, invited Ayub and Shastri to the Soviet Central Asian city of Tashkent to forge a post-war settlement. The two parties met in Tashkent on January 4, 1966. With considerable dexterity and an amalgam of persuasion and cajolery, Kosygin induced the two sides to reach a settlement. On January 10, after a near-collapse of the talks, the two sides declared that

[A]ll armed personnel of the two countries shall be withdrawn not later than February 25, 1966 to positions they held prior to August 5, 1965, and both sides shall observe the ceasefire terms on the ceasefire line.[38]

Under the terms of the Tashkent Agreement not only did the two sides agree to a ceasefire and return to the *status quo ante*, they also agreed to abjure from the use of force to settle outstanding disputes. The agreement represented important concessions from both sides. The Indians withdrew from a number of strategic positions that they had captured in Azad Kashmir, two of which were significant: the Haji Pir Pass and the town of Tithwal.[39] The Pakistanis also gave up some of their territorial gains.

The Aftermath of the War

The war obviously failed to resolve the Kashmir dispute. It did, however, have a number of unintended consequences for the politics of the region, and for India and Pakistan. At a regional level, the United States largely disengaged itself from South Asia in the aftermath of the war. American withdrawal from the region permitted the Soviets to expand their influence in the region and to curb Chinese efforts to play a significant role. At another level, the war set a precedent for future Indo-Pakistani wars: Indian and Pakistani commanders relied on similar and mostly British battle tactics, lacked significant firepower, and did not engage in any significant tactical innovation.[40]

The consequences of the war for India were not far reaching. Its military, while not distinguishing itself, nevertheless performed far more creditably than it had in the 1962 border war with China. The Indian armed forces also did not suffer significant casualties. On the other hand, much to the dismay and chagrin of the higher echelons of the military and, in fact, over their objections, the few territorial gains made during the war were traded away at Tashkent.[41]

The war undermined a series of cherished Pakistani beliefs. Its assumption that a significant window of opportunity had opened to wrest Kashmir from India proved to be deeply flawed. Despite India's weak defence of its domain in the Rann of Kutch, it showed little hesitation in militarily responding to Pakistani incursions in Kashmir.

The Pakistanis had also made a fundamentally flawed inference about the existence and extent of pro-Pakistani sentiment in Jammu and Kashmir. Many Kashmiri Muslims in the Valley may well have been unhappy with aspects of Indian rule, but such disenchantment did not necessarily translate into widespread support for Kashmir's merger with Pakistan. This unwarranted inference of extant Kashmiri support helped undermine 'Operation Gibraltar' from the outset.

Other Pakistani beliefs also proved to be both militarily and politically costly. For example, much to the surprise of Pakistani planners, Indian forces crossed the international border in Punjab in the prosecution of Indian war aims. This Indian action, in particular, came as a considerable shock to Pakistani decision-makers. In later years, Pakistan would seek to significantly strengthen its defences along this corridor to blunt any future Indian offensive.

The war also had certain unanticipated consequences for the future of the security and stability of the subcontinent. Most significantly, the West Pakistani elites' decision to leave East Pakistan only lightly defended stoked the embers of Bengali sub-nationalism. Significant number of Bengalis were already unhappy with the imposition of Urdu as the national language, inadequate Bengali representation in the civil services and the armed forces, and the disproportionate allocation of foreign assistance to West Pakistan. These incendiary conditions in East Pakistan would flare up within the next several years into civil war, which evolved into the third Indo-Pakistani war.

Notes

1. Mohammed Ayub Khan, *Friends Not Masters* (London: Oxford University Press, 1966).

2. Zulfiquar Ali Bhutto, *The Myth of Independence* (London: Oxford University Press, 1969).

3. Iqbal Akhund, *Memoirs of a Bystander: A Life in Diplomacy* (Karachi: Oxford University Press, 1997). Of course, the question of 'self-determination' is hardly unproblematic. The Pakistanis and their supporters on the Kashmir question do not address how the rights of 'nested minorities,' namely the Buddhists and the Hindus, would be addressed in an independent Kashmir.

4. The evolution of the Indian position at the United Nations is discussed at some length in Joseph Korbel, *Danger in Kashmir* (Princeton: Princeton University Press, 1954).

5. Dennis Kux, *India and the United States: Estranged Democracies* (Washington, D.C.: National Defense University Press, 1993).

6. For the most complete and dispassionate account of the conflict, see Steven Hoffmann, *India and the China Crisis* (Berkeley: University of California Press, 1990).

7. Much of the following discussion has been drawn from Sumit Ganguly, *The Crisis in Kashmir: Portents of War, Hopes of Peace* (Cambridge: Cambridge University Press; and Washington, D.C.: Woodrow Wilson Center Press, 1999).

8. See 'Telegram from Embassy in India to the Department of State,' January 19, 1963, in Louis J. Smith and Glenn W. Lafantasie, eds, *Foreign Relations of the United States [FRUS], 1961–1963*, Volume 19 (Washington, D.C.: US Government Printing Office, 1996), pp. 477–478.

9. It needs to be recalled that under the terms of the Delhi Accord signed between Sheikh Mohammed Abdullah and Prime Minister Jawaharlal Nehru, India had agreed to grant Kashmir autonomy in all matters except in the areas of defence, foreign affairs and communications. The terms of the Delhi Accord were steadily eroded after the dismissal and incarceration of Sheikh Abdullah in 1953. For a discussion of the Delhi Accord and the dismissal of Abdullah see Jyoti Bhusan Das Gupta, *Jammu and Kashmir* (The Hague: Martinus Nijhoff, 1969).

10. Memorandum from Secretary of State Rusk to President Kennedy, 'Attachment, "Elements of A Settlement",' *FRUS, 1961–1963*, Volume 19, p. 534.

11. Ayub Khan, *Friends Not Masters*, p. 158.

12. Mohammed Ayub Khan, *Pakistan Perspectives* (Washington, D.C.: Embassy of Pakistan, 1965), p. 76.

13. Many Indian security analysts argue that Nehru was the victim of inappropriate political and strategic advice from Ambassador Galbraith. Galbraith states in his memoirs that he advised Nehru not to use the Indian air force in an offensive capacity, in order to prevent a Chinese recourse to horizontal escalation along the Himalayan frontier. See John Kenneth Galbraith, *A Life in Our Times* (Boston: Houghton Mifflin, 1981).

14. For a fuller discussion of the budgetary impact of the Sino-Indian border war see Raju G.C. Thomas, *The Defense of India* (Delhi: Macmillan, 1978).

15. T. V. Paul, *Asymmetric Conflicts: War Initiation by Weaker Powers* (Cambridge: Cambridge University Press, 1994), p. 107.

16. Asghar Khan, *The First Round* (Ghaziabad: Vikas Publishers, 1979).

17. The Indians' perception of the severity of the threat from China was, in fact, so great that the Indian government took the extraordinary step of convening a separate military planning group outside the control of the military chiefs of staff. This group comprised officers from all three services, and they reported directly to the Ministry of Defence. They were entrusted with the task of assessing the overall defence needs of the country. In the end the work of this group amounted to little because their recommendations far exceeded the financial capacity of the government. See P.C. Lal, *Some Problems of Defence* (New Delhi: United Services Institute of India, 1977).

18. Military Correspondent, *Dawn* (Karachi), November 28, 1964.

19. For an early discussion of various strategies of deterrence, see Glenn Snyder, *Deterrence and Defense* (Princeton: Princeton University Press, 1961).

20. Nehru, as cited in Paul, *Asymmetric Conflicts*, p. 109.

21. Prime Minister Lal Bahadur Shastri, Lok Sabha Debates, April 28, 1965.

22. Mohammed Ayub Khan, *Speeches and Statements* (Karachi: Din Muhammadi Press, 1965), p. 200.

23. For a fuller discussion see Lorne J. Kavic, *India's Quest for Security* (Berkeley: University of California Press, 1967).

24. Kavic, *India's Quest*, p. 86.

25. Mohammad Musa, *My Version: India-Pakistan War 1965* (Lahore: Wajidalis, 1983).

26. The concept of a 'limited probe' is derived from the work of Alexander George and Richard Smoke, *Deterrence in American Foreign Policy* (New York: Columbia University Press, 1974). This concept calls for an adversary to make a limited and reversible incursion into an adversary's territory to clarify the latter's commitment to defend territory.

27. Paul, *Asymmetric Conflicts*.

28. For a detailed account of the Hazratbal episode, see Ganguly, *Crisis in Kashmir*.

29. Khan, *Pakistan Perspectives*.

30. Khan, *The First Round*, pp. 75–76.

31. For an early discussion of the British theory of 'martial races' see Stephen P. Cohen, *The Indian Army* (Berkeley: University of California Press, 1967).

32. Russell Brines, *The Indo-Pakistani Conflict* (New York: Pall Mall, 1968).

33. The *mujahideen* were lightly armed civilian reserves. The *razakars* were a paramilitary force under army control. See Brines, *Indo-Pakistani Conflict*.

34. Harbaksh Singh, *War Despatches: Indo-Pak Conflict 1965* (New Delhi: Lancer International, 1991).

35. Musa, *My Version*.

36. Personal communication with a former American military attaché to New Delhi, Washington, D.C., August 1982.

37. Brines, *Indo-Pakistani Conflict*.

38. Text of the Tashkent Declaration, January 10, 1966.

39. Brines, *Indo-Pakistani Conflict*.

40. Leo Heiman, 'Defence Pattern,' *Seminar* (New Delhi), July 1966, pp. 35–39.

41. A recently declassified Indian Ministry of Defence study demonstrates in painstaking detail how shortcomings in military planning, the timidity of senior commanders, and logistical problems hobbled Indian military operations during the war. The report is available at http://www.timesofindia.com/today/pagewars.htm.

Chapter Three

The Bangladesh War

The origins of the 1971 war were markedly different from those of the two previous Indo-Pakistani conflicts. Whereas Pakistan initiated the first two wars, India began the third. Pakistan's decision to resort to war on the first two occasions stemmed from false optimism and perceived windows of opportunity. The origins of the 1971 war, however, were more complex.

The underlying precipitants of the 1971 conflict were rooted in the exigencies of Pakistani domestic politics—the failure of federative arrangements within the Pakistani polity.[1] In the aftermath of Pakistan's first democratic election in October 1970, a long-standing demand for regional autonomy gathered considerable force in East Pakistan. Soon thereafter negotiations over power-sharing reached a deadlock. Unable to break this deadlock, the military regime of General Yahya Khan resorted to the extensive use of deadly force against the East Pakistani population (which was primarily ethnically Bengali), thereby precipitating a full-scale civil war by March-April 1971.[2]

The civil war contributed to the flight of some 10 million refugees into India over the course of the succeeding few months. Indian policy-makers, faced with this unprecedented human influx, calculated that it was cheaper to resort to war against their long-time adversary than to passively absorb the refugees into their own turgid population. India characterized its decision to intervene in East Pakistan as a form of humanitarian intervention. There is little question that Indian intervention did help put an end to further loss of life in the military crackdown in East Pakistan. India's motivation for intervening in this crisis, however, can be more forthrightly explained in terms of its desire to exploit a window of opportunity.[3] Indian decision-makers saw an excellent moment to not only materially weaken Pakistan in a war but also to attack its very ideological foundation. A vivisected Pakistan would pose less of a threat to India's security because India would not be faced with a potential two-front conflict in the event of another war. More important, however, demonstrating the inability of Pakistan to cohere as a state on the basis of Islam alone would fundamentally undercut Pakistan's time-honoured irredentist claim to Kashmir. If the bonds of Islam could not ensure national integration, then what claim, if any, did Pakistan have to the Muslim-majority state of Kashmir?

As this chapter will show, the 1971 war fundamentally altered the political geography of the subcontinent. It led to the break-up of Pakistan and the emergence of a new state, Bangladesh. It also drew India closer to the Soviet Union, a relationship that would serve as a strategic hedge for India against future Chinese malfeasance. The war and its outcomes would also lead the United States to distance itself from the affairs of the subcontinent for a considerable span of time. Yet the central problem of Kashmir, despite efforts at its resolution in the post-war settlement at Simla, would remain unresolved and would dog Indo-Pakistani relations into the next century.

The Tenuous Bonds of Pakistan

Despite the putative bond of Islam, significant differences existed between East and West Pakistan. The relationship between the two wings of the country was one of fundamental social, economic, and political inequity. Each of these categories requires some discussion.

One of the social irritants was language. The Bengali-speaking population of East Pakistan had long resented the status of Urdu as the national language of Pakistan. With their rich linguistic and intellectual heritage, the Bengalis felt that the imposition of Urdu was an affront to their history and their identity.[4] This resentment had generated linguistic riots as early as 1952. Subsequently, despite continuing reproaches and protests, various national regimes in West Pakistan had shown scant interest in assuaging the frustration of the Bengalis.

In the economic arena, East Pakistanis faced considerable discrimination. East Pakistan, for instance, with its population of 75 million, had 7,600 doctors; West Pakistan, populated by 55 million, enjoyed the services of 12,400 physicians. Similar disparities existed in educational investments. Between 1947 and 1969, the number of colleges in West Pakistan grew from 40 to 271, but in East Pakistan their number expanded from 50 to only 162. Of the foreign assistance provided by the United States to Pakistan, 66 per cent was disbursed in the West.

Finally, in the critical political-military realm, East Pakistani representation was also blatantly inequitable. In 1971, at the onset of the civil war, despite the fact that they constituted 54 per cent of the total population of Pakistan, Bengalis were a mere 5 per cent of the officer corps in the army, 15 per cent in the air force, and 20 per cent in the navy. In 1965, there was a single Bengali major-general out of 16 Pakistanis holding that rank.[5] In the elite civil service, Bengali representation in 1970 amounted to only 16 per cent, despite a 162 per cent increase in college enrollment in East Pakistan over the preceding decade.[6]

These disparities were hardly surprising given the views that the West Pakistani elite had of their East Pakistani compatriots. The following quotation from the work of Pakistani dictator Mohammed Ayub Khan aptly captures widely-held sentiments:

East Bengalis, who constitute the bulk of the population, probably belong to the very original Indian races. It would be no exaggeration to say that up to the creation of Pakistan, they had not known any real freedom or sovereignty. They have been in turn ruled either by the caste Hindus, Moghuls, Pathans, or the British. In addition, they have been and are still under considerable Hindu cultural and linguistic influence. As such they have all the inhibitions of down-trodden races and have not yet found it possible to adjust psychologically to the requirements of new-born freedom. Their popular complexes, exclusiveness, suspicion and a sort of defensive aggressiveness probably emerge from this historical background. Prudence, therefore, demands that these factors should be recognized and catered for and they be helped so as to feel equal partners and prove an asset.[7]

Pakistan after the 1965 War

Political developments within Pakistan in the mid-1960s would bring all these disparities and tensions between the two wings of the state to the fore. The problems started almost immediately after the second Indo-Pakistani war over Kashmir. The military stalemate that resulted from the 1965 war proved costly for the Pakistani military regime of President Ayub. Ayub's foreign minister, Zulfiquar Ali Bhutto, one of the architects of the 1965 war, successfully stoked popular discontent against Ayub in the aftermath of the war. In 1967, Bhutto had formed a political party, the Pakistan People's Party (PPP), which had a vaguely socialist agenda.

Bhutto exploited popular sentiment against the Tashkent Agreement as students rioted in a number of major cities. Two conservative religious parties, the Nizam-i-Islam and the Muslim League Council, that were hostile to the Ayub regime, had encouraged and prodded the students to protest the terms of the Tashkent Agreement.[8] In marked contrast to the behaviour of these parties, the Awami League, based in East Pakistan, and the pro-Soviet National Awami Party, also with a mostly East Pakistani political constituency, refrained from criticizing the agreement. These two parties did not harbour the same passion about the Kashmir issue as did their West Pakistani compatriots, and they also realized that East Pakistan had escaped largely unscathed primarily due to Indian sufferance and not because the eastern wing of the country had been resolutely defended during the war.[9]

Between 1965 and 1968 Ayub faced a string of challenges to his power and authority. Apart from mounting popular protests against his regime, even trusted members of the ruling circle broke away from him. Dr Mahbubul Haq, for example, the principal economist on Ayub's Planning Commission, resigned in April 1968 and then began publicly to raise serious questions about the economic development strategy that he had presided over while on the Planning Commission. He contended that although the strategy had contributed to growth it had also deepened economic inequities in Pakistan. The opposition parties, of course, used this damning disclosure to roundly attack the already faltering regime.[10]

As challenges to his rule became more widespread, Ayub made some last-minute attempts at political conciliation. For one thing, he released the widely popular East Pakistani politician, Sheikh Mujibur Rehman, from custody. Sheikh Mujib, as he was popularly known, was the leader of the Awami League, a party that commanded considerable political support in East Pakistan. The military regime had incarcerated Mujib in 1966 because of his putative involvement in the so-called Agartala Conspiracy Case. The government charged that Mujib, along with three junior Bengali civil servants and twenty-four junior officials, had met with Indian officials in the north-eastern Indian town of Agartala, the capital of the state of Tripura, to plot the secession of East Pakistan.[11]

In a last-ditch effort to reach political accommodation, Ayub convened a round-table conference in early 1969. Though Ayub and the conferees agreed on the need to end military rule and resurrect parliamentary democracy, they reached a deadlock over the implementation of a set of demands that had been promulgated by Mujib for several years. The measures embedded in this so-called Six-

Point Programme were widely popular in East Pakistan. In essence, it called for the creation of a polity that would be based on parliamentary democracy with universal adult franchise, limiting the powers of the federal government to the areas of defence and foreign policy, providing for mutually convertible but separate currencies for the two wings of the country, ensuring provincial control over fiscal policies, guaranteeing regional control over foreign-exchange earnings, and extending the right of federal units to maintain paramilitary forces for the purposes of guaranteeing national security.[12]

In the wake of the failure of the round-table conference, violence erupted again. As popular discontent mounted against his regime, Ayub was overthrown in a military coup on March 26, 1969.[13] Gen. Agha Muhammad Yahya Khan, the chief of army staff, took over as the president of Pakistan and the chief martial law administrator, thereby, contravening the terms of the 1962 Constitution. According to constitutional precepts, power should have been devolved to the speaker of the National Assembly in the event of the president's resignation.

Yahya, like Ayub, passed a flurry of administrative *diktats* designed to address a number of endemic problems. These ordinances promised stiff penalties for corruption, inefficiency, and subversive activities. Yahya also suspended the 'Fundamental Rights' embodied in the 1962 Constitution and placed the decisions of military courts beyond the scrutiny of civil courts.[14] Shortly after assuming power he also committed himself to holding free and fair elections in October 1970. In an attempt to assuage regional grievances about the political dominance of Punjabis, Yahya agreed to dismantle the 'One Unit' scheme that had merged the provinces of Baluchistan, the Northwest Frontier, Punjab, and Sind. This move delighted the East Pakistanis, because it meant that their province would now occupy the majority of the seats in the National Assembly, reflecting East Pakistan's larger population base.

Finally, to create conducive conditions for holding an election, on January 1, 1970, Yahya passed Martial Law Regulation Number 60, which permitted the resumption of political activity. Another ordinance soon followed permitting public rallies for electoral purposes. Yahya simultaneously started negotiations with Mujib, Bhutto, and various other political leaders about the restoration of civilian and democratic rule. The task before him was complex. The Islamic right-wing parties in Pakistan, such as the Jamaat-i-Islami, the Jamaat-ul-Ulema-i-Islam, and the Jamaat-ul-Ulema-i-Pakistan, favoured strong, centralized government with an Islamic constitution. The non–Awami League parties in East Pakistan wanted greater autonomy but were disinclined to support Mujib's radical Six-Point Programme. Bhutto and the PPP made vague statements about their commitment to socialism and Islam. They also expressed reservations about Westminister-style democracy but did not clarify their views on issues of power-sharing between the two wings of Pakistan.[15]

After much discussion with the various parties Yahya issued the Legal Framework Order (LFO) on March 31, 1970. The LFO embodied five key principles designed to guide any political arrangements that emerged from the elections and the end of military rule: that the constitution of Pakistan would be based on the ideology of Islam, that the country would have a democratic constitution, that Pakistan's territorial integrity would be upheld, that statutory provisions in the new constitution would seek to end the disparities between the two wings of the state, and that new institutional arrangements would ensure that the various provinces of Pakistan could have the maximum possible autonomy without compromising the ability of the federal government to ensure the territorial integrity of the country.[16] One other feature of the LFO merits discussion. Yahya, like most military rulers, left himself a legal loophole in the event the outcome of the elections was not entirely to his liking. The LFO gave him, as president and chief martial law administrator, the right to dissolve the National Assembly if it drafted a constitution that was not to his satisfaction either in whole or in part. Much later, Bhutto commented on this feature of the LFO:

[The LFO] sought to retain the supremacy of Martial Law and at the same time provided, under this shadow, for a National Assembly to frame the country's Constitution by the people's representatives. The order also imposed a limit on the sovereignty of the National Assembly by giving the President the authority to refuse to authenticate the Constitution passed by the Assembly. Perhaps it was not appreciated at that time that it would not have been possible for an individual, no matter how great his power, to reject without democratic sanction the decision of the National Assembly.[17]

The Awami League and other political parties in East Pakistan were also unhappy with many of the strictures of the LFO. They, nevertheless, campaigned with considerable vigour. The Awami League, in particular, refused to abandon its Six-Point Programme and indeed made it a centerpiece of the election campaign. The regime, for its part, remained firm in the belief, based on flawed intelligence estimates, that the Awami League did not enjoy widespread popular support across East Pakistan. Its intelligence reports had led it to conclude that at best the League would win sixty to seventy seats and possibly as few as forty-six seats. In the words of a prominent Pakistani military historian, 'Their assessment of the results of the forthcoming election was, therefore, based upon wishful thinking and self-generated hopes.'[18]

The election had to be postponed from October to early December 1970 as a consequence of a flood in August and a devastating cyclone in November, both of which hit East Pakistan. These two disasters had brought considerable hardship for the population and had contributed to much social and economic dislocation. The disaster relief operations of the regime in Islamabad were inadequate for the task. Not surprisingly, the hostility toward the West that already pervaded East Pakistan hardened in the wake of these two natural calamities. An American official who was present in East Pakistan on the eve of the election described the failure of the central government to mitigate the consequences of these two cataclysms as 'a mandate from heaven' for the Awami League.[19]

The results of the elections were quite lopsided and utterly belied the roseate expectations of Yahya's regime. The Awami League won every seat that it contested in East Pakistan, ending up with 160 of a possible 162 East Pakistani seats in parliament. In the West, Bhutto's PPP also fared well, winning 88 out of a possible 138 seats. The electoral outcomes placed the military regime and Bhutto in a quandary. They now had to countenance the prospect of genuine power-sharing with their East Pakistani counterparts. As early as December 20, in defiance of the results, Bhutto in a public speech made clear his party's unwillingness to occupy the opposition benches for the next five years. In the same speech, he categorically stated that no constitution could be framed nor a government formed at the national level without the consent of the PPP.[20]

Bhutto's intransigence only hardened Mujib's position. In a fateful speech on January 3, 1971, before a massive crowd of supporters at the Race Course in Dacca (Dhaka), Mujib declared that the new constitution of Pakistan had to be framed on the basis of his Six-Point Programme. In Yahya's view, Mujib's declaration was tantamount to sedition.[21] Nevertheless, he went to Dacca in mid-January to meet Mujib and other members of the Awami League. During this meeting Mujib categorically told Yahya that unless the National Assembly was convened with dispatch the electorate of East Pakistan would develop serious doubts about the willingness of the central government to honour the results of the election. According to one source, he even told Yahya that 'dire consequences' might ensue from the postponement of the convening of the National Assembly.[22]

In the interim, Yahya visited Bhutto at his family estate in Larkana, Sind. There, Bhutto reinforced the misgivings of the army about Mujib and the Awami League. More to the point, he emphasized that the degree of autonomy that Mujib was seeking for the East would amount to virtual secession.

Yahya's willingness to travel to Bhutto's estate raised further doubts in the minds of the Bengali leadership about the president's impartiality.[23] Not surprisingly, when Bhutto and a delegation from the PPP visited Dacca on January 27, Mujib proved to be utterly unmovable on the matter of the Six-Point Programme. Also at this meeting, Mujib pressed the military governor of East Pakistan, Adm. Syed Muhammad Ahsan, for an early seating of the National Assembly. Faced with this substantial pressure from Mujib, on February 13 Yahya announced that the National Assembly would be convened in Dacca on March 3, 1971.

Bhutto, however, remained utterly unreconciled to sharing power with the Awami League on the basis of Mujib's programme. He appeared willing to concede to some of the demands but would not accept them as a whole. He also asserted that he would not attend the first meeting of the National Assembly if it were convened on March 3, 1971. In an attempt to bolster his own bargaining position, Bhutto sought to develop a common West Pakistani opposition to the Six-Point Programme. His efforts, however, proved largely unsuccessful.[24]

In deference to Bhutto's demands, Yahya decided to hold a meeting of his key advisers on February 22. Despite the advice of some of his closest aides, on February 23 he made up his mind to postpone the meeting of the National Assembly once again unless Mujib showed some willingness to concede to his key demands. At the February 22 meeting, he also seriously discussed the prospect of re-imposing martial law in an attempt to intimidate the Awami League into submission. Several of his advisers forthrightly argued against the imposition of martial law. In the end, he instructed Adm. Ahsan, Gen. Rao Farman Ali, and Gen. Sahibzada Yakub Khan to meet Mujib on February 28 to inform him of the decision to postpone the seating of the National Assembly.[25]

Mujib, not surprisingly, was appalled at this decision and warned that he might lose control over the more zealous and radical members of his party. On March 2, Yahya, in a broadcast over Radio Pakistan, spelled out his rationale for postponing the seating of the National Assembly. Predictably, apart from alluding to Bhutto's concerns, he blamed India for the delay:

The position briefly is that the major party of West Pakistan, namely the Pakistan People's Party, as well as certain other political parties, have declared their intention not to attend the National Assembly session on the third of March 1971. In addition, the general situation of tension created by India has further complicated the whole position.[26]

In the aftermath of the postponement of the National Assembly's initial session, the pace of events in East Pakistan took on an increasingly rapid tempo. On March 4, Mujib called for a general strike across East Pakistan. The response to his call was overwhelming: it paralyzed the economy of the East. Mujib had started, what he described as, a 'non-violent, non-cooperation' movement, but this movement quickly became violent and, according to one observer, 'between March 3 and March 25, the central Government's writ did not run in East Pakistan.'[27] The Pakistani military responded to the agitation with characteristic harshness, resorting to indiscriminate firing in some areas. The stage was being quickly set for a full-scale confrontation between the Awami League supporters and the Pakistani military junta. The intransigence of Bhutto and his tacit support from key segments of the Pakistani military leadership had set the Pakistani state on the path of civil war.

The Failure of the Dacca Dialogue

Yahya made a final trip to Dacca on March 15, 1971. The atmosphere at the time of this meeting was miasmic. Mujib had made a series of public statements indicating that his patience was at an end. He had also started to make public statements that suggested secession was now a possibility. Some of Yahya's more astute generals, most notably Rao Farman Ali, had already warned him about the futility of a military solution to the problem.

The negotiations between Mujib and Yahya started on March 16. The initial discussions proved somewhat hopeful despite the milieu of distrust. Yahya, among other matters, promised to look into the matter of police shootings and agreed that the army should return to the barracks as long as civil order was not disturbed. The two sides also agreed that martial law should be lifted, that two committees should be created, one for each of the two wings of Pakistan, to draft provisions for a new constitution, that Yahya should continue as president while the committees met, and that a constitution should be drafted in the National Assembly after the two regional committees had completed their preparatory work.[28]

The initial progress slackened once Bhutto was persuaded to join the talks. Bhutto's presence and his unwillingness to cooperate with the Awami League drove the talks rapidly toward deadlock. Much of the contention between the three parties centred on the specific terms of a federal bargain between the two wings of Pakistan and the need for (or the lack of) two separate constitutional committees. The final meeting was held on March 24 and concluded without a resolution. Faced with this impasse, Yahya gave orders to Gen. Tikka Khan and Gen. Rao Farman Ali to undertake military action to restore order and central authority in East Pakistan.[29] The stage was now set for the military crackdown.

The Tragedy of 'Operation Searchlight'

The military operation launched on the night of March 25 was known as 'Operation Searchlight.' Focused on the Bengali population of Dacca and its environs, its purpose was to decimate the likely sources of political opposition to the military regime in West Pakistan.[30] The brutality and scale of this military operation against a civilian population was unparalleled in the history of South Asia. For example, the army killed substantial members of defenceless students on the campus of Dacca University, which was perceived to be a hotbed of resistance to the military regime.

At the time of the military crackdown, the total troop strength of the Pakistani army in the East was four infantry brigades. There were also six field artillery regiments, several independent field and heavy-mortar batteries, and some light anti-aircraft artillery. In addition, one regiment of American Chaffee tanks and one independent squadron of Chaffee and Russian PT-76 tanks were based there. The Pakistani air force's eastern wing was composed of some twenty-five Sabre jet fighters and some transport aircraft and helicopters.[31] Out of these five were East Bengal battalions staffed mostly by Bengali officers. The East Pakistan Rifles supplemented these forces. Prior to the onset of Operation Searchlight, the West Pakistani military leadership had ensured that these Bengali-staffed forces were suitably dispersed throughout East Pakistan to lessen the prospects of concerted resistance.[32]

On the external front, the Pakistanis had concentrated much of their firepower near India's most vulnerable areas, especially near the 'chicken's neck' of the Siliguri corridor in Bengal and in the area where the Indian state of Tripura abutted Burma. Most of the Pakistani armoured forces were concentrated in a bulge between the towns of Hilli and Gaibunda near the then independent principality of Sikkim.[33] At the narrowest point in this sector, the Pakistani forces were a mere 32 kilometres from the deployments of the Chinese People's Liberation Army at the strategic Nathu Pass. The Pakistani infantry was concentrated to produce a pattern of 'strongpoint' defences. Accordingly, they were garrisoned at Sylhet, Mymensingh, Akhaura, Comilla, Maynamati, and Laksham. From many of these garrisons Pakistan could strike at highly vulnerable areas of the Indian state of Assam.[34]

The Drift toward War

Shortly after the crackdown, thousands of refugees fled from East Pakistan into India. By mid-May the number of refugees in India had grown to an estimated ten million. The presence of the refugees in West Bengal and in other northeastern Indian states was both an economic and a political onus for the government in New Delhi. India, a poor country, already sandbagged with a turgid population, could not afford to permanently absorb another ten million disadvantaged individuals. Furthermore, the long-term presence of the refugees would pose an equally serious political problem: the refugees, most of whom were Muslims, would change the demographic composition of key border states and thereby heighten the prospect of communal discord. Many of these near-destitute individuals were also potential prey for the radical communist and ethnic separatist groups that were active in India's northeastern states.

In addition to posing this political and economic problem, the refugee situation also provided India with an important opportunity. If a political solution could not be forged in East Pakistan, the eventual return of the refugees would be unlikely. Under these circumstances, India would be within its rights to use force to change the political dispensation in East Pakistan. A former Indian foreign secretary and one-time ambassador to Pakistan, J.N. Dixit, has summarized India's calculations for intervening in the crisis in East Pakistan with considerable candour:

The two wings of Pakistan with an intervening stretch of a thousand miles of the Indian Republic was a geographical and political incongruity. India was also getting a little tired of having to confront and possibly fight Pakistan on two fronts whenever a conflict situation arose, specially so when the eastern front would strategically attract a China-Pakistan nexus. So if the people of East Pakistan, because of their socio-ethnic and linguistic considerations and in the face of the obstinate negation of their aspirations, wished secession from Pakistan and independence, India had no objection. If Indian endorsement and support resulted in this new entity being friendly to India, it was all to the good. A non-hostile Bangladesh instead of a hostile East Pakistan was considered desirable. Given the encouragement being offered off and on to the centrifugal forces in India's north-eastern states from East Pakistani bases, it was natural for India to support the liberation movement, which, in addition, had powerful humanistic rationale in the context of Pakistan's denial of democratic rights to the Bengalis and their military crackdown.[35]

Indian Decision-Making

The developments in East Pakistan had an immediate impact on India because of the refugee influx. The initial Indian response, though sharp, was circumspect.[36] The leadership in New Delhi wanted to avoid the impression that it was ready to promptly provide support to the Bengali resistance in East Pakistan.[37] This caution, however, did not last long: in mid-April India allowed the establishment of an Awami League office near Calcutta and, on April 17, permitted the announcement of a 'government in exile' from Baidyanath Tala, popularly referred to as 'Mujibnagar.'[38] By April 18, the Pakistani deputy high commission in Park Circus, Calcutta was taken over by a Bengali defector, and from that point on, it served as the de facto mission of Bangladesh to India. A number of prominent Awami League officials, including Tajuddin Ahmed, Nazrul Islam, Mansur Ali, and Col. M.A.G. Osmani, also took refuge in Calcutta. They were all comfortably housed in a government-owned property on Shakespeare Sarani, a prominent Calcutta thoroughfare.

Once the political leadership was safely ensconced in Calcutta, India started to arm, train, and provide sanctuaries to the 'Mukti Bahini' (literally, 'liberation force'), a Bengali guerilla force, along the border areas. The Mukti Bahini was composed of students, civil servants, and former members of the East Pakistan Rifles (EPR). They were placed under the command of Col. Osmani, a retired East Pakistani army officer. During the conduct of the military operations in East Pakistan, the Mukti Bahini played a vital role in harrying the Pakistani forces, engaging in acts of espionage and sabotage, and killing collaborators.[39]

On the Verge of Intervention

Long before India could actively contemplate war against Pakistan, a number of key political and military considerations had to be taken into account. The reasons for such circumspection were both political and strategic. India had been caught somewhat flat-footed by the turn of events in East Pakistan. Consequently, it had to take stock of the emerging situation before it formulated an appropriate response. Although many in the political opposition quite predictably criticized the government for its putatively weak response, several prominent political figures and former military officers counselled restraint. They feared that supporting a secessionist movement in East Pakistan could come back to haunt India, which faced a number of such demands on its own soil. Others in the Indian foreign policy bureaucracy feared the possible adverse repercussions that such an intervention might have on India's delicate relations with the Muslim Arab world.[40]

Furthermore, as early as late March of 1971, the Political Affairs Committee (PAC) of India's Union Cabinet had met with the three Indian military chiefs of staff to discuss a possible military response to the crisis. During this meeting the service chiefs had categorically stated that a number of organizational and logistical hurdles had to be overcome before any military action in East Pakistan could be seriously contemplated, let alone undertaken. The chief of army staff, Gen. S.H.F.J. Manekshaw, in particular, emphasized that at least two divisions of the Indian army were deployed in 'aid to the civil' responsibilities in the disturbed state of West Bengal. Another two divisions were tied down in counter-insurgency operations against the Mizo and Naga rebels in India's troubled northeast. The air force chief also indicated that there were far too few air bases in the eastern sector from which significant strikes could be made into East Pakistan. Finally, all the service chiefs underscored the deltaic topography of the region, which would force the Indians to wait at least until October, when the monsoon rains would end, to commence any large-scale military action.[41]

Shortly after this meeting, K. Subrahmanyam, a senior civil servant with long experience in defence issues and the director of an influential, government-funded think tank in New Delhi, the Institute of Defence Studies and Analyses, made a spirited strategic and political argument for Indian military intervention in East Pakistan. At a seminar titled 'Bangladesh and India's National Security,' held under the auspices of the Indian Council of World Affairs on March 31, 1971, in New Delhi, Subrahmanyam forcefully argued in favour of Indian intervention. His argument was three-pronged. First, he contended that the costs of absorbing the refugees would far exceed the costs of a war with Pakistan. Second, he held that since China had no direct stake in the conflict, Beijing was unlikely to intervene. Third, he felt that a policy of inaction would simply encourage the military regime in Pakistan to act with impunity against its minority citizens and push them into India.[42] Even though the contents of the seminar were meant to be off the record, they were quickly made public.[43]

Subrahmanyam's views slowly but surely came to prevail in the key decision-making circles in New Delhi. Nonetheless, the government felt compelled to at least appear to have exhausted all diplomatic options before resorting to military intervention. Additionally, it had to contend with the very practical matter of building up its forces before attempting a large scale military venture against a long-standing adversary.

In an attempt to demonstrate India's willingness to seek a political solution to the crisis in East Pakistan and along its borders, Prime Minister Indira Gandhi organized a major diplomatic effort, dispatching her minister for external affairs, Sardar Swaran Singh, on a tour of a number of foreign cities, including Moscow, Bonn, Paris, London, Ottawa, and Washington, D.C. Singh's brief was to apprise the key states in the global community of the burden that India faced as a consequence of the refugee crisis. Simultaneously, he sought to mobilize international public opinion to pressure Pakistan to create conditions conducive to their return. India's efforts were not entirely in vain. On June 21, 1971, the Aid Pakistan Consortium voted to cut off multilateral economic assistance to Pakistan until a modicum of political stability returned to the East. Within a month thereafter, the US House Foreign Affairs Committee also voted to cut off all American bilateral assistance to Pakistan.[44]

Other developments during this period were far less propitious for India. Among other matters, and quite coincidentally, President Richard Nixon's national security adviser, Henry Kissinger, had embarked on his strategy to establish full-fledged diplomatic relations with the People's Republic of China.[45] Pakistan had played a critical role in Kissinger's effort: key Pakistani decision-makers had arranged for Kissinger to travel to Islamabad in July 1971 and then, under the pretext of illness, to secretly fly to Beijing for negotiations.[46]

Pakistan's historic ties with the United States had previously come under some strain under Prime Minister Bhutto, especially because of his professed socialist inclinations and his overtures toward China. Now, however, as Pakistan's ties with China proved most useful to the Nixon administration, the United States viewed Pakistan in an entirely new light. Additionally, Nixon also had a personal animus toward Indira Gandhi, whom he found both cold and distant. Consequently, as the political situation in the subcontinent continued to deteriorate, the Nixon administration adopted a markedly pro-Pakistani stance.[47]

Nevertheless, before his clandestine trip to China, Kissinger did stop in New Delhi to meet Foreign Secretary T.N. Kaul. During their meeting, Kissinger reportedly assured Kaul that improvements in Sino-American relations would not come at a cost to the Indo-American relationship, nor would the United States tolerate any Chinese malfeasance toward India.[48]

These assurances, however, proved less than enduring. Shortly after his visit to Beijing, Kissinger told L.K. Jha, the Indian ambassador to the United States, that it was his understanding that the Chinese would intervene on Pakistan's behalf should India decide to attack Pakistan. More to the point, he said that India could not count on American assistance in such an eventuality.[49] Faced with this shift in the American position, the Indians promptly moved to improve relations with China. To this end, D.P. Dhar, the chairman of the Policy Planning Group in the Indian Ministry of External Affairs, held secret talks with the Chinese ambassador in Moscow toward the end of July.[50] These talks, however, got him nowhere. It did not take the Indian leadership long to realize that they had to protect the nation's northern borders from a possible Chinese incursion in the event a war with Pakistan became unavoidable.

The emergent Sino-American rapprochement and the important change in America's willingness to aid India in the event of a Chinese attack led Indian decision-makers to turn to the Soviet Union. Moscow, also wary of the new Sino-American nexus, found it useful to forge a new relationship with India. Consequently, on August 9, 1971, while Andrei Gromyko, the Soviet foreign minister, was on a state visit to New Delhi, India and the Soviet Union signed their 'Treaty of Peace, Friendship, and Cooperation,'[51] a twenty-year-long arrangement. One of the key clauses in the treaty, embodied in Article 9, made clear that attack on either party would automatically lead to joint consultations to remove the threat.[52] Most importantly, this treaty granted India the support of a veto-wielding superpower in the UN Security Council in the event of a possible motion to censure its actions against Pakistan. It is also believed that the Soviet ambassador to India assured New Delhi that in the event of a Chinese attack on India, the Soviets would exert military pressure on the Chinese in Xinjiang province.[53]

Despite the reassurance that was embedded in the treaty against possible international pressures on India either from the United States in the Security Council or from China along India's borders, the Soviets continued to behave in a most circumspect fashion in dealing with the crisis in East Pakistan. In large part, this caution stemmed from Moscow's desire not to undermine the process of détente with the United States.[54] The Indian leadership nevertheless kept up its pressure on the Soviet Union to more fully embrace the Indian assessment of the crisis in the subcontinent. Indira Gandhi visited Moscow in late September 1971 and met General Secretary Leonid Brezhnev, Supreme Soviet Chairman Nikolai Podgorny, and Council of Ministers Chairman Alexei Kosygin. The Soviets still failed to fully endorse India's position during this visit. This was apparent from the scrupulous language of the joint communique issued at the end of Indira Gandhi's visit, which primarily alluded to the refugee burden that India now had to shoulder but did not upbraid Pakistan for the actions that had contributed to the crisis in the first place.[55]

To make India's case before the major Western powers Indira Gandhi decided to undertake a whirlwind tour of their capitals in October. While in the United States, she persuaded the Nixon administration to stop the transfer of any further weaponry to Pakistan.[56] Just prior to this visit she no doubt drew some comfort from a perceptible shift in the Soviet position on the crisis. Soviet Deputy Foreign Minister Nikolai Firiubin, when he visited New Delhi for consultations under the aegis of the recently signed treaty, made clear to her that the Soviets shared the Indian position on the unfolding crisis in East Pakistan.[57]

The Pakistan-China Link

While Indira Gandhi was visiting the capitals of the Western world, Zulfiquar Ali Bhutto led a high-level military delegation to China. The delegation included, among others, Air Marshal Rahim Khan, the chief of the Pakistani air force; Lt.-Gen. Gul Hasan, the army chief of staff; and Adm. Rashid Khan, the navy chief of staff. This visit was no doubt designed to elicit some support from China as the crisis significantly worsened. Whatever comfort the Pakistanis may have hoped to find in Beijing, it was less than forthcoming. The Chinese proved willing to assist Pakistan in the most general fashion but would not incur any material costs or risks. The Chinese foreign minister, Chi P'eng-fei, stated during the visit,

Our Pakistan [sic] friends may rest assured that should Pakistan be subjected to foreign aggression, the Chinese Government and people will always resolutely support the Pakistan Government and people in their just struggle to defend their state sovereignty and national independence.[58]

Privately, it is believed that Chi told his Pakistani interlocutors that they should find a 'national' solution to the crisis in the subcontinent.[59] The Chinese had no doubt decided that it was not in their interest to become embroiled in this subcontinental crisis, especially in light of the new Indo-Soviet nexus. Pakistani analysts acknowledge that the fear of antagonizing the Soviet Union led China to limit its support for Pakistan's position to verbal exhortations and little else.[60] Yet Pakistani officials, especially President Yahya Khan, believed that the Chinese would come to Pakistan's assistance because of his 'grand role' in acting as an interlocutor between the United States and China.[61] Unfortunately, the structure of political decision-making in Pakistan precluded others from informing him that neither the Chinese nor the Americans would act to materially alter the balance of military forces on the subcontinent. False optimism had again taken its toll.

On the other hand, New Delhi quite correctly assessed that the Chinese support for Pakistan was mostly in the verbal realm and that little material assistance would be forthcoming.[62] Now India had somewhat greater latitude to pursue military action in East Pakistan when the moment was propitious. More to the point, India had exhausted most diplomatic efforts to secure the release of Sheikh Mujibur Rehman and enable the return of the substantial refugee population; its justification for resorting to force was growing ever stronger.

The Onset of War

By late October India had started to exert steady military pressure on Pakistan. On November 22, Indian forces along the border areas of East Pakistan had started to provide artillery fire to protect the Mukti Bahini forces as they conducted operations within East Pakistan and then sought refuge in Indian territory. The Pakistani military regime found this form of sustained Indian involvement increasingly intolerable; it felt compelled to act.

The war formally started with an Israeli-style pre-emptive air attack by Pakistan on India's northern air bases on December 3, 1971. The attack failed miserably on all counts. The Indian Air Force (IAF), which had anticipated such an attack, had removed its aircraft from open locations and had placed them in specially reinforced concrete bunkers. The IAF retaliated the next day, striking a number of West Pakistani air bases, including those at Islamabad, Sargodha, and Karachi.[63] At the same time the Indians carried out a naval bombardment of Karachi, Pakistan's most important port. The attack on Karachi had two goals: to destroy vital oil installations at the port and to blockade the harbour for the entire course of the war. Both objectives were fully achieved in this coordinated land-air action.

In the eastern sector, the IAF's operations were even more successful. Close to half of the Pakistani air force's aircraft were destroyed on the ground or in air combat. Other aircraft were put out of commission because the IAF pockmarked most of the key airfields using MiG-21 aircraft and thousand-pound bombs.[64]

The Indian navy also played a substantial role in the war. In additional to attacking Karachi with Soviet-built Osa-class missile boats in early December, the navy attacked oil storage facilities at Jewani and Gawadar on the Makran coast near the Iranian border.[65] By mid-December the navy had succeeded in establishing a virtual naval blockade between the two wings of Pakistan.[66]

The American scholar John Mearsheimer has characterized the Indian military strategy in the eastern sector as a 'blitzkreig.'[67] This involved making a sharp, quick set of incursions using mechanized armour. These thrusts would bypass the enemy's 'strongpoint' defences and seize as much territory as possible in the initial onslaught. Subsequently, reserve Indian forces would surround these beleaguered garrisons and induce their surrender.

The Indian land forces that struck in the east were drawn primarily from the army's Eastern Command. The force was composed of six divisions, including the 8th, 23rd, and 57th army divisions, supported by bridge-building platoons and eight infantry battalions of the Mukti Bahini. The Indian forces were primarily under the operational command of Lt. Gen. Sagat Singh. This incursion was directed against the headquarters of the Pakistani 14th Division, located near Ashuganj, and the 39th Division, at Chandpur. As these land attacks took place against the Pakistani forces, the IAF quickly destroyed the small Pakistani Air Force (PAF) contingent in East Pakistan and put the Dacca airfield out of commission.

By December 6, 1971, the Indian forces, in concert with the Mukti Bahini, succeeded in establishing two possible avenues for a final assault on Dacca: from the east across the Meghna River, and from the north out of the Indian state of Meghalaya. Initially, the Indian forces were stopped at the Meghna, as all the bridges had been blown up. However, they managed to make an unopposed crossing through the use of local river craft and helicopters. By December 8, these forces had managed to reach the outskirts of Dacca. The forces from the north, however, had already reached Dacca, having bypassed a Pakistani infantry brigade that was supported by a squadron of tanks. On December 11, Indian paratroop units reinforced the advancing formations and, on December 12, in a fierce battle, they defeated the Pakistani brigade that they had by passed earlier. By December 13 the Indian forces regrouped and prepared for a final assault on Dacca on December 16.

On December 15, Gen. A.A.K. Niazi, the commander of the Pakistani forces in the eastern sector, had sought a conditional cease-fire. His Indian counterpart, Lt. Gen. Jagjit Singh Aurora, the commanding officer for the Eastern Command, had rebuffed this offer. By December 16, the Pakistani forces were routed and the Indian army entered Dacca. On December 17, Prime Minister Indira Gandhi ordered a unilateral cease-fire that was to go into effect that evening at 8 p.m. The same day, President Yahya Khan ordered the Pakistani forces to reciprocate, thereby bringing the war to a close.[68]

In the middle of the war, the Nixon administration, in a half-hearted attempt to demonstrate its reliability to Yahya and his regime, sent a naval task force, led by the U.S.S. *Enterprise* and carrying some 2,000 marines from its station off the coast of Vietnam, toward the Bay of Bengal.[69] Ostensibly, this task force was sent in to rescue American civilians trapped in Dacca. In the event, by the time that the task force reached the outer waters of the bay, the war was over.

Henry Kissinger later claimed that he and President Nixon had sent in the task force to prevent India from dismembering West Pakistan.[70] Yet no evidence exists that any Indian decision-maker even contemplated a further vivisection of Pakistan. Kissinger's propensity to see every regional conflict through the prism of superpower conflict led him to believe that India was acting as an agent of the Soviet Union.[71] This explains his false conclusion that there was a Soviet-Indian design to dismember Pakistan, an American ally.

The Aftermath of the War and the Simla Accord

After the war, Prime Minister Indira Gandhi of India and President Zulfiquar Ali Bhutto met in the former British colonial summer capital of Simla to reach a post-war settlement.[72] Only a handful of details, some of which are contradictory, have emerged about the negotiations at Simla. Prior to the leaders' meeting, preparatory talks were held at the Pakistani hill station of Murree. The final negotiations took place at Simla between June 28 and July 2, 1972.

The Indian delegation included the foreign secretary, T.N. Kaul, and P.N. Haksar, a senior Indian Administrative Service (IAS) officer who was a trusted aide to Indira Gandhi and served as a key official in the Prime Minister's Office. Initially included in the Indian delegation was D.P. Dhar, another aide in the Prime Minister's Office with close ties to Mrs Gandhi, but Dhar dropped out prior to the start of the Simla negotiations owing to ill health. Representing the Ministry of External Affairs was Ashok Chib, a joint secretary. Bhutto's principal negotiator was Aziz Ahmed, a senior Pakistani civil servant and the secretary-general of Pakistan's Ministry of Foreign Affairs. Ahmed was assisted by Rafi Raza, a Pakistani barrister and a special assistant to Bhutto. The final member of the Pakistani team was another Pakistani foreign service officer, Abdul Sattar, who subsequently became foreign secretary (and would, three decades later, be appointed foreign minister under the military dictatorship of Gen. Pervez Musharraf).

India had a number of key objectives at this meeting. Principal among them were the Pakistani acceptance of bilateral negotiations as the sole mechanism for resolving outstanding disputes with India, the normalization of diplomatic relations between the two countries, the repatriation of all prisoners of war, and Pakistani acceptance of the inviolability of all existing frontiers with India.[73] The last objective, in effect, would have settled the Kashmir dispute along the 1948 cease-fire line, possibly with minor modifications.

Pakistan had four major objectives and, thanks to some skilled diplomacy, achieved them in large measure. These objectives were to secure a release of the 93,000 Pakistani prisoners of war, to prevent Bangladesh from holding a war crimes trial against captured Pakistani officers and other ranks, to retrieve the 5,000 square miles of territory that it had lost to India in the western sector, and to ensure that its long-standing position on the Kashmir dispute was not fundamentally altered.[74]

The accord that was reached had a number of salient features. All prisoners of war were repatriated, most of them Pakistani. The two sides agreed to restore diplomatic relations and reiterated their commitment to abjure from the use of force in settling the Kashmir dispute.[75] They also changed the nomenclature for the 1948 cease-fire line in Kashmir, which had been reaffirmed in 1971, to the Line of Control (LoC).

There is a widespread belief in Indian political and diplomatic circles that Prime Minister Indira Gandhi and President Bhutto reached an informal agreement at Simla to divide Kashmir along the LoC. Bhutto, it is claimed, contended that, as the leader of a defeated nation, he could ill afford to make such a drastic concession. In effect, he held that making such a concession would be tantamount to political suicide.[76] However, according to Indian interlocutors, he did agree that when conditions were more conducive to such a settlement he would be willing to take the necessary step to transform the LoC into a *de jure* international border. It is also claimed that in pursuit of this end, Bhutto agreed to take steps to integrate into Pakistan those areas of Kashmir that Pakistan controlled and other related territories within the federal jurisdiction of Pakistan. While Bhutto did thereafter detach the Northern Areas of the old princely state of Jammu and Kashmir and integrate them into the federal territories of Pakistan, he did not accomplish much else along these lines, as he became embroiled in a domestic controversy after about the middle of 1976.[77]

Pakistani interlocutors deny that any such informal agreement was reached at the Simla conference.[78] On the contrary, they insist that Pakistan had to negotiate the treaty under considerable duress but did not even agree to any territorial concessions whatsoever.

Conclusions

In the wake of the 1971 war India emerged as the dominant power on the subcontinent. At an ideological level, Pakistan's claim to Kashmir was effectively demolished. For even at the peak of the Bangladesh crisis, the Muslim population of Kashmir showed scant interest in undermining India's war making efforts in the western sector. Had they chosen to wreak havoc within Kashmir, India's ability to conduct military operations from the state along the western front would have been severely hobbled. If, as Pakistani propaganda had long claimed, the Kashmiri Muslims were entirely disaffected from India, why then did they fail to promptly rally to Pakistan's cause?

Furthermore, and more importantly, the secessionist movement in Bangladesh demonstrated that adherence to a common faith—Islam— could not be the sole basis of state-building in South Asia. Other facets of ethnic identity, especially language, exerted as much if not greater power as a foundation for state-building. Pakistani apologists, however, continued to propagate the view that Muhammed Ali Jinnah's 'two-nation theory,' propounding that the Muslims and Hindus of South Asia constituted two distinct, primordial nations, had not been discredited. Even though now three sovereign states existed on the subcontinent, supporters of Jinnah's theory argued that the states of Pakistan and Bangladesh were nevertheless Muslim-majority states, thereby vindicating the principle embodied in the original Pakistan resolution of 1940.[79]

At a strategic level, the Indian political leadership demonstrated that, like Pakistan in 1965, it was loath to pass up a vital window of opportunity.[80] Internal developments within Pakistan caused a refugee crisis for India, which posed for New Delhi both a threat and an opportunity. In addition to presenting a severe economic burden, the presence of the refugees threatened political stability amid scarce employment, housing, and educational opportunities, and could have strengthened the neophyte Marxist guerillas in India's northeast. But the refugees also posed an opportunity for India to create an international political question centred on their return that India could then use to effect the dismemberment of Pakistan.

The 1971 war also had profound psychological implications for the Indian polity. Even though the Indian armed forces had performed creditably in the 1965 war with Pakistan, the outcome of that war had been far from decisive. After the 1971 war Indians were able to discard the sense of humiliation that had so haunted them after the disastrous Sino-Indian border war of 1962.[81]

After the 1971 war, Bhutto turned Pakistan away from a preoccupation with India and Kashmir, seeking instead to focus his attention on improving relations with the Arab Muslim world. India's overwhelming conventional military superiority over Pakistan and its demonstrated military prowess made any further military ventures by Pakistan against India untenable. Yet the Pakistani military establishment proved fundamentally unable to come to terms with its own flawed strategic assessments, its acute complicity in the misrule of the country, and its poor battlefield performance against India. The military continued to blame external forces and factors and individual political leaders for their own limitations. The analysis of a prominent Pakistani general of the military regime's colossal errors of judgment in East Pakistan reveals this persistent inability to confront reality:

In the final analysis, Pakistan's internal mismanagement, the treachery of Sheikh Mujibur Rehman, the over-ambitiousness of Mr Bhutto, and the inept leadership of General Yahya Khan contributed to converting East Pakistan into Bangladesh, no less than the covert and overt aggression committed by India.[82]

Historical scholarship on the causes of the war is also deeply problematic, as the following excerpt shows:

The same Bengali Hindu was responsible for the backwardness of East Pakistan. But, hiding the story of his two-century sins, atrocities, and pillage, he used 'Bengali nationalism' to punish innocent West Pakistanis for sins they had not committed.[83]

The structural dimensions of Pakistan's deeply-flawed priorities, choices, and policies in contributing to the East Pakistan crisis and the emergence of Bangladesh are left unexamined in most Pakistani analyses. Instead, the collapse of the Pakistani polity is simply blamed on the professional laxity and flawed personalities of particular individuals— and, of course, Indian and, more specifically, 'Hindu' perfidy. This inability to confront the fundamental mistakes of policy formulation and policy choices continues to haunt Pakistani decision-making. The debility of most of Pakistan's institutions, with the obvious exception of the army, continues to undermine access to alternative views, an honest discussion of past errors, and a dispassionate analysis of historical epochs and political choices. Long after the war, particular regimes heaped scorn and blame on individual choices and acts rather than confronting the structural flaws that hobble the Pakistani polity.[84]

On the other side of the border, following the war, India continued to strengthen its relationship with the Soviet Union. The Soviets now came to see their relationship with India as a useful counterpoint to the emergent US-China nexus. Also, the international image of the Soviets was burnished by having a large, democratic, Third World state as a quasi-ally. From the Indian standpoint, the Soviet relationship served as a vital guarantee against possible Chinese misbehaviour.

The United States distanced itself from South Asia. Senator Daniel Patrick Moynihan, a former Harvard professor who became US ambassador to India after the 1971 war, aptly described American policy toward India as one of 'benign neglect.' Despite the lack of US interest in India, Indira Gandhi remained obsessed with supposed American machinations against her country. She magnified the significance of the sailing of the *U.S.S. Enterprise* into the Bay of Bengal during the 1971 crisis. On more than one occasion she suggested that the United States and the Central Intelligence Agency were intent on destabilizing India.[85]

The euphoria of India's decisive victory over Pakistan lasted for a considerable span of time. Between 1972 and 1983, various governments in New Delhi showed skill, tact, and intelligence in dealing with the internal dimensions of the Kashmir problem. From 1984 onward, however, they returned to the extraordinary clumsiness, thoughtlessness, and downright deceit that had characterized domestic policy toward Kashmir in the 1950s and 1960s. These highly uneven policies of accommodation and manipulation ultimately culminated in an ethno-religious insurgency in December 1989 that once again gave Pakistan a chance to pry Kashmir out of the Indian union. As the insurgency gathered strength in early 1990, some of the more astute and thoughtful Indian decision makers would privately question the sagacity of India's 1971 intervention in the internal politics of Pakistan.[86]

Notes

1. The most succinct early account of the circumstances surrounding the Pakistani civil war and the creation of Bangladesh is Robert Jackson, *South Asian Crisis: India-Pakistan-Bangladesh* (London: Chatto and Windus for the International Institute for Strategic Studies, 1975). Also see Herbert Feldman, *The End and the Beginning: Pakistan, 1969–1971* (Karachi: Oxford University Press, 1976). The classic study on this subject remains Rounaq Jahan, *Pakistan: Failure in National Integration* (New York: Columbia University Press, 1972).

2. The Government of Pakistan, shortly after the conclusion of the 1971 war, conducted its own internal analysis of the military debacle in East Pakistan. The commission that carried out the review was chaired by the former chief justice of East Pakistan, Hamoodur Rahman. His report, completed in October 1974 but kept secret for two and a half decades, deals at considerable length with the charges of atrocities committed by the West Pakistani military in East Pakistan. The full text of the 'Hamoodur Rahman Report' was made available by the magazine *India Today* (New Delhi) in September 2000. See http://www.news.india-today.com/ntoday/extra/71war/index.shtml

3. For the most comprehensive account of Indian decision-making see Richard Sisson and Leo E. Rose, *War and Secession: India, Pakistan, the United States, and the Creation of Bangladesh* (Berkeley: University of California Press, 1990).

4. It is pertinent to note that in the 1951 census Bengalis constituted some 56 per cent of the population of Pakistan. A useful discussion of language policy in Pakistan is found in Tariq Rahman, *Language and Politics in Pakistan* (Karachi: Oxford University Press, 1996).

5. S.L. Menezes, *Fidelity and Honor: The Indian Army from the Seventeenth to the Twenty-First Century* (New Delhi: Viking, 1993).

6. See Sisson and Rose, *War and Secession*.

7. Mohammed Ayub Khan, *Friends Not Masters: A Political Biography* (Oxford: Oxford University Press, 1967).

8. For a discussion of the politics of this period, see Lawrence Ziring, *Politics in Pakistan: The Ayub Khan Era* (Syracuse: Syracuse University Press, 1971).

9. Interview with US State Department official, Washington, D.C., July 1982.

10. Ian Talbott, *Pakistan: A Modern History* (New York: St. Martin's Press, 1994).

11. Sisson and Rose, *War and Secession*. Sisson and Rose argue that although Mujib and various of his supporters did have contacts with Indian intelligence officials, no 'conspiracy' for secession ever existed.

12. Sheikh Mujibur Rehman, *Bangladesh, My Bangladesh* (New Delhi: Orient Longman, 1972), pp. 129–148.

13. For the details surrounding the plotting of the coup against Ayub, see Hasan Zaheer, *The Separation of East Pakistan: The Rise and Realization of Bengali Muslim Nationalism* (Karachi: Oxford University Press, 1994).

14. Talbott, *Pakistan: A Modern History*.

15. For a discussion of the electoral posture of the various political parties see G. W. Choudhury, *The Last Days of United Pakistan* (Bloomington: Indiana University Press, 1974).

16. Choudhury, *Last Days*.

17. Zulfiquar Ali Bhutto, *The Great Tragedy* (Karachi: Vision Publications, 1971).

18. Fazal Muqueem Khan, *Pakistan's Crisis in Leadership* (Islamabad: Muqueem National Book Foundation, 1973).

19. Interview with a former US National Security Council official with responsibility for South Asia, May 1983, Washington, D.C.

20. Bhutto, as quoted in *The Pakistan Times*, December 21, 1970.

21. Zaheer, *Separation*.

22. Choudhury, *Last Days*.

23. Zaheer, *Separation*.

24. Sisson and Rose, *War and Secession*.

25. Zaheer, *Separation*.

26. Yahya Khan, as quoted in *The Pakistan Observer*, March 2, 1971.

27. Choudhury, *Last Days*, p. 158.

28. Sisson and Rose, *War and Secession*.

29. For the precise details of the negotiations, see Sisson and Rose, *War and Secession*.

30. The best journalistic account of Operation Searchlight can be found in Anthony Mascarhenas, *The Rape of Bangladesh* (Delhi: Vikas, 1971).

31. J.F.R. Jacob, *Surrender at Dacca: Birth of a Nation* (New Delhi: Manohar, 1997).

32. Jacob, *Surrender*.

33. In 1975 Sikkim chose to merge itself with India; it is now a state in the Indian Union.

34. Much of this discussion has been derived from Pran Chopra, *India's Second Liberation* (New Delhi: Vikas Publishing House, 1973).

35. J.N. Dixit, *Anatomy of a Flawed Inheritance* (New Delhi: Konark, 1995), pp. 23–24.

36. Sisson and Rose, *War and Secession*.

37. Sisson and Rose, *War and Secession*.

38. Jacob, *Surrender*.

39. For discussions of the role of the Mukti Bahini during the war, see Talukder Maniruzzaman, *The Bangladesh Revolution and Its Aftermath* (Dacca: Bangladesh Books International, 1980), and Jahan, *Pakistan*.

40. Sisson and Rose, *War and Secession*.

41. D.K. Palit, *The Lightning Campaign* (Salisbury, UK: Compton Press, 1972).

42. K. Subrahmanyam, *Bangladesh and India's Security* (Dehra Dun: Palit and Dutt, 1972), pp. 98–99.

43. Personal interview with K. Subrahmanyam, Bangkok, August 2000. Subrahmanyam was also reprimanded by the then defence secretary, K.B. Lall, for making these remarks.

44. Jackson, *South Asian Crisis*.

45. For a highly informed discussion of the politics surrounding Kissinger's gambit to establish diplomatic relations with China, see Walter Isaacson, *Kissinger: A Biography* (New York: Simon and Schuster, 1992).

46. A detailed account of this episode can be found in Dennis Kux, *Disenchanted Allies: The United States and Pakistan, 1945–2000* (Baltimore: Johns Hopkins University Press; and Washington, D.C.: Woodrow Wilson Center Press, 2001).

47. The tilt toward Pakistan during the 1971 crisis is best explored in Christopher Van Hollen, 'Geopolitics Misapplied: The Tilt Policy Revisited,' *Asian Survey*, Volume 20, Number 4, April 1980.

48. T. N. Kaul, *The Kissinger Years* (New Delhi: Arnold Heinemann, 1980), p. 48. Kissinger's memoirs confirm that he gave Kaul such an assurance. See Henry Kissinger, *The White House Years* (Boston: Little, Brown, and Company, 1979).

49. G.W. Choudhury, *India, Pakistan and the Major Powers* (New York: The Free Press, 1975)

50. Peter J.S. Duncan, *The Soviet Union and India* (New York: Council on Foreign Relations, 1989), p. 20. Also see Robert Horn, *Soviet-Indian Relations: Issues and Influence* (New York: Praeger, 1982).

51. Linda Racioppi, *Soviet Policy towards South Asia since 1970* (Cambridge: Cambridge University Press, 1994), p. 78; also see the discussion in Ramesh Thakur and Carlyle A. Thayer, *Soviet Relations with India and Vietnam, 1945–1992* (New Delhi: Oxford University Press, 1993).

52. The text of the Treaty of Peace, Friendship, and Cooperation between India and the Soviet Union can be found in the Appendix.

53. Jack Anderson, *The Anderson Papers* (New York: Random House, 1973).

54. Surjit Mansingh, *India's Search for Power: Indira Gandhi's Foreign Policy, 1966–1982* (New Delhi: Sage Publications, 1984).

55. Racioppi, *Soviet Policy.*

56. Her success was clearly limited. Some arms continued to trickle into Pakistan from the United States despite a formal congressional ban. Interview with senior State Department South Asia analyst, Washington, D.C., January 1983.

57. Racioppi, *Soviet Policy.*

58. Chi P'eng-fei, as quoted in K. Subrahmanyam and Mohammed Ayoob, *The Liberation War* (New Delhi: S. Chand and Company, 1972), p. 205. The inability of the Pakistani leadership under Gen. Yahya Khan to come to terms with its international isolation is made clear in the Hamoodur Commission Report, which states that, 'All the Governments friendly to Pakistan, especially Iran, *China* [emphasis added] and the USA, had made clear to Gen Yahya that they would not be in a position to render any physical assistance to Pakistan in the event of an armed conflict with India. However, the significance of this international situation was unfortunately completely lost on Gen Yahya Khan and his associates. They blundered ahead, oblivious of the fatal consequences of their international isolation.' International Aspect, paragraph 14, Justice Hamdoodur Commission Report as available at http://www.news.india-today.com/ntoday/extra/71war/index.shtml

59. Choudhury, *Last Days*, p. 219.

60. S.M. Burke and Lawrence Ziring, *Pakistan's Foreign Policy: An Historical Analysis* (Karachi: Oxford University Press, 1990), p. 404. For an alternative formulation by a Pakistani scholar see Hasan-Askari Rizvi, *Pakistan and the Geostrategic Environment: A Study of Foreign Policy* (New York: St. Martin's Press, 1993).

61. G.W. Choudhury, *India, Pakistan and the Great Powers* (New York: Free Press, 1975).

62. Gen. Manekshaw had nonetheless advised Prime Minister Indira Gandhi that he would not want to commence any military operations until the Himalayan passes became snowbound, in order to reduce the possibilities of Chinese mischief-making on India's northern borders.

63. Pran Chopra, *India's Second Liberation* (Delhi: Vikas Publications, 1973).

64. Chopra, *India's Second Liberation.*

65. S.N. Kohli, *We Dared: Maritime Operations in the 1971 Indo-Pak War* (New Delhi: Lancer International, 1989).

66. Ranjit Rai, *A Nation and Its Navy at War* (New Delhi: Lancer International, 1987).

67. John Mearsheimer, *Conventional Deterrence* (Ithaca: Cornell University Press, 1984).

68. Much of the foregoing description of the war has been drawn from Sumit Ganguly, *The Origins of War in South Asia: The Indo-Pakistani Conflicts Since 1947*, 2nd ed. (Boulder: Westview Press, 1994).

69. Roger Morris, *Uncertain Greatness: Henry Kissinger and American Foreign Policy* (New York: Harper and Row, 1977).

70. Kissinger, *White House Years*.

71. Van Hollen, 'Geopolitics Misapplied: The Tilt Policy Revisited.'

72. President Yahya Khan had been forced to resign in shame after the military defeat; Bhutto was then declared president and chief martial law administrator.

73. Imtiaz H. Bokhari and Thomas Perry Thornton, *The 1972 Simla Agreement: An Asymmetrical Negotiation* (Washington, D.C.: Johns Hopkins Foreign Policy Institute, 1988).

74. Dixit, *Anatomy*.

75. It is useful to note that, contrary to popular belief, the Tashkent Agreement of 1966 had affirmed that the two sides would not resort to force to settle the Kashmir question.

76. D.P. Dhar, 'LoC as Border: Bhutto's Deal with Mrs. Gandhi,' *Times of India*, April 4, 1995.

77. Dixit, *Anatomy*.

78. Abdul Sattar, 'Simla Pact: Negotiation Under Duress,' *Regional Studies* (Islamabad), Volume XIII, Number 4, Autumn 1995. Also see Khalid Mahmud Arif, *Working with Zia: Pakistan's Power Politics, 1977–1988* (Karachi: Oxford University Press, 1995).

79. Burke and Ziring, *Pakistan's Foreign Policy*.

80. Unlike Pakistan in 1965, however, India's perceptions in 1971 were not clouded by false optimism or misperception.

81. On this point see the discussion in Steven Hoffmann, 'Anticipation, Disaster, Victory,' *Asian Survey*, Volume 12, Number 11, November 1972.

82. Arif, *Working with Zia*.

83. S. Husain and M.A. Hasan, *Mukhzum Mutalliyah-i-Pakistan* (A Survey of Pakistan) (Lahore: Kitab Khana Danishwuran, 1981).

84. For a brief discussion of the seemingly endemic structural flaws of the Pakistani polity, see Sumit Ganguly, 'Pakistan's Never-Ending Story: Why the October Coup Was No Surprise,' *Foreign Affairs*, Volume 79, Number 2, March-April 2000.

85. For a particularly strident critique of Indian foreign policy under Nehru and Indira Gandhi, see Shashi Tharoor, *Reasons of State: Political Development and India's Foreign Policy under Indira Gandhi, 1966–1977* (New Delhi: Vikas, 1982).

86. Interview with senior retired Indian diplomat, New Delhi, December 1990.

Chapter Four

From Crisis to Crisis

After the Simla Agreement, South Asia saw a period of relative peace. Pakistan's crushing military defeat in 1971 laid to rest the tired myth of Pakistani military superiority. Also, following its break-up in 1971, the Pakistani political leadership of Zulfiquar Ali Bhutto remained preoccupied with the myriad tasks of domestic political consolidation.[1] Simultaneously, India's overwhelming conventional superiority significantly limited the serious consideration of yet another military confrontation. This period of stability, however, drew to a close with the end of the decade.

The Soviet Invasion of Afghanistan

The Soviet invasion and subsequent occupation of Afghanistan in December 1979 had profound consequences for the security of both India and Pakistan. Pakistan was now faced with two potentially hostile states on its borders. The Soviet-installed regime of Babrak Karmal was expected to be unfriendly toward Pakistan, and Pakistan's relations with India (and the United States) had been strained in the aftermath of Gen. Muhammad Zia-ul-Haq's overthrow and subsequent execution of Zulfiquar Ali Bhutto.

Consequently, Zia's regime found itself in a quandary in early 1980. This strategic quandary would not last long, however. Dextrous diplomacy on Zia's part would turn a potentially adverse strategic milieu into a strategic near-windfall for his regime. Through a series of adroit diplomatic moves, Zia managed not only to alter Pakistan's seemingly parlous security environment but also to bolster the security of his own regime.[2]

To summarize how he went about this, which has been ably detailed by other authors,[3] shortly after the Soviet invasion of Afghanistan, President Jimmy Carter, who was in the final days of his ill-fated administration, offered Pakistan $400 million in the form of military and economic assistance to bolster the regime's willingness to stand up to the Soviets. As is well known today, Zia dismissed Carter's offer as 'peanuts.'[4] In dismissing the offer the general made a sagacious calculation: another American administration, one with a more conservative ideological orientation, would be far more forthcoming in addressing Pakistan's perceived strategic needs and vulnerabilities. His calculations proved prescient: with Carter's electoral defeat in November 1980 and the advent to power of the ideologically-charged Reagan administration, Pakistan became the recipient of substantial American military and economic assistance. This new security relationship enabled Zia to bolster his own position while significantly upgrading Pakistan's military capabilities.[5] Of course, the renewal of a US-Pakistani arms-transfer relationship had important repercussions in India, which, after some initial but futile efforts to reassure Pakistan, moved with some dispatch to strengthen its own military relationship with the Soviet Union.

The Soviet invasion of Afghanistan came as a stunning surprise not only to the United States and the Western world, but also to the states of the subcontinent. India, which had forged a robust relationship with the Soviet Union in the years following the 1971 war with Pakistan, was no less surprised by the invasion than were the states in the Atlantic alliance.[6] Although some pro-Soviet ideologues could be found within the Congress Party and in the Ministry of External Affairs, the Indo-Soviet relationship was based more on strategic considerations than on strong ideological affinity.[7] The Soviets were keen on countering Chinese and American influence in South Asia and accordingly had sought to limit Sino-Indian rapprochement and any significant improvement in Indo-US relations. India, on its part, had developed a deep distrust of Chinese intentions and military capabilities after the 1962 border war. Despite fitful improvements in relations since the now-famous 'Mao smile' of 1970, Sino-Indian relations remained strained.[8] The already-frayed but mildly-improved relationship had most recently been strained in the aftermath of the Chinese attack on Vietnam in 1978. This attack took place during the visit of the Janata Party government's foreign minister, Atal Behari Vajpayee, to Beijing.[9] The Chinese had especially provoked the ire of the Indian leadership when they had declared that they were 'teaching

Vietnam a lesson' just as they had taught another country a similar one in 1962. Consequently, a diplomatic consensus existed across party lines in New Delhi that the Soviet-Indian relationship constituted a vital strategic hedge against possible Chinese military malfeasance in the future. The Indian elite's deep-seated distrust of American interests and intentions in South Asia also helped bolster the Indo-Soviet relationship.[10]

India Reacts to the Soviet Invasion

The Soviet invasion of Afghanistan came in the midst of a political interregnum in India. Indira Gandhi had been ousted from the prime ministership in the first election after her draconian, ill-advised 'state of emergency.'[11] The subsequent Janata Party regime of Prime Minister Morarji Desai had collapsed, and an interim prime minister, Charan Singh, a politician with rural roots and no particular interest in or knowledge of foreign affairs, was in office. Nevertheless, Charan Singh publicly expressed the view that the Soviet invasion of Afghanistan would have 'far-reaching and adverse consequences' for South Asia.[12] Privately, he sharply upbraided the Soviet ambassador to India, Yuri Vorontsov, for contributing to a new set of regional tensions.[13] Simultaneously, the Indian Ministry of External Affairs expressed its misgivings to the American ambassador, Robert Goheen, about the renewed American willingness to supply weapons to Pakistan. Charan Singh also wrote to President Jimmy Carter spelling out his concerns about the American decision to lift the existing arms embargo on Pakistan, imposed after the 1971 war.

Charan Singh's diplomatic overtures toward the Soviet Union and the United States were of brief duration. In the mid-term elections of January 1980, Indira Gandhi and the Congress Party made a triumphant return. The Indian public opinion on the Soviet invasion changed swiftly as a consequence of the change in regime in New Delhi. A significant number of Indira Gandhi's closest political advisers in the foreign policy bureaucracy held staunchly pro-Soviet and anti-American sentiments, and they acted with alacrity to restore more amicable relations with the Soviet Union. Others, while lacking great ideological affinity for the Soviet Union, nevertheless were disturbed by the potential renewal of the US-Pakistan military nexus. Accordingly, they felt that it was critical to court the Soviet Union to ensure that India maintained a substantial military edge over Pakistan. To this end, they argued that the benefits of a continued Indo-Soviet relationship far outweighed any international disapprobation that India would suffer from its equivocal position on the Soviet invasion and occupation of Afghanistan.[14]

The Soviets, in turn, anxious not to alienate India, moved with considerable dispatch to address India's concerns while staunchly defending their actions in Afghanistan. Specifically, they sent Foreign Minister Andrei Gromyko to New Delhi in March 1980 to explain the Soviet position on the Afghan question.[15] The Indians, while warmly greeting Gromyko, nevertheless refused to fully and publicly endorse the Soviet position on the subject. In an attempt to further assuage Indian concerns, especially in light of the likely resurgence of a US-Pakistan military relationship, the Soviets offered India an exceptionally generous arms package in May 1980. This deal amounted to $1.63 billion in the form of credits payable over a period of 10 to 15 years.[16] The arms-transfer package included MiG-25 'Foxbat' aircraft and T-72 tanks.[17]

The Soviet largesse toward India came with a significant political price attached, however. In exchange for continued Soviet transfers of substantial amounts of sophisticated weaponry, India had to maintain a studious silence on the question of Afghanistan during the UN General Assembly debates. The Indian unwillingness to condemn the Soviet presence in Afghanistan markedly strained its relations with the United States and other Western powers.

India's relations with Pakistan deteriorated dramatically as American military assistance to Pakistan became an inevitability. Zia, with characteristic dexterity, in an attempt to cultivate a conciliatory international image, offered India a 'no-war pact' in September 1981.[18] The Indian political leadership promptly rejected this offer and instead asked Pakistan for a more comprehensive peace treaty, assuring Pakistan that it would not exploit the latter's security anxieties. Zia's military regime, unsurprisingly, evinced little interest in the Indian attempts at reassurance.[19]

The failure of Indian efforts to reassure Pakistan led its decision-makers to adopt a fairly strident position on the transformation of the security environment in the subcontinent. Though privately holding the Soviets responsible for the genesis of the crisis, Indian officials focused most of their public criticism on the United States for renewing the arms-transfer relationship with Pakistan and thereby prompting an arms competition in the region. These Indian criticisms only served to exacerbate Indo-US relations.

The first breakthrough in Indo-US relations came when Prime

Minister Indira Gandhi met President Ronald Reagan at a North-South Summit in Cancun in October 1981.[20] Following this meeting, Indian spokesmen curbed their strident anti-American rhetoric, and the United States eased up on its anti-Indian stances on multilateral lending to India.

Following Indira Gandhi's assassination in October 1984, her son, Rajiv Gandhi, a political neophyte, succeeded her as prime minister. India's foreign policy orientation did not change dramatically under Rajiv Gandhi. Like his grandfather, Jawaharlal Nehru, and his mother had, Rajiv retained the foreign policy portfolio. The junior position in the Ministry of External Affairs went to K. Natwar Singh, a former Indian foreign service officer with an inveterate hatred of the United States, a deep distrust of Pakistan, and a fondness for the Soviet Union.[21]

In June 1985, Rajiv Gandhi visited the United States. During this visit he sought to allay American misgivings about India's close relationship with the Soviet Union. Even after Rajiv Gandhi's visit, however, Indo-US relations remained strained over the question of India's position on the Soviet presence in Afghanistan, the supply of American weaponry to Pakistan, and other global issues.[22] These differences persisted despite a new American willingness to provide important technologies to India—from computers to aircraft engines. The differences were accentuated when the United States considered selling Pakistan the Hawkeye EC-2 Advanced Warning and Control Systems (AWACS) aircraft. Indian analysts vociferously argued that these aircraft would confer significant battlefield advantages to the Pakistani military in any confrontation with India.[23]

The Chill of Siachen

In the early 1980s Indo-Pakistani relations worsened for reasons independent of the consequences of the Soviet invasion of Afghanistan. The principal reason for this deterioration in relations was a dispute over the Siachen Glacier, located in the Karakoram Range in the disputed state of Jammu and Kashmir. The glacier is 75 kilometres long, varies in width from 2 to 8 kilometres and is over 300 metres deep—the second largest glacier in Asia. The total area covered by the glacier is approximately 10,000 square kilometres. The surface temperature on the glacier can drop as low as minus 40 degrees Celsius in the winter and blizzards in the area can generate winds up to 150 knots. Not surprisingly, the region is often popularly referred to as the 'third pole.'[24]

The dispute stemmed from the inadequate demarcation of the

Cease-Fire Line in the wake of the cease-fire agreement in 1949. As Samina Ahmed and Varun Sahni have written:

The CFL ran along the international India-Pakistan border and then north and northeast until the map grid-point NJ 9842, located near the Shyok river at the base of the Saltoro mountain range. Because no Indian or Pakistani troops were present in the geographically inhospitable northeastern areas beyond NJ 9842, the CFL was not delineated as far as the Chinese border. Both sides agreed, in the vague language that lies at the root of the Siachen dispute, that the CFL extends to the terminal point, NJ 9842, and 'thence north to the glaciers.'[25]

Even after the 1965 and 1971 wars, no attempt was made to extend the CFL and subsequently the Line of Control to the glacier. The precise factors that contributed to the militarization of the undemarcated area of the glacier are difficult to pinpoint. It is clear that India did deploy troops on the glacier first to establish its claim. On the other hand, there is evidence that prior Pakistani efforts to stake a claim to the glacier prompted the pre-emptive Indian action in April 1984. Lt-Gen. M.L. Chibber, the head of the Northern Command at the time, has provided the most complete account of the Indian action.[26] According to Chibber, the Indian military operation, code-named 'Meghdoot' (Cloud Messenger), resulted from intelligence reports that Pakistan was planning to establish a military operation to claim the glacier. Faced with the Indian military presence on the glacier, Pakistan launched its own military operation, 'Abadeel' (Swallow), in April 1984.[27]

Despite attempts at disengagement, Indian and Pakistani troops remain stationed in this extraordinarily inhospitable terrain, sustaining more injuries and losses through frostbite and pulmonary oedema than from each other's artillery shells.[28] What exactly is the strategic significance of Siachen? The principal importance of the glacier appears to be its location. As one observer has written:

The Siachen Glacier Complex which abuts the Indo-Tibetan border along the disputed territory of Aksai Chin on the one side, the Shaksgam Valley (which India regards as illegally ceded by Pakistan to China) to the north-west, and the Northern 9842 triangle, is a wedge that separates a closer Sino-Pak territorial nexus. Additionally, the strategic importance to India of its stand in the Siachen Glacier dispute is that it is in accordance with the accepted international principle of watershed. India also wants to apply this principle to its disputed Himalayan borders with China.[29]

Despite the substantial material and human costs of stationing troops at these altitudes it is unlikely that either side will be willing to make substantial concessions on this dispute. The prospects of conflict resolution probably further diminished after the 1999 Pakistani incursion across the LoC in Kargil, Dras, and Batalik (see Chapter 6). From the standpoint of Indian security analysts, a successful Pakistani incursion in Kargil could have cut off the strategic Srinagar-Leh Highway, which India relies on to supply its troops in Siachen.[30]

Brasstacks and Loose Tongues

American military assistance to Pakistan certainly contributed to its security. However, it also emboldened Zia to exploit India's weaknesses. In the late 1980s, when the indigenous Sikh insurgency peaked in India's Punjab, Zia sought to raise the costs of the insurgency for the Indian state by covertly aiding the insurgents.

The origins of this Khalistani separatist insurgency are quite complex, rooted as they are in a number of historical and contemporary factors. A number of excellent studies trace the origins of the movement, which are beyond the scope of this chapter.[31] But by the late 1980s entire sections of the Punjab were aflame. Khalistani terrorist activity, as well as the heavy-handed tactics of the Indian state designed to suppress the insurgency, was taking a daily human toll.[32]

It is against this backdrop of continuing turmoil and Pakistani-abetted violence in Punjab that India launched a military exercise code-named 'Brasstacks.' This exercise was the brainchild of Gen. Krishnaswami Sundarji, the talented, if swaggering, chief of staff of the Indian army. The exercise had a number of purposes, military and political. At a military level, it was designed to test the combat readiness of a number of newly inducted mechanized units of the Indian army. It was also intended to test an indigenously designed command, control, communications, and intelligence network. Finally, it was geared to ascertain the viability of a new conventional deterrence strategy that Sundarji had fashioned.[33]

In addition to the explicitly military dimensions of this exercise, it was also laden with political significance. Pakistan's support for the Sikh insurgency in the Punjab had piqued a number of key Indian decision-makers. As a consequence, some officials within the national government in New Delhi felt that a message should be conveyed to Pakistan that despite India's counter-insurgency commitments in Punjab, its army was still in a position to inflict considerable military costs on Pakistan.[34] Thus, embedded in the Brasstacks military exercise was a element of coercive diplomacy.

The size and complexity of Brasstacks was without parallel in independent India's history. It was comparable in size to the North Atlantic Treaty Organization's and the Warsaw Pact's exercises during the Cold War. Apart from the dimensions of the exercise, it was also held along an east-west axis (thus pointing toward Pakistan) instead of the usual north-south axis in the state of Rajasthan.[35]

The size and location of the exercise caused anxiety in Islamabad. Worse still, when Pakistani prime minister Mohammed Khan Junejo attempted to elicit information about the dimensions of the exercise from Rajiv Gandhi at a meeting of the South Asian Association for Regional Cooperation in Bangalore, India, he received only sketchy information and inaccurate figures.[36] Unable to obtain sufficient reassurance of the goals and significance of this impending Indian military exercise, the Pakistanis decided to bolster their own scheduled military exercises, 'Saf-e-Shikan' and 'Flying Horse.'[37] Accordingly, even after the completion of their planned exercises in November and December 1986, the Pakistani forces did not return to their normal peacetime cantonments but remained in battle-ready stations near the Indo-Pakistani border in the Bahawalpur sector in Punjab. Later, these forces were moved to Bhatinda and Firozpur. The Pakistani air force also remained on alert despite the completion of its own military exercise, 'Highmark'.

The continued deployment of the Pakistani armoured divisions after the completion of the military exercises caused considerable concern in New Delhi. New Delhi's anxieties were threefold: first, the Pakistani forces were so arrayed that they could, in a pincer movement, cut off their Indian counterparts in strategic areas; second, a demonstration of force by Pakistan along sensitive border areas in Punjab could embolden the Khalistani terrorists, who might think they were to receive overt military support; and third, access to Kashmir could be interdicted by the Pakistani forces.

The crisis erupted in mid-January when Indian intelligence sources learned that the Pakistani forces had not returned to their peace stations after their exercises but had moved toward border positions in Punjab and Kashmir. Fearing an impending Pakistani attack, India decided to respond in kind and also moved troops into forward positions in Punjab and Kashmir. By late January, these moves and counter-moves had placed the two states on a confrontation course.

Fearing the prospect of a general war and under the orders of Rajiv Gandhi, who now was in a state of panic, the Indian minister of state for external affairs, Natwar Singh, called in Humayun Khan, the Pakistani

high commissioner to New Delhi, on January 23 to express India's misgivings about the Pakistani troop deployments.[38] Singh also warned
Khan that India would take appropriate steps if the Pakistani troops
were not withdrawn from their forward deployments. Khan promptly
contacted Islamabad and had the Pakistani vice chief of army staff
contact Sundarji through the Indian director-general of military operations. On the same day, the Indian minister of state for defence, Arun
Singh, met John Gunther Dean, the American ambassador to New
Delhi. During this meeting Singh shared his worries about the location
of particular Pakistani troop and armour deployments. Following this
conversation, Dean passed on Singh's concerns to the Pakistanis and
suggested that they open a dialogue with the Indians.

At about the same time, in Islamabad, Zain Noorani, the Pakistani
minister of state for foreign affairs, summoned the Indian high commissioner, S.K. Singh, to convey his concerns about the Indian troop
deployments.[39] Shortly after these meetings, the prime ministers of the
two countries, in a telephone conversation, agreed to scale down
the spiral of tensions. Accordingly, at the end of January, a Pakistani
delegation headed by Foreign Secretary Abdul Sattar visited New Delhi
to negotiate an end to the crisis. These secretary-level talks lasted from
January 31 to February 4 and led to a mutual exchange of proposals for
defusing the crisis and for designing a set of confidence and security
building measures (CSBMs) to avoid future tensions.[40]

There is widespread speculation that this crisis had a nuclear
dimension. Much of the speculation swirls around an interview that
Abdul Quadir Khan, one of Pakistan's principal nuclear scientists, gave
to Kuldip Nayar, a prominent Indian journalist, on January 28. In
this interview, published in *The Observer* of London on March 1, Khan
stated, 'Nobody can undo Pakistan or take us for granted. We are here
to stay and let it be clear that we shall use the bomb if our existence is
threatened.'[41]

It remains unclear if this interview constituted an attempt at nuclear
signalling. If indeed it was carrying such a message, it had little effect
on the evolution and settlement of the crisis, because by mid-February
the tensions had already started to abate. Regardless of the message
that may have been encoded in this statement, it did mark a new epoch
for the presence and role of nuclear weapons in South Asia. Even though
Khan subsequently claimed that he had been inveigled into making
that statement, American and Indian decision-makers took his warning
seriously. Both the United States and India started to re-assess their

view of the state of the Pakistani nuclear weapons programme after this episode.[42] Indian decision-makers, in particular, came to assume that Pakistan had crossed an important threshold in its quest for nuclear weapons.

Kashmir Flares Again

No unambiguous evidence can be adduced to demonstrate that Pakistan felt more secure vis-à-vis India after it crossed that nuclear threshold in 1987. However, it is not unreasonable to infer that Pakistan's acquisition of an incipient nuclear capability and the communication of that information to India further emboldened Pakistani military decision-makers. Any Indian defence planner would now have to take into account Pakistan's nuclear weapons potential in the event of a future confrontation.

The role of nuclear weapons in a crisis would soon become manifest in the context of Kashmir. After the Simla Agreement, the Kashmir issue had not loomed large in Indo-Pakistani relations. The Pakistani leadership under Zulfiquar Ali Bhutto, though hardly reconciled to the status quo, realized that it could do little to wrest Kashmir back from India. Consequently, the Pakistani leadership ritualistically raised the Kashmir question at the United Nations but did not actively seek to foment discord within Kashmir.

Indeed, in the 1970s the opportunity for Pakistani mischief-making in Kashmir was significantly limited. The government of India had finally moved to grant the Kashmiris a fair political dispensation; a new generation of young, politically conscious Kashmiris came to believe that they were finally being treated as full citizens of India with the right of democratic dissent.[43] Tragically, this new and more democratic political order would not last long. Short-sighted policies on the part of various regimes in New Delhi would undermine the brief emergence of genuinely democratic politics in the state and create conducive conditions for the rise of an ethno-religious insurgency in December 1989. Thanks to those myopic policies, India is continuing to pay a high price in blood and treasure in Kashmir.

As Pakistan turned away from Kashmir in the aftermath of the 1971 war, India moved with considerable dispatch to integrate Kashmir into the Indian Union. To this end, Prime Minister Indira Gandhi, flush after her decisive victory over Pakistan, felt confident enough to start negotiations with Sheikh Mohammed Abdullah about the future status of Kashmir in the Indian Union. Abdullah's initial response to Indira Gandhi's overtures was not particularly enthusiastic. After his house arrest for the better part of a decade and enforced exile from Kashmir since his release, his hostility toward Indira Gandhi's attempts to re-open negotiations with him was not entirely unexpected. At one point, he grandiloquently stated, 'Throw my body in the Arabian Sea. Do not bury me in a slave country.'[44]

Nevertheless, she persisted in this endeavour and enlisted the support of Balraj Puri, a long-time Kashmiri activist, for forging ties with Abdullah. After much persuasion, Abdullah sent one of his trusted lieutenants, Mirza Afzal Beg, to start negotiations with Indira Gandhi's representative, G.P. Parthasarathy. Once the Beg-Parthasarathy negotiations started in earnest, Abdullah made clear that his central concern was the 'quantum of autonomy' that the Indian central government was prepared to grant to Kashmir. In effect, he was now willing to abandon any secessionist agenda that he may have once harboured.

Under the aegis of the Beg-Parthasarathy accord, Abdullah was allowed to return to Kashmir and resume normal political activity. The government of India also agreed to examine a number of legislative provisions that had been passed over the decades and alter them to grant Kashmir a greater degree of autonomy within the Indian Union. Kashmiris, young and old, welcomed the ageing 'lion of Kashmir' back to his home ground. Even a younger, better-educated, and more politically savvy generation of Kashmiris saw his return as an emblem of a new, positive relationship between the state and the central government.[45] This hope, however, would be extinguished within a decade and with the most dire consequences for Kashmir and the Indian Union.

Kashmiris went to the polls in 1977. This election is widely considered to have been free of political taint. At the time, Indira Gandhi was out of office following the post-'emergency' national elections. The Janata Party prime minister, Morarji Desai, personally assured Sheikh Abdullah that no electoral malfeasance would be permitted in Kashmir and that the Kashmiris would be allowed to exercise their right of adult franchise without any form of intimidation or skullduggery. Desai's promise was realized, and free and fair elections were conducted in the state. The people of Kashmir came to believe that a new political dispensation had finally emerged in their state where the right to adult franchise would not be undermined or compromised.[46]

In this election Sheikh Mohammed Abdullah won a decisive and overwhelming victory, and his party, the National Conference, returned to power. Despite Abdullah's triumphant return to Kashmiri politics, his tenure was short: he died on September 8, 1982. Prior to his demise, he had successfully inducted his son, Farooq Abdullah, into his cabinet as the state's minister for health. Farooq had spent the bulk of his professional life as a physician in London. Unlike his father, who had grown up and come to political maturity in the rough-and-tumble world of Indian politics, Farooq was a political neophyte. Even though his father had drawn him into the web of Kashmir's politics, he lacked his father's political acumen and knew little about the folkways of political life in Kashmir or in India. Nevertheless, thanks to his family's standing in the politics of the state, Farooq experienced little difficulty in winning the first election that he campaigned for in 1983. Sadly Farooq's triumph, too, would prove to be limited. A variety of factors contributed to his political eclipse shortly after he assumed office.[47]

To understand the reasons behind Farooq's dramatic political misfortunes it is necessary to have some sense of the political backdrop in the subcontinent in the early 1980s. During this period, Indira Gandhi was increasingly facing challenges to the dominance of the Congress Party. In large part, as has been well documented elsewhere, key decisions on her part had contributed to the decline of the party and to the challenges that it now faced in a number of different parts of India.[48] She had a propensity to see the rise of these new political forces as fundamental threats to her standing in the country and, by extension, to the security and integrity of the Indian state. Most of these movements, whether in Punjab or in Assam, started out as demands for greater regional autonomy. Her unwillingness to concede to these demands for varying degrees of regional autonomy and her deep-seated hostility to the growth of regional power centres only made these movements more intransigent. As their rhetoric and positions hardened, she assumed an increasingly unyielding position, thereby worsening matters. Kashmir under Farooq Abdullah fell prey to this pattern of Indira Gandhi's attempts (and later those of her son and political heir, Rajiv Gandhi) to shoehorn the Congress Party into states where it had little organization and even less political standing.

The critical turning point in Kashmir's fortunes came in the aftermath of the deeply-flawed local elections of 1987. In this election, at the instance of Rajiv Gandhi, Farooq Abdullah forged an alliance with the Congress Party to contest the elections. Widespread fraud and skullduggery characterized this election. Voters were intimidated, opposition politicians were harassed, and ballot boxes were tampered. The resultant

National Conference–Congress alliance that came to power consequently lacked legitimacy. Past generations of Kashmiris, who had lacked political sophistication, had tolerated similar malfeasances. A new generation of Kashmiris had now emerged in the state who were far more politically conscious. They proved far less willing to passively acquiesce to the corruption of the electoral process. Lacking an alternative model of social protest such as mass-based civil disobedience, they resorted to violence.[49] Very quickly their protests took on an explicitly secessionist tenor.

Protests, demonstrations, bombings, and other violent incidents swept across the Valley throughout much of 1988 and 1989. These incidents ultimately culminated in the kidnapping of Rubiya Sayeed, the daughter of the Union home minister, Mufti Mohammed Sayeed, on December 8 in Srinagar, the capital of Jammu and Kashmir. The perpetrators of the act were members of the Jammu and Kashmir Liberation Front (JKLF), a nominally secular secessionist organization, formed in 1976. To secure the release of Rubiya Sayeed the government of Vishwanath Pratap Singh acceded to the demands of the JKLF, releasing five political activists who had been incarcerated on various charges.[50] The government's willingness to concede emboldened the insurgents, and very soon the Valley was aflame.

The Crisis of 1990

It is against this backdrop of growing centre-state tensions and the outbreak of insurgency in Kashmir in December 1989 that the next crisis in Indo-Pakistani relations erupted. Much has been written about the crisis of 1990. Unfortunately, a good deal of this literature is polemical.[51] What follows is an attempt at reconstructing the events as they unfolded.

As discussed earlier in this chapter, a tide of violence and unrest had been sweeping through the Valley in 1989. The tide had crested in December 1989 and, since then, the Valley has been trapped in a state of constant turbulence. It is against this backdrop of upheaval and turmoil that the newly elected national government of Prime Minister V.P. Singh encountered its first crisis.

It is difficult to pinpoint a precise starting date for the crisis. However, the situation in Kashmir had started a steady slide toward anarchy in January–February 1990. An Indian civil servant, Jagmohan Malhotra, who had previously been a governor of the state, had been re-appointed since the resignation of Farooq Abdullah in January 1990. In his previous stint Jagmohan had demonstrated that he could be a tough-minded but reasonably competent administrator. On this occasion, however, he failed to grasp the depth of disaffection that existed in the state against any regime in New Delhi. Worse still, his propensity to see the disturbed situation in the state almost exclusively as a Pakistani-instigated law and order problem was a fundamental error of judgment.[52]

Kashmir's descent into political chaos ironically came during a time of improving relations between India and Pakistan. During the previous two years, Prime Ministers Benazir Bhutto and Rajiv Gandhi had worked on a political rapprochement. The new prime minister, V. P. Singh, who had assumed office in early December 1989, was also interested in continuing this process. His foreign minister, Inder Kumar Gujral, was a staunch advocate of improved relations with Pakistan. The abrupt political uprising in Kashmir derailed these fitful attempts at ameliorating the Indo-Pakistan relationship.[53]

Within Pakistan, Benazir Bhutto, whom significant segments of the Pakistani military had long distrusted, now felt compelled to do a volte-face in terms of relations with India because of rising anti-Indian sentiment within Pakistani society. After the outbreak of the Kashmir uprising she decided to openly advocate the 'self-determination' of the Kashmiris and to condemn India's harsh response to the insurgency.[54] As the conflict in Kashmir intensified, opposition parties continued to outbid Benazir on the question of Kashmir, leading her to ratchet up her inflammatory political rhetoric.[55]

Two compelling reasons, in turn, had emboldened the Pakistani military to aid the insurgency in Kashmir despite the possibility of Indian military escalation. At one level, the spontaneous outbreak of the insurgency in Kashmir, Indian claims to the contrary notwithstanding, had taken the Pakistani national leadership by surprise.[56] Now they saw an excellent opportunity to impose significant material and other costs on India at little cost to themselves. At another level, they believed that their incipient nuclear capabilities had effectively neutralized whatever conventional military advantages India possessed.[57] Key Indian decision makers, however, indicated that India's conventional and nuclear capabilities still gave it an edge over Pakistan and that if Pakistani support for the insurgents continued, India would be forced to retaliate despite the possible risks of escalation.[58]

The war of words and troop movements on both sides continued through much of 1990, raising concerns in Washington, D.C., and other western capitals about the increased likelihood of the outbreak of war in South Asia. These fears in no small measure stemmed from specific developments in the subcontinent. Specifically, the Pakistani political leadership of Benazir Bhutto started to publicly call for 'azadi' ('freedom') for the Kashmiris as the violence in Kashmir started to gather force. Faced with these developments, Prime Minister V.P. Singh permitted the Indian Army to move three divisions from the eastern sector to the west. One division was then stationed in Punjab, one in Kashmir and a third along an unspecified portion of the international border. Simultaneously, the army also moved some heavy artillery toward border positions. The Indian Air Force also curtailed leaves and placed its radar installations into wartime positions. The Pakistanis, in turn, also mobilized forces, moving one division from Multan in Pakistani Punjab toward the international border. Neither side, however, moved its strike formations.[59]

In early April, as the exchange of hostile rhetoric between New Delhi and Islamabad escalated, key signs started to emerge that the prospect of war in the region was by no means a distant possibility. Prime Minister V.P. Singh urged Indians to strengthen their resolve as evidence emerged of Pakistani troop movements along the Line of Control (LoC) in Kashmir. In a public speech Singh derided Benazir Bhutto's statement about fighting a thousand-year war against India and commented that it remained to be seen if Pakistan could last even a thousand hours in a war with India. In the same speech he called upon Indians to be 'psychologically prepared' for war with Pakistan.[60]

Singh's tough rhetoric against Pakistan was not merely a response to Benazir's intransigent statements. Domestically, his coalition government depended on the jingoistic Bharatiya Janata Party (BJP) for political support in parliament. Consequently, to demonstrate his willingness to stand up to Pakistani provocation, Singh felt compelled to heighten his rhetoric. His government also decided to increase defence spending in light of the developments in Kashmir and also because of the growing tensions with Pakistan. Shortly thereafter, the Indian defence ministry released its annual report, which highlighted new and growing threats from both Pakistan and the People's Republic of China.[61]

These mutually intemperate statements from the two national capitals and troop movements along a sensitive border area took place against a background of growing political instability and violence within the Kashmir Valley. The insurgents intensified their activities and India increased its troop strength to quell the rebels.[62] In mid-April 1990, Pakistan accused India of massing a strike force comprising several infantry divisions, one armoured division, and three or four armoured brigades some 80 kilometres from the Indo-Pakistani border in Rajasthan, between Bikaner and Suratgarh.[63] Pakistan responded militarily to these alleged Indian moves: toward the end of April it started to call up its military reserves. Key Pakistani officials also publicly affirmed their ability to 'meet any challenge' that their country faced from India's forces.[64]

Matters simply worsened as the month drew to a close despite attempts to defuse the unfolding crisis at the foreign ministry level.[65] Within India, hawkish analysts argued that war with Pakistan was likely even as other, more moderate voices called for restraint. A former Indian vice-chief of army staff admitted that a form of 'war psychosis' was developing in India, while also making clear that India would fight with vigour if war was thrust upon it.[66] Fortunately, toward the end of the month, both sides decided to pull away from the brink.

In part, this de-escalation stemmed from the discussions between the two foreign ministers, Inder Kumar Gujral of India and Shahibzada Yakub Khan of Pakistan, held in New York toward the end of April. The two sides did not reach any substantive agreements in these talks but they did agree on the need to exercise mutual restraint in both words and actions.[67] Subsequently, the Pakistani foreign minister, while publicly disagreeing with his Indian counterpart's assertion that the Simla Agreement had superceded the United Nations plebiscite resolutions of 1948 and 1949, nevertheless acknowledged the utility of continued bilateral negotiations with India.[68]

Despite this seeming willingness to de-escalate the crisis, tensions between the two states continued apace during the month of May. As these tensions continued to mount, concern within the United States grew about the possible dangers of a nuclear war in South Asia. Western newspapers were the first to sound the tocsin about the danger of a nuclear conflagration in South Asia. In mid-May amid growing concerns about the possibility of a war between India and Pakistan, Robert Gates, the US deputy national security adviser, accompanied by Richard Haass, a member of the National Security Council staff, visited New Delhi and Islamabad.[69] Reportedly, in New Delhi the American team counselled restraint in Kashmir and in Islamabad informed the Pakistani leadership that in every Indo-Pakistani war-game that the United States had simulated, Pakistan had lost. Consequently, it was in Pakistan's interest to desist from any further escalation in Kashmir.[70]

The concern about a full-scale war between India and Pakistan was so great in many foreign capitals that even after the Gates-Haass mission, President George H.W. Bush of the United States and President Mikhail

Gorbachev of the Soviet Union felt compelled to issue a joint statement urging restraint over Kashmir.[71]

Continuing Tensions

Even though war did not ensue in 1990, Indo-Pakistani relations remained strained throughout the decade. The situation in Kashmir continued to deteriorate throughout the early 1990s. India routinely accused Pakistan of blatant interference in India's internal affairs and repeatedly called on Pakistan to stop its support to the various insurgent groups operating in Kashmir. Pakistan, in turn, persistently accused India of denying the Kashmiris their right of 'self-determination' and of systematic human rights violations. Simultaneously, Pakistani officials denied that they were providing any form of material assistance to the insurgents.

On the nuclear front, as the decade unfolded, both states came under considerable pressure from the United States and a number of its key allies to dispense with their nuclear weapons programmes. Neither India nor Pakistan paid much heed to these demands. Indian spokespersons continued to argue that India would not abandon its nuclear capabilities until some time bound plan for global disarmament was achieved. Pakistan, for its part, argued that it could ill afford to give up its nuclear weapons programme in the face of India's possession of nuclear capabilities along with its overwhelming conventional superiority. Consequently, little progress was made on the nuclear front in the subcontinent. The ambiguous status of the respective nuclear weapons programmes, of course, came to a close in May 1998 when India and Pakistan each tested a series of nuclear weapons.[72]

Notes

1. A useful discussion can be found in Anwar H. Syed, *The Discourse and Politics of Zulfiquar Ali Bhutto* (New York: St Martin's Press, 1992)

2. For a broader discussion of regime security in fragile post-colonial states see Mohammed Ayoob, *The Third World Security Predicament* (Boulder: Lynne Rienner, 1995).

3. See, for example, Dennis Kux, *Disenchanted Allies: The United States and Pakistan, 1947–2000* (Baltimore: Johns Hopkins University Press; and Washington, D.C.: Woodrow Wilson Center Press, 2001).

4. See S. Nihal Singh, *The Yogi and the Bear* (New Delhi: Allied Publishers, 1986).

5. For a quasi-official Pakistani account of the discussions between the

United States and Pakistan on the Afghanistan question see Khalid Mahmud Arif, *Working with Zia: Pakistan's Power Politics, 1977–1988* (Karachi: Oxford University Press, 1995).

6. For an excellent survey of Indo-Soviet relations since the 1971 war, see Robert Horn, *Soviet-Indian Relations: Issues and Influence* (New York: Praeger, 1982).

7. The best treatment of the history of Indo-Soviet relations remains Robert Donaldson, *Soviet Policy towards India: Ideology and Strategy* (Cambridge: Harvard University Press, 1974); also see the excellent treatment of Soviet aid policy toward India in Richard B. Remnek, *Soviet Scholars and Soviet Foreign Policy: A Case Study in Soviet Policy towards India* (Durham, N.C.: Carolina Academic Press, 1975).

8. The 'Mao smile' refers to a critical event that took place on May 1, 1970, when Chairman Mao Zedong warmly greeted Brajesh Mishra, the Indian chargé d'affaires of the embassy in Beijing, in the receiving line at the May Day celebrations in New Delhi. For a discussion of the political circumstances surrounding the 'Mao smile' and the subsequent diplomatic minuet in Sino-Indian relations after the 1962 war see Sumit Ganguly, 'The Sino-Indian Border Talks: A View from New Delhi, 1981–1989,' *Asian Survey* 29, Number 12, December 1989.

9. Vajpayee in 1998 became the prime minister in the Bharatiya Janata Party's coalition government.

10. The distrust of the United States is discussed in Surjit Mansingh, *India's Quest for Power: Indira Gandhi's Foreign Policy* (New Delhi: Sage Publications, 1984).

11. For a useful set of discussions of Indira Gandhi's declaration of the 'state of emergency' see Henry Hart, ed., *Indira Gandhi's India: A Political System Reappraised* (Boulder: Westview Press, 1976).

12. Bhabani Sen Gupta, *The USSR in Asia: An Interperceptional Study of Soviet-Asian Relations* (New Delhi: Young Asia Publications, 1980).

13. Interview with senior Indian diplomat, New York, November 1995.

14. Interview with Indian defence journalist and political commentator, New Delhi, July 1988.

15. For an excellent analysis of the Afghanistan question as an issue in Soviet-Indian relations see Robert Horn, 'Afghanistan and the Soviet-Indian Influence Relationship,' *Asian Survey*, Volume 23, Number 3, March 1983.

16. Horn, *Soviet-Indian Relations: Issues and Influence.*

17. Peter J.S. Duncan, *The Soviet Union and India* (New York: Council on Foreign Relations, 1989), p. 47.

18. India had initially made the 'no-war' pact offer to Pakistan in 1949. The Pakistani leadership had, at that time, rejected it out of hand. For a discussion of the history of the 'no-war' pact, see Douglas Makeig, 'War, No-War and the India-Pakistan Negotiating Process,' *Pacific Affairs*, Volume 60, Number 2 (Summer 1987), pp. 271–294.

19. On this diplomatic minuet see G. S. Bhargava, *South Asian Security after Afghanistan* (Lexington: D.C. Heath and Company, 1983).

20. For a useful discussion in the shift that occurred in Indo-US relations in the wake of the Cancun Summit see Dennis Kux, *India and the United States, 1947–1990: Estranged Democracies* (Washington, D.C.: National Defense University Press, 1992).

21. Based upon personal interviews, New York, October 1986.

22. Kux, *India and the United States.*

23. Kux, *India and the United States.*

24. Raspal S. Khosa, 'The Siachen Glacier Dispute: Imbroglio on the Roof of the World,' *Contemporary South Asia*, Volume 8, Number 2, 1999.

25. Samina Ahmed and Varun Sahni, 'Freezing the Fighting: Military Disengagement on the Siachen Glacier,' *Cooperative Monitoring Centre Occasional Papers* (Albuquerque: Sandia National Laboratories, 1998).

26. Lt. Gen. (retd.) M.L. Chibber, 'Siachen—The Untold Story (A Personal Account),' *Indian Defense Review*, January 1990.

27. Khosa, 'Siachen Glacier Dispute,' p. 195.

28. For a discussion of the various attempts at disengagement see A.G. Noorani, 'Easing the Indo-Pakistani Dialogue on Kashmir: Confidence-Building Measures for the Siachen Glacier, Sir Creek and the Wular Barrage,' Occasional Paper 16 (Washington, D.C: The Henry L. Stimson Center, April 1994)

29. Khosa, 'Siachen Glacier Dispute,' p. 199.

30. Jasjit Singh, 'Pakistan's Fourth War,' *Strategic Analysis*, Volume 23, Number 5, August 1999.

31. The term 'Khalistan' literally means 'land of the pure' and was the name given by the insurgents to the independent nation-state they wished to create by seceding from India. For the historical setting to the Khalistani movement see Rajiv A. Kapur, *Sikh Separatism: The Politics of Faith* (London: Allen and Unwin, 1986); and Harjot Singh Oberoi, *The Construction of Religious Boundaries: Culture, Identity, and Diversity in the Sikh Tradition* (Chicago: University of Chicago Press, 1994). For the more contemporary dimensions of the movement and the subsequent insurgency see Mark Tully and Satish Jacob, *Amritsar: Mrs Gandhi's Last Battle* (London: Jonathan Cape, 1985); for an account of the politics of Khalistani terror see Paul Wallace, 'Political Violence and Terrorism in India: The Crisis of Identity,' in Martha Crenshaw, ed., *Terrorism in Context* (University Park: Pennsylvania State University Press, 1995).

32. For a vivid journalistic account of the Punjab insurgency and the harsh counter-insurgency tactics of the Indian state see Steve Coll, *On the Grand Trunk Road: A Journey into South Asia* (New York: Times Books, 1994).

33. The strategy was a near mirror-image of American writing on deterrence. Pared to the bone, the strategy had three components: the requisite military capabilities to 'dissuade' an adversary for undertaking hostile action,

the means to effectively communicate the existence of these capabilities to the adversary, and the necessary political will to use these forces. For an early analysis of the Brasstacks crisis and Gen. Sundarji's concept of 'dissuasion,' see Sumit Ganguly, 'Getting Down to Brass Tacks,' *The World and I*, May 1987, pp. 100–104.

34. Interview with Indian diplomat, New York City, March 1988.

35. For a detailed discussion of Brasstacks see Kanti Bajpai, P.R. Chari, Pervaiz Iqbal Cheema, Stephen P. Cohen, and Sumit Ganguly, *Brasstacks and Beyond: Perception and the Management of Crisis in South Asia* (New Delhi: Manohar Books, 1995).

36. Bajpai et al., *Brasstacks*.

37. Bajpai et al., *Brasstacks*.

38. Interview with former Indian defence ministry senior official, September 1995.

39. Bajpai et al., *Brasstacks*.

40. For a discussion of these and other CSBMs in the region see Sumit Ganguly and Ted Greenwood, eds, *Mending Fences: Confidence and Security-Building Measures in South Asia* (Boulder: Westview Press, 1997).

41. *The Observer* (London), March 1, 1987. Pakistani had been developing nuclear weapons since 1972, but had never publicly admitted this programme.

42. For a discussion of the aftermath of the Khan interview see George Perkovich, *India's Nuclear Bomb* (Berkeley: University of California Press, 1999).

43. For a trenchant discussion of this issue see Sten Widmalm, *Democracy and Violent Separatism in India: Kashmir in Comparative Perspective* (Uppsala, Sweden: Department of Government, Uppsala University, 1997).

44. Interview with Balraj Puri, Washington, D.C., March 1994.

45. Based upon personal interviews with Kashmiris. Also see Widmalm, *Democracy*.

46. Unfortunately, a series of regimes in New Delhi had long tolerated corrupt regimes in Jammu and Kashmir as long as their leaders did not raise the secessionist bogey. For an extended discussion of New Delhi's complicity in supporting the dubious practices of a number of Kashmiri regimes see Sumit Ganguly, *The Crisis in Kashmir: Portents of War, Hopes of Peace* (Cambridge: Cambridge University Press, and Washington, D.C.: Woodrow Wilson Center Press, 1999).

47. A good account of the political backdrop to Farooq's troubles with Indira Gandhi can be found in M.J. Akbar, *Kashmir: Behind the Vale* (New Delhi: Vikas, 1971).

48. See, for example, the discussion in Paul R. Brass, *The Politics of India after Independence* (Cambridge: Cambridge University Press, 1990).

49. An alternative model of social and political protest was not embedded in the political culture of Kashmir for a number of compelling reasons. Historically, Kashmir had not been integrated into the Indian nationalist

movement which, had heavily relied on grassroots, civil disobedience as the principal mode of political agitation. Subsequently, Kashmiri leaders, with the possible exception of Sheikh Abdullah, had made few efforts to encourage such widespread social and political mobilization.

50. Pankaj Pachauri, 'Abduction Anguish,' *India Today*, December 31, 1989, pp. 38–41.

51. Much of this literature is of the sensational variety. See, for example, William E. Burrows and Robert Windrem, *Critical Mass: The Dangerous Race for Superweapons in a Fragmenting World* (New York: Simon and Schuster, 1994). The most disturbing article dealing with the 1990 crisis remains Seymour M. Hersh, 'On the Nuclear Edge,' *New Yorker*, March 29, 1993. Also see Michael Krepon and Mishi Faruqee, eds, *Conflict Prevention and Confidence Building Measures in South Asia: The 1990 Crisis*, Occasional Paper No.1 (Washington, D.C.: Henry L. Stimson Center, 1990).

52. For Jagmohan's views of the situation and his responses see his *My Frozen Turbulence in Kashmir* (New Delhi: Allied Publishers, 1993).

53. S. Viswam and Salamat Ali, 'Vale of Tears,' *Far Eastern Economic Review*, February 8, 1990, pp. 19–20.

54. Madhu Jain, 'Raising the Stakes,' *India Today*, February 28, 1990, pp. 27–29.

55. Lyce Doucet, BBC World Service, 'Opposition Warns Government on Kashmir Issue,' London, BBC World Service in English, 02:15 GMT, March 24, 1990, as reported in *Foreign Broadcast Information Service, Near East and South Asia*, FBIS-NES-90–061, March 29, 1990.

56. For Indian views that the insurgency was the result of Pakistani instigation and sponsorship, see *Facets of a Proxy War* (New Delhi: Government of India, 1993).

57. For a thoughtful assessment of the India-Pakistan military balance, see Dilip Bobb and Raj Chengappa, 'War Games,' *India Today*, February 28, 1990, pp. 22–27.

58. Dilip Bobb and Raj Chengappa, 'If Pushed Beyond a Point by Pakistan, We Will Retaliate,' *India Today*, April 30, 1990, pp. 76–77.

59. Based upon interview with senior, retired Indian Air Force officer, February 2000.

60. United News of India, 'VP Urges Nation to be Ready as Pak Troops Move to Border,' *Times of India*, April 11, 1990, p. 1.

61. Pratap Chakravarti, 'AFP Reports Further Details,' Hong Kong Agence France Presse in English, 11:14 GMT, March 30, 1990, as reported in *Foreign Broadcast Information Service: Near East and South Asia*, FBIS-NES-90–062, March 30, 1990.

62. Associated Press, 'Violence in Kashmir Is Intensified and India Sends in 1,000 Troops,' *New York Times*, April 12, 1990, p. A4.

63. Salamat Ali, 'Will Words Lead to War?' *Far Eastern Economic Review*, April 26, 1990, pp. 10–11.

64. V.K. Dethe, 'Pakistan Calling up Reserves,' *Times of India*, April 24, 1990, p. 3.

65. Press Trust of India, 'Gujral-Yakub Talks on Wed,' *Times of India*, April 24, 1990, p. 3.

66. For hawkish views, see Press Trust of India, 'Indo-Pak War Likely: Experts,' *Times of India*, April 26, 1990, p. 5; for a call for restraint see A.M. Vohra, 'Indo-Pak Rhetoric Has to be Cooled,' *Times of India*, April 25, 1990, p. 5.

67. Gautam Adhikari, 'War Threat Recedes,' *Times of India*, April 27, 1990, pp. 1, 9.

68. The Times of India News Service, 'Yakub Tones Down J and K Rhetoric,' *Times of India*, April 27, 1990, p. 9.

69. James Adams, 'Pakistan Nuclear War Threat,' *Sunday Times* (London), May 27, 1990, p. 1.

70. On this point, see the discussion in Devin Hagerty, *The Consequences of Nuclear Proliferation: Lessons from South Asia* (Cambridge: MIT Press, 1998), pp. 150–52.

71. Doyle McManus, 'Kashmir Issue May Draw a Summit Plea,' *Los Angeles Times*, June 1, 1990, from Lexis-Nexis.

72. For a discussion of the nuclear dimension of this crisis and the subsequent evolution of the nuclear doctrines of the two states, see Waheguru Pal Singh Sidhu, 'India's Nuclear Use Doctrine,' and Zafar Iqbal Cheema, 'Pakistan's Nuclear Use Doctrine and Command and Control,' in Peter R. Lavoy, Scott D. Sagan, and James J.Wirtz, eds, *Planning the Unthinkable: How New Powers Will Use Nuclear, Biological, and Chemical Weapons* (Ithaca: Cornell University Press, 2000).

Chapter Five

The Nuclear Dimension

After years of dissembling about its precise nuclear status, India tested a series of five nuclear devices at the Pokhran test site in the state of Rajasthan on May 11 and 13, 1998.[1] Pakistan, after about two weeks of deliberation, followed suit on May 28 and 30, 1998. Indian spokesmen were quick to declare that the tests were not directed toward any particular country. Pakistani decision-makers, however, made clear that their tests were a direct reaction to the Indian tests. Reactions to the Indian and Pakistani tests from the global community were almost uniformly critical.[2]

In this chapter, I will explore the ramifications of the Indian and Pakistani nuclear tests of May 1998 for the future security and stability of the region. Has the overt nuclearization of the region reduced the likelihood of war in the region or is the region now more war-prone?

Interestingly, India's and Pakistan's nuclear programmes, which developed somewhat in tandem, were impelled by quite different factors. The roots of the Indian programme are a bit deeper and more complex, and it evolved as a result of various international and domestic factors. At an international level, India's misgivings about a nuclear-armed China and India's quest for great-power status have proven to be powerful incentives. Domestically, a bureaucratic-scientific-technological complex has also propelled the programme.

Popular assumptions aside, the Pakistani programme did not arise after the first Indian nuclear test in 1974 (also conducted at Pokhran in the Rajasthan desert). On the contrary, the origins of the Pakistani programme can be directly traced to the country's military defeat at the hands of India in the 1971 war. The consequent break-up of Pakistan induced a deep sense of insecurity in the minds of the Pakistani decision-making and political elite. Cognizant of their military's structural inability to cope with significant Indian conventional superiority, the Pakistani elite chose to invest in a nuclear weapons option.[3] Its rationale was simple: Pakistani possession of nuclear weapons would deter any Indian attempt to further vivisect the country in a future regional crisis. Of course, the Indian nuclear test of 1974 provided a further impetus to the Pakistani programme.

The Development of the Indian Nuclear Programme

The Indian nuclear programme has long historical antecedents.[4] The origins of the programme can actually be traced to the pre-independence era, when a young Indian nuclear physicist, Homi Bhaba, who had trained under Ernest Rutherford at Cambridge University, returned to India in 1944. Bhaba convinced the wealthy, philanthropic Tata family of the potential uses of nuclear energy. Accordingly, with financial assistance from the Tatas, in 1945, the Tata Institute of Fundamental Research was created in Bombay with Bhaba as its first director. Bhaba then successfully persuaded India's first prime minister, Jawaharlal Nehru, to create a Department of Atomic Energy (DAE) in 1948. Persuading Nehru to make such a commitment was not a difficult task; the prime minister, who had a scientific bent, was already convinced of the potential uses of nuclear power in an energy-deficient country.[5]

Under Bhaba's tutelage in the 1950s, the DAE fashioned a three-stage nuclear energy programme. It sought to use indigenous sources of uranium to produce plutonium possibly both for weapons and for nuclear energy. The plutonium, in turn, was to be used in fast-breeder reactors to generate more plutonium and uranium 233 from thorium. The resulting uranium 233 was then used in breeder reactors to convert thorium into more uranium 233. The DAE chose to rely on thorium because of the significant deposits of natural thorium in the south Indian state of Kerala.

Bhaba's efforts were explicitly directed toward the goal of complete mastery and indigenization of the nuclear fuel cycle. It is also quite possible that Bhaba sought to lay the infrastructural foundations of a nuclear weapons programme in the event the political leadership chose to pursue such an option.[6] At a political level, however, Nehru remained opposed to India's development of nuclear weapons. Indeed, in virtually all his public pronouncements on nuclear-related issues, Nehru made clear his opposition to nuclear weapons. In 1954, for instance, he called for a worldwide cessation of all nuclear tests.[7] His opposition to the nuclear option for India drew in part from his acute concern about the opportunity costs of defence spending in a poor, developing nation facing myriad socio-economic challenges.[8]

A shift in Indian elite and popular opinion on the question of nuclear weapons came in the wake of the 1962 Sino-Indian border war. The border dispute, which had been festering for about a decade, had culminated in a brief but vicious border war in October 1962. Indian forces were largely unprepared for the Chinese onslaught and suffered substantial casualties. India also lost some 14,000 square miles that it had claimed along its Himalayan border.[9] Not surprisingly, in the aftermath of this military debacle, Nehru, now in his waning days, was forced to concede to a cacophony of demands at home for increased defence spending. Indeed, after the war, India embarked on a significant defence modernization programme that called for the creation of an 825,000-man army equipped with ten mountain divisions, the development of a 45-squadron air force with supersonic aircraft, and the upgrading of India's naval facilities.

These plans were barely being implemented when the first Chinese nuclear explosion took place at Lop Nor in October 1964. The political fallout in India over the Chinese nuclear explosion cannot be underestimated. Prime Minister Lal Bahadur Shastri, who had inherited Nehru's mantle, faced extraordinary pressures to abandon India's commitment not to develop nuclear weapons. Certain right-wing parties, most notably the pro-American Swatantra Party, argued that India should also dispense with its commitment to non-alignment, whereby it had scrupulously avoided cozying up to either the Warsaw Pact or the US-led North Atlantic Treaty Organisation, and seek the support of the West.[10] Despite substantial pressure, Shastri did not concede to any of the demands. He did, however, state that India would now be willing to conduct nuclear tests for peaceful purposes. He also directed the chiefs of staff of the Indian armed forces to evaluate the new Chinese nuclear threat.

Their study, which was completed in 1966 after Shastri's demise, concluded that the principal threat emanating from China remained in the conventional realm. The nuclear threat, the authors of the study concluded, would have to be handled through adroit diplomacy and reliance on the goodwill of the great powers. Not surprisingly, the Indian political leadership under Prime Minister Indira Gandhi made a concerted effort to obtain a nuclear guarantee from the United Kingdom, the United States, and the Soviet Union. The outcome of this enterprise proved chastening to the Indian elite: none of the great powers proved willing to provide such a guarantee. The failure to obtain an assurance from the great powers only increased pressure on Prime Minister Indira Gandhi's government to reassess the country's nuclear stance.

To some extent, India's nuclear diplomacy shifted ground as the decade drew to a close. Specifically, in 1966, the Indian delegate to the Eighteenth National Disarmament Commission, Vishnu Trivedi, cogently argued that India would accede to the nascent Nuclear Nonproliferation Treaty only if the nuclear weapons states undertook reciprocal measures to reduce and ultimately eliminate their nuclear arsenals. At a domestic level, India also indicated that it reserved the right to carry out nuclear explosions for peaceful purposes.[11]

'The Buddha Is Smiling'[12]

The Indian decision to break the nuclear taboo came shortly after the 1971 war with Pakistan and was precipitated by two sets of factors. Thanks to the efforts of Bhaba and his successors, India had mastered most of the elements of the nuclear fuel cycle; the requisite scientific base was in place for pursuing a nuclear weapons option. Additionally, India's humiliating defeat at Chinese hands in the 1962 war loomed large in the minds of Indian decision-makers. In addition to these underlying forces, more immediate concerns pushed India over the nuclear precipice. Flush with India's trouncing of Pakistan in the 1971 war, Indira Gandhi wanted to bolster India's new-found regional power status through the acquisition of a demonstrated nuclear weapons capability.

As the elation of this military victory dissipated, however, she faced the onerous tasks of governing the country under conditions of economic distress and concomitant political instability. The economic problems, in large measure, stemmed from the abrupt rise in global oil prices after the Arab-Israeli War of October 1973. The detonation of a nuclear device in 1974 did little to address India's vast socio-economic problems, but it proved to be a short-term panacea for Mrs Gandhi's beleaguered government. Many in India saw the detonation of the device as a striking scientific and technological feat. The event conveyed to them some sense of governmental efficacy and national self-esteem.[13]

The reactions of the international community to the Indian 'peaceful nuclear explosion' were mixed. Of the industrialized countries, only France congratulated India on the successful test. Much of the developing world expressed vicarious pleasure at India's successful breaching of an exclusive club. The United States and Canada, however, took a dim view of the Indian test. The United States suspended transfers of fuel to the General Electric–built nuclear power plant at Tarapur. The Canadians cut off all nuclear cooperation with India on the alleged grounds that India had diverted nuclear fuel from a Canadian-assisted research reactor.[14] In 1975, American pressure led to the creation of the London Suppliers Group, an organization of advanced industrial states that would monitor and limit the spread of dual-use nuclear technology.

The international community's disapprobation over the Indian nuclear test and the restrictions that followed had two important consequences for the Indian programme. On the one hand, there is little question that both the civilian nuclear industry, as well as the weapons programme, suffered from the loss of various forms of international cooperation. On the other hand, the Indian nuclear complex, perforce, became more self-reliant.

Pakistan's Nuclear Development

The origins of the Pakistani nuclear programme are markedly different from those of India's. Unlike Nehru, who saw a critical role for modern science in boosting India's development, the post-independence Pakistani leadership evinced little interest in harnessing the power of the atom. The initial concerns of Pakistan's leadership focussed on the substantial problems of the maintenance of domestic order and the pursuit of national consolidation. Indeed it was not until after the Eisenhower administration launched its 'Atoms for Peace' programme in December 1953 that Pakistan's leadership sought to develop a small nuclear research programme. In October 1954, the Pakistani government expressed an interest in the development of nuclear energy. About two years later the Pakistan Atomic Energy Commission (PAEC) was formed, with Dr Nazir Ahmad, a Cambridge-trained physicist, at its head.

Pakistan's decision to develop a nuclear device came much later.[15] In the aftermath of the humiliating defeat at Indian hands in 1971, President Zulfiquar Ali Bhutto met with a group of Pakistani scientists in Multan to press for the development of a nuclear bomb.[16] Bhutto no doubt calculated that India's overwhelming conventional superiority and size would place Pakistan at a significant military disadvantage in any future conflict. Consequently, the acquisition of nuclear weapons could deter a future Indian intervention in Pakistan's remaining territory.

Pakistan's attempt to bolster its own security through the acquisition of a nuclear weapons capability in the wake of the 1971 war was compelling. Customarily, states have two possible means of guaranteeing their security in the anarchic international environment.[17] One involves some form of self-help, and the other requires the forging of an alliance. After the 1971 war, and the resultant loss of East Pakistan (now Bangladesh), the Pakistani economy was in the doldrums. Pakistan could ill afford to devote substantial resources to strengthening its conventional forces. Simultaneously, in Pakistani eyes, the United States had proven to be a singularly unreliable ally for failing to prevent the breakup of Pakistan.[18] Under these trying circumstances the pursuit of a nuclear weapons option was seen as a possible strategic panacea.

Shortly after Bhutto's decision to pursue the development of nuclear weapons, the Indian nuclear test provided an additional impetus. Five months later, in October 1974, Pakistan signed a contract with France for a plutonium reprocessing plant designed to produce fuel for a series of nuclear power plants. An able Pakistani metallurgist, Abdul Qadir Khan, who had obtained substantial knowledge of a centrifuge enrichment process during his stint with URENCO, a Dutch consortium, returned to Pakistan in late 1975. Bhutto put Khan in charge of a secret programme to manufacture nuclear weapons. During the latter part of the decade, it is believed that the enterprising Khan made a series of clandestine purchases of technological components to fashion a small, pilot enrichment plant. Subsequently, a larger installation was developed at Kahuta, near Islamabad.[19]

Pakistan's clandestine activities and a proposed French nuclear reactor sale to Pakistan attracted the attention of the Jimmy Carter administration in Washington. The US Congress and the administration accordingly pushed through the Symington and Glenn Amendments to the Foreign Assistance Act. The Symington Amendment effectively prohibited the United States from providing foreign assistance to countries that imported uranium-enrichment technologies without accepting full-scope International Atomic Energy Agency (IAEA) safeguards. The Glenn Amendment sought to limit the sales of reprocessing technology or the receipt of uranium-enrichment plants. It also barred assistance to countries that imported plutonium-reprocessing technologies without the appropriate IAEA safeguards. Simultaneously, the Carter administration exerted considerable diplomatic pressure on the French to abandon the proposed transfer of reactor technology. In the end, the United States prevailed.

The Pakistani commitment to acquire nuclear weapons, nevertheless, did not waver. In fact, following the overthrow of Zulfiquar Ali Bhutto in a military coup in July 1977, the new military dictatorship of

Gen. Mohammed Zia-ul-Haq pursued the nuclear programme with renewed vigour. At a public level, however, Zia continued to deny that Pakistan was making any effort to acquire or manufacture nuclear weapons.

The United States' stringent efforts to prevent Pakistan from acquiring nuclear weapons dissipated somewhat in the wake of the Soviet invasion of Afghanistan in December 1979. The exigencies of dislodging the Soviets from Afghanistan necessitated placing the nuclear non-proliferation issue aside. This policy was accentuated under the Ronald Reagan administration, which obtained waivers of both the Symington and Glenn Amendments in its effort to court Pakistan to funnel US aid to the Afghan resistance. During this period Pakistan became the beneficiary of substantial US military assistance.[20] Not unexpectedly, India utilized its relationship with the Soviet Union to strengthen its own arsenal and maintain its conventional superiority vis-à-vis Pakistan.[21]

Despite the Reagan administration's virtual abandonment of the non-proliferation agenda, key individuals in the US Congress sought to maintain some elements of the non-proliferation agenda. For example, in 1985, the US Congress passed the Solarz Amendment, which barred American assistance to countries seeking to illegally import nuclear commodities for use in nuclear weapons.[22] Subsequently, in an attempt to maintain the American role in Pakistan, the US executive branch fashioned an agreement with Congress in the form of the Pressler Amendment. The tightly worded language of the Pressler Amendment required the president of the United States to certify that Pakistan 'did not possess a nuclear explosive device' to enable the latter to be eligible for American assistance. Unlike the previous amendments, the Pressler Amendment did not have any waiver provisions. Throughout the Afghan war, the Reagan and the George H.W. Bush administrations certified to Congress that Pakistan was adhering to the Pressler standard. As the Afghan war drew to a close, in 1990, the Bush administration finally failed to wink at the Pressler standard. Accordingly, all US assistance to Pakistan was suspended.

Despite the eventual restrictions of the Pressler Amendment, the Afghan war and the concomitant exigencies of US policy priorities had provided a significant respite for the Pakistani nuclear programme. During this period, Pakistan made substantial gains in its pursuit of a full-fledged nuclear weapons option.[23]

The final Pakistani decision to conduct nuclear tests came in the aftermath of the Indian nuclear tests of May 1998. Pakistani decision-makers, most notably Prime Minister Muhammad Nawaz Sharif, on the advice of the professional military, felt compelled to carry out a set of six nuclear tests to demonstrate that it could match India's nuclear prowess. Some have argued that an intemperate statement on the part of L.K. Advani, the Indian Home Minister, made shortly after the Indian nuclear tests, prodded an anxious Pakistani politico-military establishment to cross the nuclear Rubicon.[24]

A More Unstable Region?

It is virtually an article of faith among members of the global and, in particular, the American nuclear non-proliferation communities that the Indian and Pakistani nuclear tests have made the region more prone to war.[25] Indian and Pakistani decision-makers, on the other hand, have, with almost equal force, argued that the likelihood of full-scale war in the region is now highly unlikely specifically *because* of the emergence of a crude form of nuclear deterrence.[26] They contend that if nuclear deterrence preserved the peace between the two adversarial blocs during the Cold War, a similar strategic arrangement can also emerge in South Asia. Which of these two analyses constitutes a more accurate assessment of the situation that now obtains on the subcontinent?

Both propositions are open to question. The new-found anxieties of the non-proliferation community notwithstanding, India and Pakistan have been nuclear-armed rivals for well over a decade; they just were not *declared* nuclear powers. As argued in Chapter 4, the two sides lived through two military crises, in 1987 and 1990, at least one of which had a nuclear component. The events of May 1998 simply made their covert nuclear programmes overt. Even the ballistic missile programmes and the quest for other delivery systems on the part of both sides were well under way before the 1998 tests.[27] Consequently, in terms of material capabilities, the nuclear tests of 1998 did not significantly alter the strategic balance in South Asia. The major difference that the tests made was to end the 'tacit bargaining' with nuclear weapons. Now both sides had to explicitly take cognizance of the nuclear capabilities of the other.[28]

But has stable deterrence arrived in South Asia, as many Indians and Pakistanis would argue? It may well be too early to make that claim with any degree of certainty. Clearly, neither side has the requisite capability to pursue a decapitating first strike against the other. Consequently, either side, if contemplating a nuclear or conventional attack on the other's nuclear capabilities, must take into account the possibility of a nuclear response from the other. As long as these conditions prevail, most sensible decision-makers will refrain from nuclear sabre-rattling, let alone contemplating an attack on the other's nuclear forces.

Why, then, should deterrence not work in South Asia? One argument holds that the extremely short flight times of ballistic missiles in the region make the situation extremely dangerous. In a crisis, if one side received false warning of an impending missile attack it would be under extraordinary pressure to launch its missiles for fear of immediate decapitation.[29] The same argument also suggests that the acute tension and hostility that prevail in the region enhance the possibility of misperception and inadvertent nuclear use. This argument does not stand up to careful historical scrutiny, however. For example, Soviet missiles could also have struck American forces in West Germany during the Cold War in fairly short order, leaving the United States very little time to retaliate.[30] Tensions between the superpowers during the Cold War also ran very high and were punctuated by a number of grave crises.[31]

Evidence from other conflict-ridden relationships also offers reason for a more sanguine conclusion about the Indo-Pakistani nuclear dyad. China and the Soviet Union, for instance, fought a major border war in 1969 along the Ussuri River. At that time both states had nuclear weapons and the requisite means of delivery.[32] Furthermore, Chinese Communist Party chairman Mao Zedong was not averse to using significant force in the context of either domestic or external politics.[33] The Soviet leader, Leonid Brezhnev, had also exhibited a capacity to use force, both near and far from the borders of his country, based on the defence of ideological principles.[34]

The more serious issues in the region are the possibilities of technological error and misperception. Until India and Pakistan successfully embed their nuclear weapons in robust command, control, communications, and intelligence infrastructure, the risk of inadvertent or, worse, unauthorized usage will persist.[35] Ironically, American non-proliferation policy, in its single-minded zeal to prevent the proliferation of nuclear weapons, also prohibits the transfer of certain technologies that might mitigate the dangers of accidental nuclear war. [36]

The 1999 war between India and Pakistan in Kargil offers one useful test of the two competing positions about nuclear stability and instability in South Asia.[37] Despite the overt nuclearization of the region, an undeclared war did take place. However, no reliable evidence has yet emerged that either side contemplated a resort to nuclear weapons during this conflict. More to the point, unlike in the 1965 war, when Pakistan attacked India in Kashmir, in 1999 India did not resort to prompt horizontal escalation. Instead, it carefully limited the war to a particular arena and did not even attempt to cross the Line of Control into Pakistani territory after dislodging the Pakistani troops from its own lands.

There is little question that one of the principal reasons for the Indian restraint was the acute awareness of Indian defence officials that their adversary possessed nuclear weapons and would resort to their use if its vital interests or assets were jeopardized.[38] For the foreseeable future then, the overt nuclearization of the region may have contributed to nuclear security on the subcontinent while increasing the likelihood of lower-level engagements. This 'stability/instability' paradox will be discussed further in the next chapter, which examines in detail the war in Kargil.

Notes

1. Much of this chapter has been adapted from Sumit Ganguly, 'Nuclear Proliferation in South Asia: Origins, Consequences and Prospects,' in Shalendra Sharma, ed., *The Asia-Pacific in the New Millennium* (Berkeley: Institute of East Asian Studies, 2000). This chapter will not attempt to trace the origins of the Indian and Pakistani nuclear programmes in detail. This task has been performed elsewhere with varying degrees of reliability and accuracy. On the origins and evolution of the Indian nuclear programme see Itty Abraham, *The Making of India's Atomic Bomb* (London: Zed Press, 1998); Raj Chengappa, *Weapons of Peace* (New Delhi: Harper Collins, 2000); George Perkovich, *India's Nuclear Bomb* (Berkeley: University of California Press, 1999); and Sumit Ganguly, 'India's Pathway to Pokhran II: The Origins and Sources of India's Nuclear Weapons Program,' *International Security*, Volume 23, Number 4 (Spring 1999), pp. 148–177. For an assessment of competing arguments see Sumit Ganguly, 'Explaining Indian Nuclear Policy,' *Current History*, Volume 98, Number 632 (December 1999), pp. 438–440. For a superb discussion of the likely future of the Indian nuclear programme, see Ashley J. Tellis, *India's Emerging Nuclear Posture: Between Recessed Deterrent and Ready Arsenal* (Santa Monica: Rand Corporation, 2001).

Less information is available about the Pakistani nuclear weapons programme. For a useful treatment see Samina Ahmed, 'Pakistan's Nuclear Weapons Program: Turning Points and Nuclear Choices,' *International Security*, Volume 23, Number 4 (Spring 1999), pp. 178–204. Also see Ziba Moshaver, *Nuclear Weapons Proliferation in the Indian Subcontinent* (New York: St. Martin's Press, 1991). For a discussion of how the overt posession of nuclear weapons by India and Pakistan is likely to affect stability in the region see Ashley J. Tellis, *The Changing Political-Military Environment in South Asia* (Santa Monica: Rand Corporation, 2001).

2. For a sampling of adverse reactions to the Indian and Pakistani nuclear tests, see the various articles in 'India Bombs the Ban,' *Bulletin of the Atomic Scientists*, Volume 54, Number 4 (July/August 1998).

3. Zulfiquar Ali Bhutto, *The Myth of Independence* (London: Oxford University Press, 1969).

4. For an early analysis of the Indian nuclear weapons programme see Sumit Ganguly, 'Why India Joined the Nuclear Club,' *Bulletin of the Atomic Scientists*, Volume 39, Number 4 (April 1983), pp. 30–33.

5. Ganguly, 'Why India Joined the Nuclear Club,' p. 30.

6. Personal communication with a retired senior International Atomic Energy Agency official, February 1995, Oxford, United Kingdom. Also see Shayam Bhatia, *India's Nuclear Bomb* (Ghaziabad: Vikas Publishing House, 1979). Bhatia contends that Bhaba discussed his interest in pursuing nuclear weapons with an eminent British physicist, Lord P.M.S. Blackett.

7. Moshaver, *Nuclear Weapons in the Indian Subcontinent*, 1991.

8. Nehru's views about the military and defence spending are discussed in Sumit Ganguly, 'From the Defence of the Nation to Aid to the Civil: The Army in Contemporary India,' *Journal of Asian and African Affairs*, Volume 26, Numbers 1–2 (1991). Also see the excellent treatment in Veena Kukreja, *Civil-Military Relations in South Asia: Pakistan, Bangladesh and India* (New Delhi: Sage Publications, 1991).

9. The best account of the Sino-Indian border war can be found in Steven Hoffmann, *India and the China Crisis* (Berkeley: University of California Press, 1990).

10. For an account of this debate see G.G. Mirchandani, *India's Nuclear Dilemma* (New Delhi: Popular Book Services, 1968).

11. Bhatia, *India's Nuclear Bomb*.

12. This was the pre-arranged coded telegraphic message that was sent by the scientists at Pokhran to Indira Gandhi indicating the successful completion of the nuclear test. See Roberta Wohlstetter, *The Buddha Smiles: Absent-Minded Peaceful Aid and the Indian Bomb* (Los Angeles: Pan Heuristics, 1977).

13. For a discussion of Indian reactions to the nuclear test see Surjit Mansingh, *India's Search for Power: Indira Gandhi's Foreign Policy 1966–1982* (New Delhi: Sage Publications, 1984), pp. 98–99.

14. For an excellent discussion of the Indo-US tussle over fuel for the Tarapur reactor see Brahma Chellaney, *Nuclear Proliferation: The US Conflict* (New Delhi: Orient Longman, 1993).

15. For a thoughtful discussion of Pakistan's nuclear choices see Samina Ahmed, 'Pakistan's Nuclear Weapons Programme.'

16. Steve Weissman and Herbert Krosney, *The Islamic Bomb* (New York: Times Books, 1981).

17. For the standard statement of this position see Kenneth Waltz, *Theory of International Politics* (Reading, Mass.: Addison-Wesley, 1979).

18. The best description and analysis of the American role in the 1971

war is Richard Sisson and Leo E. Rose, *War and Secession: Pakistan, India, and the Creation of Bangladesh* (Berkeley: University of California Press, 1990).

19. Weissman and Krosney, *Islamic Bomb*.

20. The initial tranche amounted to $3.2 billion over five years.

21. Robert Horn, *Soviet-Indian Relations: Issues and Influence* (New York: Praeger, 1979); also see Jerome M. Conley, *Indo-Russian Military Cooperation: Lessons and Options for US Policy in South Asia* (Lanham: Lexington Books, 2001).

22. The Solarz Amendment came in the wake of the arrest in the United States of a Pakistani national, Arshad Pervez, who had been attempting to export krytons, essentially triggering devices for nuclear weapons, to Pakistan.

23. On this point see Mitchell Reiss, *Bridled Ambition: Why Countries Constrain Their Nuclear Capabilities* (Washington, D.C.: Woodrow Wilson Center Press, 1995).

24. Harish Khare, 'Roll Back Proxy War, Pak Told,' *The Hindu*, May 19, 1998. For Pakistani reactions to Advani's remarks see Amit Baruah, 'Pak. Reacts Sharply to Advani's Statement,' *The Hindu*, May 20, 1998.

25. Craig R. Whitney, 'Five Nations Join in Plea to Pakistan and India,' *New York Times*, June 6, 1998, p. 4.; also see *Proceedings of the 2000 Carnegie International Non-Proliferation Conference, March 16–17, 2000* (Washington, D.C.: Carnegie Endowment for International Peace, 2000).

26. On this issue see the chapters in Jasjit Singh, ed., *Nuclear India* (New Delhi: Knowledge World, 1998), and Amitabh Mattoo, ed., *India's Nuclear Deterrent: Pokhran II and Beyond* (New Delhi: Har-Anand Publications, 1999). Also see John F. Burns, 'Leaders in India and in Pakistan Tone Down Crisis,' *New York Times*, May 30, 1998, pp. A1, A5; a further discussion can be found in Pratap Bhanu Mehta, 'Exploding Myths,' *The New Republic*, June 8, 1998, pp. 17–19.

27. Raj Chengappa, *Weapons of Peace: The Secret Story of India's Quest to be a Nuclear Power* (New Delhi: HarperCollins, 2000).

28. Neil Joeck, 'Nuclear Relations in South Asia,' in Joseph Cirincione, ed., *Repairing the Regime*, text available at http://www.ceip.org/programs/npp/RegimeSouthAsia.htm.

29. Some of these issues are raised in Gregory S. Jones, *From Testing to Deploying Nuclear Forces: The Hard Choices Facing India and Pakistan* (Santa Monica: Rand Corporation, 1998).

30. Admittedly, an important difference was that in the Western European context the two sides had extensive surveillance and intelligence capabilities, which are not yet present in the Indo-Pakistani context.

31. Scott D. Sagan, *Moving Targets: Nuclear Strategy and National Security* (Princeton: Princeton University Press, 1989); also see Raymond Garthoff, *Detente and Confrontation: American-Soviet Relations from Nixon to Reagan* (Washington, D.C.: Brookings Institution, 1985).

32. Harrison Salisbury, *The Coming War between Russia and China* (New York: Norton, 1969).

33. The brutality of the Chinese regime under Mao can be gauged from the horrors of the 'Great Leap Forward,' Mao's misguided attempt to transform the Chinese economy and polity between 1958 and 1962. For two excellent accounts see Jasper Becker, *Hungry Ghosts: Mao's Secret Famine* (New York: Henry Holt and Company, 1966), and Jean-Luc Domenach (Translated by A.M. Berrett), *The Origins of the Great Leap Forward: The Case of One Chinese Province* (Boulder: Westview, 1995).

34. Some sense of the Soviet willingness to use force beyond its national borders in the defence of ideological principles can be ascertained from Henry S. Bradsher, *Afghanistan and the Soviet Union* (Durham: Duke University Press, 1983).

35. Shaun Gregory, 'A Formidable Challenge: Nuclear Command and Control in South Asia,' *Disarmament Diplomacy*, Number 54 (February 2001), pp. 2–4.

36. For the most comprehensive treatment of the likely evolution of the Indian nuclear weapons programme see Ashley Tellis, *India's Emerging Nuclear Posture: Between Recessed Deterrent and Ready Arsenal* (Santa Monica: Rand Corporation, 2001).

37. The larger debate about whether or not nuclear weapons contribute to stability or the lack thereof is explored in Scott D. Sagan and Kenneth N. Waltz, *The Spread of Nuclear Weapons: A Debate* (New York: W.W. Norton and Company, 1995).

38. Interview with senior Indian general, October 2000.

Chapter Six

The Kargil War

Between April and June 1999, India and Pakistan almost plunged into another full-scale war along the Line of Control (LoC) in Kashmir. The conflict can be traced to the Pakistani attempt to infiltrate regular troops from the Northern Light Infantry and Kashmiri insurgents across a 150-kilometre stretch of the LoC at three points in Batalik, Dras, and Kargil in the spring of 1999. The intrusion proved to be a complete surprise for Indian military and intelligence officials, who had failed to anticipate a Pakistani military incursion across a most inhospitable terrain.[1]

The background to this conflict requires some discussion. After the Indian and Pakistani nuclear tests of 1998, both countries had come under significant pressure from the United States and many of the other major powers to reduce bilateral tensions in South Asia. The pervasive belief in New Delhi and Islamabad that their overt acquisition of nuclear capabilities had significantly reduced the likelihood of war was not shared in other international capitals. In fact, a number of key American and other officials had underscored the increased risk of nuclear war in the region, given its conflict prone history.[2]

It is impossible to adduce incontrovertible evidence that these pressures led Pakistani prime minister Muhammed Nawaz Sharif and his Indian counterpart, Atal Behari Vajpayee, to attempt the improvement in Indo-Pakistani relations that was seen in early 1999.[3] However, it is not unreasonable to infer that the widespread international condemnation of the Indian and Pakistani tests and the imposition of a raft of economic sanctions against both countries had induced the two leaders to initiate a dialogue on a series of outstanding issues.

In February 1999, Vajpayee with much fanfare had personally

inaugurated a bus service between the border cities of Amritsar in India and Lahore in Pakistan. At the end of this bus trip, the two prime ministers signed an agreement at Lahore, the capital of the Pakistani state of Punjab, reiterating the principles embodied in a number of previous agreements, including the Simla Agreement of 1971. No doubt with a view toward addressing the professed concern of the great powers, most notably the United States, about the dangers of nuclear war in the region, the agreement also called upon the two sides to

take immediate steps for reducing the risk of accidental or unauthorized use of nuclear weapons and discuss concepts and doctrines with a view to elaborating measures for confidence building in the nuclear and conventional fields, aimed at prevention of conflict.[4]

Indian officials had placed much hope in the Lahore process and genuinely believed that Prime Minister Nawaz Sharif was interested in ushering in a new era in Indo-Pakistani relations. They genuinely believed that it was in the mutual interest of both countries to work toward a pragmatic settlement of many outstanding disputes and felt that the moment was ripe to take steps toward those ends.

An End to Goodwill

Despite the positive and cooperative sentiments expressed in the Lahore Agreement and in the weeks thereafter, the Pakistani military, with the acquiescence of Nawaz Sharif, planned a military operation in Kashmir designed to revive the Kashmir issue on the international agenda and possibly jump-start the flagging insurgency.[5] Again, the all-too-familiar propensity of assuming eternal support without seeking proper confirmation characterized Pakistani decision-making.[6]

A combination of Pakistani false optimism and Indian complacency contributed to the Kargil crisis of the summer of 1999. Pakistani decision-makers made a number of unwarranted assumptions about the likely response of the global community, particularly the United States, when they embarked on a bold manoeuvre to breach the LoC. They believed that even if they initiated a conflict along the LoC, it would be difficult for the great powers to accurately pin responsibility on Pakistan and, in any case, the United States would be loath to support the Indian position. The latter belief stemmed from the Pakistani assessment of past American behaviour during Indo-Pakistani conflicts and tensions.

Indian obliviousness to the possibility of a Pakistani attempt to breach the LoC in the Kargil sector provided the requisite opportunity for Pakistan to undertake this enterprise. In fairness, this sector, according to military sources, is exceedingly difficult to adequately patrol because of the harsh and inhospitable terrain. Poor weather conditions also limit reconnaissance activities, and heavy snows, especially in the winter months, render movement exceedingly difficult, if not impossible.[7]

The events unfolded as follows. On May 5, the Indian army's 121st Brigade sent out a routine reconnaissance patrol in the Kaksar area along the LoC in Kashmir. The purpose of this patrol was to ascertain if the snows had melted sufficiently to enable the Indian forces to re-occupy the mountain redoubts that they normally abandoned in the winter months. The patrol was never heard from again. It was probably ambushed and all its members killed.

Shortly thereafter, as a consequence of the disappearance of the patrol, and increased reconnaissance, the commanders of the 121st Brigade estimated that there were approximately 100 hostile intruders in the mountain peaks near Kargil. They also concluded that their brigade had sufficient capabilities to dislodge the intruders. By May 15, their assessment of the strength of the intruders was dramatically revised upward, to some 800 intruders. The military authorities soon found that these groups had also breached the LoC in Mushkoh Valley, Kaksar, and Batalik.[8] Not until the last week of May did the Indian army realize that these hostile actors—regular Pakistani forces and Kashmiri insurgents—had occupied as many as 70 positions along the LoC. They now also came to the belated realization that well over the initial estimate of 800 men were involved in this operation. Worse still, the intruders had occupied a number of strategic salients directly above the road from Kargil to Leh and were now in a position to cut off the northern portions of Kashmir from the rest of the state. Aerial surveillance revealed that the intruders were equipped with snowmobiles, artillery and substantial stocks of supplies.

The initial Indian reaction was clumsy due to a lack of good information about the intruders' strength, disposition, and capabilities. Indian troops attempted to push their way up to heights of 16,000 feet and higher. But because of the lack of ground cover and the intruders' command of the heights, the advancing Indian troops became easy targets for Pakistani snipers and gunners. After taking substantial casualties, the Indians realized that they would need considerably greater firepower to dislodge the Pakistani intruders. Not until May 25, however, did the Indian decision-making machinery undertake a more comprehensive political-military analysis of the emergent problem. During a meeting of the high-powered Cabinet Committee on Security (CCS), a decision was taken to induct as many as three brigades into the region. Furthermore, in view of the fact that Indian troops would need acclimatization before being deployed at these altitudes, the CCS decided in the interim to permit the use of air power against the entrenched Pakistanis.[9]

Accordingly, the Indian Air Force (IAF) carried out a first round of air strikes against the peaks on May 26.[10] On May 27, the IAF launched a second round of air strikes with the objective of dislodging the intruders from Batalik, Turtuk, and Dras. During the length of 'Operation Vijay' (literally, 'operation victory'), as it was called, the IAF flew as many as 550 sorties. In conducting these air operations the IAF relied on Mirage-2000, MiG-21, MiG-23, and MiG-27 airplanes,[11] of which it lost two: a MiG-21 and a MiG-27.[12] Indian authorities insisted that all air attacks were confined to areas that India deemed to be on its side of the LoC. Pakistani officials, however, claimed that the IAF planes had crossed the LoC and had struck targets within 'Azad Kashmir.'[13]

The decision to permit the use of air power marked a significant departure from past Indian attempts to deal with Pakistani incursions along the LoC. Indeed, not since the 1971 war had air power been used in support of military operations in Kashmir.[14] The Indian forces resorted to the use of air power because they realized that it would be all but impossible to dislodge the intruders through the use of ground troops in frontal assaults, since crossing the LoC was rejected for political reasons.

With the air strikes under way, the Indian army moved post-haste to dislodge the intruders from the salients that they had come to occupy. Though Operation Vijay was eventually successful, it proved to be extraordinarily costly in both human and material terms.[15] Official sources in India stated that 487 men were killed and another 1,000 injured.[16] Unofficial accounts suggest that the casualties may have been significantly higher.[17]

Logistical, organizational and topographic limitations significantly hobbled Indian military operations. In the initial stages of the conflict troops deployed in counter insurgency operations in Kashmir were hastily moved to significantly higher altitudes, thereby seriously endangering their health. Furthermore, this drawing-down of troops engaged in counter-insurgency operations left other parts of the state vulnerable to terrorist actions. Finally, the terrain along the LoC greatly favoured the Pakistani forces.[18] Nevertheless, by early June, the Indian army had made dogged progress and had managed to recapture some 21 positions.

In launching their assaults, the Indian army brought in its Bofors howitzers and also relied on IAF sorties to soften up targets.[19] These gains were made at considerable cost, as the Indian soldiers had to assault bunkers and redoubts at considerable heights while facing punishing fire from well-entrenched, fortified positions above them.[20]

While these operations proceeded, Indian decision-makers took considerable comfort from the fact that few, if any, states were supporting the Pakistani position. Most significantly, perhaps, the United States showed little inclination to support a Pakistani effort to bring the issue before the United Nations Security Council. Indian diplomacy moved into high gear as the minister for external affairs, Jaswant Singh, while preparing to leave for China, agreed to meet with his Pakistani counterpart, Sartaj Aziz, in New Delhi.[21] Although he showed a willingness to entertain diplomatic solutions to the crisis, Prime Minister Vajpayee took a tough stance in a public speech, stating that his government would not rest until every intruder had been dislodged.[22] He also made clear that while India was prepared to hold talks with Pakistan, these discussions would be strictly confined to the resolution of the Kargil crisis.[23] Eventually, New Delhi set a date for Sartaj Aziz's visit (June 12) but insisted that the talks remain limited to Pakistan's role in precipitating the Kargil problem.[24]

The talks between Sartaj Aziz and Jaswant Singh proved infructuous. Aziz sought a 'partial de-escalation' in Kargil and made it contingent on an end to the Indian artillery barrages and air strikes. More to the point, he insisted that Pakistan had no control over the intruders. Singh, however, refused to accept any of Aziz's formulations and insisted that the Pakistanis simply withdraw their troops.[25]

Only around June 14–16 did the Indian forces manage to retake key positions near Dras and Batalik. These two positions were deemed to be of considerable importance because they overlook the principal supply route for the Indian military to the Siachen Glacier, where India and Pakistan had been fighting a costly and stalemated battle since 1984.[26] Around June 20, they managed to re-establish control over Batalik itself.[27] Some several hundred Indian troops and officers perished in this battle and at least two IAF aircraft and one helicopter were shot down.

As the hostilities showed few signs of abating, in the last week of June Gen. Anthony Zinni, the commander-in-chief of the US Central Command, visited Pakistan and pointedly told Prime Minister Sharif to call off his troops.[28] In the aftermath of Zinni's visit, Gordon Lanpher, a US deputy assistant secretary of state for South Asia, visited New Delhi to apprise his Indian counterparts of the substance of Gen. Zinni's message to Islamabad and also to counsel restraint by the Indians. According to a well-known Indian journalist and commentator, Lanpher informed the Indians that Zinni had told the Pakistanis to start a prompt withdrawal of their forces from the Kargil region. More to the point, Zinni had reportedly refused to entertain Pakistan's efforts to link the Kargil question with the broader Indo-Pakistani dispute over Kashmir.[29]

Despite Zinni's warning, the conflict continued into early July. No doubt surprised by the intensity of the Indian attacks and the inability to persuade the United States and other powers to back Pakistan, Sharif visited Washington, D.C., on July 4 in search of a face saving device.[30] Much to Sharif's surprise, President Bill Clinton was unwilling to accept Pakistan's claim that India was responsible for provoking the crisis. By not accepting the Pakistani version of the origins of the Kargil crisis, the United States helped hasten its end.[31] Unlike in the past, the United States also refused to mediate between the two parties.[32]

Although Sharif's visit to Washington underscored his realization of the scope of his misadventure, various Kashmiri groups who were participating in the Pakistani effort in Kargil showed little inclination to bring their fighting to a close. One of the principal leaders involved in the insurgency, Sayed Saluhuddin, the head of the United Jihad Council, proclaimed that Sharif's willingness to withdraw his troops was 'tantamount to stabbing the movement in the back.'[33]

The US unwillingness to mediate stood in marked contrast to the Clinton administration's propensity to intervene in a variety of regional disputes. Two factors explain in large part the American unwillingness to invest time and resources in mediating an end to this conflict. At one level, even in the post–Cold War era, South Asia has remained a fairly low priority for most American administrations. At another level, although keen on preventing a full-scale conflagration in South Asia, the United States did not have any vital interests implicated in the region. Consequently, it remained loath to step into a region riven by a long-standing dispute with little or no prospect of easy or quick resolution.

As Sharif sought American intercession to find a face-saving way out of the imbroglio, India maintained its military pressure. These efforts started to meet with success by the first week of July, when the Indians recaptured yet another strategic peak, Tiger Hill.[34] By the second week of July, the Pakistani forces were facing relentless artillery barrages and air attacks from the Indian military. A more sympathetic American response to Sharif might have emboldened him to allow the Pakistani military to persist with their plans. However, in the face of escalating losses and a paucity of international diplomatic support, Sharif was forced to reconsider the value of continuing military operations.[35] By June 9, Pakistan had offered to send a special envoy to New Delhi to discuss a de-escalation. Veteran diplomat Niaz Naik went to New Delhi to meet the principal secretary to the prime minister (and national security adviser), Brajesh Mishra, to find ways to withdraw Pakistani forces from Kargil.[36] Initially, India expressed little interest in talks but later agreed.[37]

On July 12, following his visit to Washington D.C., Sharif gave a nationwide television address in which he called for the withdrawal of the *mujahideen* from the mountain redoubts.[38] It should be noted that Sharif carefully avoided making a public statement about altering any deployments of the Pakistani army.[39] In effect, he was trying to maintain the fiction that the *mujahideen* had scaled these heights and seized the redoubts of their own accord. (Only in late July did Pakistani sources start admitting that their military forces had been deeply involved in the Kargil conflict.[40]) By July 14, the first set of infiltrators started to withdraw from their positions, ceding them to the advancing Indian forces.[41] It was only toward the end of the month, however, that the conflict finally came to a close.

As mentioned earlier, the Pakistani infiltration had in part been designed to jump-start the flagging insurgency in Kashmir. On this score the Pakistanis saw a partial success. With the withdrawal of Pakistani forces from Kargil, the insurgency within the state of Kashmir continued unabated. On July 19 insurgents struck at the village of Lihota, in the Doda District of Jammu, killing fifteen civilians. In another attack, five other villagers lost their lives.[42]

In India, which was in the midst of a national election campaign, the Pakistani climb-down was played up as a major military success.[43] It remains an open question whether or not the Indian victory in Kashmir shaped the electoral outcome. The failure to anticipate and respond suitably to the Pakistani incursions, however, did lead to some self-assessment on the part of the Indian leadership.[44]

And even as the government began its self-examination and sought to pinpoint the sources of the incursion, Indian defence planners started to draw up plans to prevent a future incursion. Among other measures, the Indian army planned to set up permanent posts every 200 yards along the LoC. It also decided to build all-weather bunkers at high altitudes, to enhance long-range patrols, and to purchase a variety of sophisticated equipment needed for mountain warfare, including direction-finding equipment, snow clothing and goggles, snowmobiles, and heating equipment.[45]

Explaining the Incursions

Why did the Pakistani army embark on this risky enterprise? Were these incursions tied to a larger political strategy or were they merely opportunistic? And what factors explain the Indian failure to anticipate the possibility of these intrusions and thereby take steps to forestall them?

The answers to these questions are complex. A number of factors can be adduced to explain the Pakistani enterprise. Some of these are firmly based on available evidence, whereas others can be substantiated only on the basis of inference and attribution. The explanations for the crisis have to be sought from two different perspectives: one deals with Islamabad's decision to attempt an infiltration across the LoC along a most difficult terrain; the other focuses on India's failure to anticipate the possibilities of Pakistani infiltration and respond in a timely and appropriate fashion.

At a tactical level, the incursion along the LoC had all the characteristics of what is referred to as a 'limited probe.'[46] This involves making a small, calibrated incursion to clarify the adversary's will and commitment to fight and defend its territory. The ability to reverse course is one of the distinguishing features of a limited probe. In effect, if the thrust runs into firm opposition, its course is reversed. The party making the probe believes that the risks associated with the probe are both calculable and controllable. The mistake that the Pakistani decision-makers made was to dramatically expand the scope of the probe once they encountered little or no opposition. This expansion of the scale of their incursion made it imperative for India to respond with considerable vigour.

The timing of the probe was not insignificant. Since the late 1990s the Pakistani-aided insurgency in Kashmir was increasingly waning. The Indian security forces had the bulk of the insurgents on the run. With the insurgents at bay, India had held three elections in the state for state-level and national offices. Turnout in these elections had varied but had resulted in a popular, elected government with some slim element of legitimacy. By 1997–98, although pockets of resistance continued to play havoc in Kashmir, a semblance of normalcy had been restored to the Valley.[47] Though most of the Muslim inhabitants of the Valley remained disaffected from the Indian state, they also lived in abject fear of the more virulent insurgent groups such as the Al-Faran, the Laskhar-e-Toiba, the Harkat-ul-Ansar (later styled the Harkat-ul-Mujahideen), and the Al-Badr.[48] The Pakistani leadership feared that this emergent normalcy in the Valley, once consolidated, would foreclose the possibility of further incitement to the insurgency.

Kashmir had also ceased to be an active issue on the international community's agenda. India's deft diplomatic and military strategies had placated the international community's interest in the issue. Diplomatically, India had managed to convince much of the external world that it had addressed problems of human rights violations, had held reasonably free and fair elections, and was now attempting to restore both law and order in the state. Militarily, its 'mailed-fist' strategy had worn down a number of the insurgent groups. Pakistan concluded that, if it wished to remain a relevant player in the Kashmir problem, it had to revive the insurgency. With the normal routes of infiltration into the Valley closed by the increased alertness and deployments of the Indian security forces, Pakistan had to choose a more remote and unlikely region to mount a serious incursion.

In making this incursion the Pakistani leadership simply assumed that the United States and other major states would step in to prevent an escalation of the crisis.[49] This belief in large measure emerged from the Pakistani assessment that the international community had become quite alarmed about the overt nuclearization of South Asia. They also believed that these states would bring concerted pressure on India to desist from taking any compellent action.[50] As in the episodes recounted in the previous chapters of this book, false optimism was at work: there is little or no evidence that the leadership had any tangible basis for their belief in international support. Even Pakistan's traditional ally, China, had distanced itself from Pakistan after 1996.[51]

Pakistan's overt nuclearization had also bolstered this sense of false optimism. Pakistani decision-makers had convinced themselves that their achievement of rough nuclear parity with India now enabled them to probe along the LoC with impunity. In their view, the Indian leadership, cognizant of Pakistan's nuclear capabilities, would decline to use overwhelming force and would also avoid a dramatic escalation or expansion of the conflict.[52]

The Pakistani behaviour in precipitating this conflict conformed closely to the expectations of the 'stability/instability paradox.'[53] This proposition holds that nuclear weapons do contribute to stability at one level, for fear of nuclear escalation. Simultaneously, however, they create incentives for conventional conflicts in peripheral areas as long as either side does not breach certain shared thresholds.

Certain Indian actions that sought to alleviate the acute tension in Indo-Pakistani relations in the wake of the 1998 tests also strengthened the Pakistani resolve to provoke a crisis. These Indian moves constituted an effort to ease pressure from the United States and other major powers over the festering Kashmir problem. These pressures to achieve better bilateral relations had grown out of a widespread belief that Indo-Pakistani border tensions in the wake of the nuclear tests had made the region a 'tinderbox' or a 'flashpoint.'[54] With the overt nuclearization of the region after May 1998, these fears were further exacerbated.

No doubt as a consequence of these demands and with a clear-cut interest in addressing them, India had initiated a dialogue with Pakistan designed to tackle the underlying sources of hostility. As discussed at the outset of this chapter, Prime Minister Vajpayee chose to visit Pakistan in February 1999. During this much-heralded visit, apart from negotiating a number of substantive agreements, Vajpayee undertook an act fraught with political symbolism: he visited the Minar-e-Sharif memorial in Lahore, a monument that celebrates the initial public call for the creation of Pakistan in 1947. At a ceremony there, Vajpayee affirmed India's acknowledgment of Pakistan's territorial integrity.

In the wake of this historic visit, many in the defence and foreign policy-making bureaucracies in New Delhi assumed that relations with Pakistan were on the mend. As a consequence, the routine gathering of intelligence on Pakistan's force deployments, movements, and likely actions was slackened. Moreover, many senior officials became caught up in the heady 'spirit of Lahore' and were unwilling to countenance the prospect of Pakistani malfeasance in Jammu and Kashmir.

Within Kashmir, the ebbing of the insurgency and the return of a modicum of normalcy had an ironic consequence: a significant slackening of the vigilance operations that had taxed the resources of the army as well as the paramilitary forces for nearly a decade. Few individuals in the higher realms of political authority believed that large-scale infiltration could again resume from Pakistan to boost the flagging insurgents.[55] They certainly could not fathom that Pakistani decision-makers would infiltrate soldiers and insurgents from Pakistan's Northern Areas at altitudes of over 16,000 feet across difficult and inhospitable terrain into the Dras-Kargil-Batalik sectors. In the same

vein, Indian analysts had also correctly assessed that the Pakistani
intruders could find little succour from the largely Shi'a and Buddhist
population of this region, whose members do not harbour significant
grievances against the Indian state. Finally, they had concluded that
India's overt nuclear status would nullify the possibilities of conventional
conflict with Pakistan. These inferences and judgments, however, proved
to be fatally flawed.

Structural limitations on intelligence-gathering in Pakistan-
controlled Kashmir and the Northern Areas, combined with these
flawed inferences and judgments, compounded the consequences of
the intelligence failure. Pakistan does not allow Indian diplomats
posted in Islamabad to visit the Northern Areas or 'Azad Kashmir.'
Consequently, intelligence gathering in this remote area is quite limited.
(By the same token, India does not easily allow Pakistani citizens to
visit relatives on the Indian side of the border.) Furthermore, after the
April 1992 overthrow of the India friendly Mohammed Najibullah regime
in Afghanistan, an important source of intelligence on the Northern
Areas had been closed.

The forms of intelligence available to Indian decision-makers were
also at fault. Intelligence analysts make a distinction between 'strategic' intelligence and 'tactical' intelligence. Strategic intelligence is
focussed on changes of policy and strategy. Tactical intelligence deals
with the likely and actual implementation of such policies and strategies. According to one authoritative account, in the lead up to the Kargil
crisis, Indian tactical intelligence proved quite weak, even though its
strategic intelligence was sound.[56]

This account, however, cannot be considered definitive. An alternative position holds that tactical intelligence about likely Pakistani
actions was indeed available as early as September 1998. India's domestic intelligence organization, the Intelligence Bureau (IB), had made
an assessment based on human sources that Pakistan was likely to test
Indian military preparedness in Kargil and other points along the LoC in
the summer. According to the same report, the newly created National
Security Council had received reports in February 1999, from both
the IB and from the Research and Analysis Wing (RAW, India's international intelligence agency), about an ongoing Pakistani military
build-up in key border areas.[57] Unfortunately, the account offering this
information does not offer any clear-cut explanations for the failure of
the higher-level Indian decision-makers to act on the available evidence.

Other evidence, while somewhat controversial, tends to support
the allegations that high-level authorities failed to act on available

tactical intelligence. As early as August 1998, Brig. Surinder Singh, the commander of the Kargil-based 121st Brigade, had submitted a report to his immediate superior, Maj.-Gen. V.S. Budhwar, the general officer commanding the Leh-based 3rd Infantry Division, warning of increased Pakistani shelling in the Kargil region.[58] Budhwar, however, refused to authorize any action to verify Singh's concerns.

Two factors may explain the failure of the higher army brass to act on Singh's misgivings about potential Pakistani malfeasance. At one level, the senior army officials had convinced themselves that the Pakistanis, as much as themselves, saw the Simla Agreement of 1972 as virtually inviolate.[59] They could envisage minor incursions along the LoC but could not countenance the possibility that Pakistan's political-military leadership would embark on a full-fledged violation of the LoC. At another level, the bulk of the forces under the 15th Corps (of which Budhwar's division was a component) were tied down in counterinsurgency operations in Kashmir. Consequently, no significant forces were available for deployment and patrolling along the LoC.

Finally, the lack of inter-organizational coordination exacerbated the intelligence failure. According to a reliable source, RAW's Aviation Research Centre has the requisite aircraft (specially equipped Boeing 707s and twin-engined Beechcraft) for the surveillance of the LoC. Unfortunately, for reasons that remain unclear, the Indian army failed to activate these assets despite RAW warnings about possible Pakistani infiltration.[60]

Flawed assumptions, limited manpower, and organizational shortcomings certainly took their toll on Indian vigilance along the LoC. The inattention of the higher political authorities to the developments in Kashmir worsened matters. No clear-cut evidence is available about the reasons for the failure of the Ministry of Defence and the Ministry of Home Affairs to focus on the prospect of a major Pakistani offensive in Kashmir. In the absence of such information, one can only surmise that the seemingly improved political climate between India and Pakistan, the distraction of many of the key players in the government with the demands of the national election campaign, and the governing inexperience of the ruling coalition contributed to the discounting of the intelligence and resulted in this monumental and costly complacency.

In the aftermath of the conflict, the Bharatiya Janata Party–led government appointed the Kargil Review Committee to examine the causes of the intelligence failure. The committee was composed of K. Subrahmanyam, a highly regarded, hawkish Indian defence analyst;

B.G. Verghese, a noted Indian journalist; Lt.-Gen. K.K. Hazari, a former vice-chief of the Indian army; and Satish Chandra, a senior diplomat. The committee conducted extensive interviews with relevant policy-makers and also toured significant border areas. On January 6, 2000, its findings were made available to the government in a classified report, which ran some 2,000 pages in 17 volumes. The government promised to eventually release a public version of the report, appropriately trimmed to prevent the leakage of sensitive information.[61] At the time of the submission of the classified report, little information about its contents was made available to the public. Journalists, however, managed to discern two general themes that undergirded the report. It criticized the lack of coordination between the plethora of intelligence and security agencies involved in securing the border, and also concluded that there had been a failure to evaluate and disseminate raw intelligence that had been gathered about Pakistani capabilities and likely intentions along the LoC.[62]

Conclusions and Prospects

The long-term repercussions from the Kargil episode are likely to be considerable. In early January 2000, Gen. V.P. Malik, the chief of army staff, declared publicly that in a future confrontation with Pakistan, India might cross the LoC.[63] Later that month, the Indian defence minister, George Fernandes, elaborated on Malik's remarks and provided a glimpse of oncoming shifts in India's military posture vis-à-vis Pakistan. In the light of the overt nuclearization of the region and the ongoing hostilities with Pakistan, he hinted at the emergence of a new doctrine of 'limited war.' Though his presentation was short on detail, Fernandes made clear that India would retain sufficient conventional capabilities to keep the nuclear threshold as high as possible.[64]

Indian military analysts are now formulating a variety of strategies to fight a conventional war against Pakistan while limiting the prospects of escalation. One such strategy would involve attacking in a wide band along the international border without making deep incursions into Pakistani territory. This form of rapid, horizontal escalation, they believe, will result only in a commensurate Pakistani conventional response, because such an action would be unlikely to threaten the fundamental viability of the Pakistani state. On the other hand, such a strategy would confer a significant advantage to India, whose substantially larger conventional forces could inflict considerable human and material costs on the Pakistani forces.[65] The ultimate goal of this strategy would be to seize as much territory as possible along the border areas and then use the captured lands as bargaining chips for Pakistani concessions in Kashmir.

This strategy, while seemingly sound, may well be fraught with considerable military and political risks. A Pakistani defence planner might not be convinced that such a strategy would not include other components, one of which might be to strike more deeply into the Pakistani heartland along vulnerable salients. Furthermore, even if India succeeded in seizing and holding significant chunks of Pakistani border territory, it would still face the problem of being continually harassed by Pakistani forces. Maintaining the security of occupied areas could stretch India's lines of communication and logistical capabilities to a breaking point. Finally, the strategy is also laden with considerable political risks. Key states in the international arena would be highly critical of such a dramatic escalation and would almost certainly seek to bring quick diplomatic and material pressure on India to end the conflict.

Did the Kargil war demonstrate that the overt nuclearization of the region has made it more war-prone? Or did the fact that India did not escalate horizontally show that the likelihood of major war in the region has actually declined? It is difficult at this stage to provide a definitive answer to that question. What is certain, however, is that limited, calibrated incursions across the LoC are still possible despite the mutual acquisition of nuclear capabilities. What South Asia may be witnessing is the emergence of the 'stability/instability' paradox discussed above. The realization on both sides of the sheer destructive power of nuclear weapons makes the prosecution of deliberate full-scale war most unlikely: neither side would wilfully start an all-out war for fear of escalation to the nuclear level.

On the other hand, each side may feel tempted to probe in peripheral areas to test the resolve of the other side, secure in the belief that the likelihood of escalation is both controllable and calculable. Episodes like Kargil may continue to occur unless certain technical, political, and institutional arrangements are put in place and, more importantly, adhered to. Given the stakes that both sides have in the Kashmir issue and their intractable positions on the subject, it is unlikely that any political solution to the conundrum will soon be found. Both sides are also likely to continue the pursuit of their nuclear weapons programmes despite ongoing American and other external pressures. Thus, the implementation of confidence- and security-building measures has taken on crucial importance.

Peering Ahead

What does the future hold for the Indo-Pakistani dispute over Kashmir? The principal hope lies in Pakistan's abandonment of its quest to wrest Kashmir from India through the use of force. All three attempts to seize Kashmir through the use of force have brought Pakistan only marginal returns. Pakistan is no better off in this endeavour than it was on January 1, 1949. Yet the configuration of Pakistani public and elite opinion, coupled with the institutional interests of the armed forces, is such that the prospects of the early abandonment of this effort are unlikely. However, Pakistani president Pervez Musharraf, in his visit to India on July 15–16, 2001, ruled out a military solution to the Kashmir dispute.[66] The inability of the Pakistani armed forces to engage in an open and honest discussion of Pakistan's political limitations, its economic weaknesses, and its social flaws prevents them from acknowledging the folly of repeatedly taking on a state with far more robust political institutions, organizational capabilities, and military prowess.[67]

Nor is India, the status quo power in the region, likely to cede much ground on the Kashmir question. In the 1990s, a series of governments successfully weathered considerable international disapprobation while they pursued harsh counter-insurgency policies in Kashmir. International criticism did lead to some changes in tactics and strategies. For example, in 1992 the Narasimha Rao government created the National Human Rights Commission (NHRC). Initially dismissed as a toothless body, the NHRC quickly achieved a degree of organizational autonomy and censured the government on a number of human rights issues, including the conditions of internment in prisons in Kashmir. The government also created the Rashtriya Rifles, an organization staffed with officers and men from the Indian army and designed to be utilized in counter-insurgency operations. The Rashtriya Rifles were created because most of the paramilitary forces previously deployed in Kashmir, especially the Border Security Force and the Central Reserve Police Force, were found wanting on a number of counts. They often resorted to the inordinate use of force, lacked discipline, and frequently were outgunned by the insurgents. Indian officials believed that a specially trained and well-disciplined force drawn from the regular Indian army would be better suited to handle the rigours of counter-insurgency operations in Kashmir.

These changes in tactics and strategy were, at best, ameliorative. They did not reflect any fundamental shift in the Indian position on the Kashmir issue. The commitment of the national government, regardless of its political or ideological orientation, to the defence of what it deems to be India's territorial integrity remains entirely intact. Some Indian officials even argue that a public shift to accept the LoC as a permanent international border, a proposal that has been made from several quarters, will entail considerable political dexterity on the part of any government in New Delhi.[68]

The extraordinary intransigence of the Indian state on the prospect of any significant territorial concessions arises from the fear of internal 'dominoes.' If Kashmir is allowed to secede, the argument runs, other disaffected states may well consider that exiting the Indian Union is a viable option. Whether these misgivings are real, imagined, or constructed is largely immaterial; they do exist and cannot be dismissed. Consequently, regardless of its political orientation or ideological colouration, any regime in New Delhi will be willing to expend further blood and treasure to maintain control over Kashmir. With increasing economic growth, India's ability to augment its military prowess will only increase.

In the end, perhaps the only practical solution to this sanguinary dispute lies in permanently dividing the state along the LoC and making significant changes in Kashmir's federal relationship with the Indian Union.[69] This solution is unlikely to find much favour with Indian or Pakistani decision-makers, most of whom are committed to maximalist positions. Those postures, however, have little or no practical possibilities of realization either at the present juncture or in the foreseeable future.

Notes

1. For particularly critical essays on India's failure to anticipate a Pakistani incursion across the LoC see *Guns and Yellow Roses: Essays on the Kargil War* (New Delhi: HarperCollins, 1999); an especially critical account of Indian intelligence-gathering and military operations is the essay in that volume by Rahul Bedi, 'A Dismal Failure.'

2. Stephen Kinzer, 'Kashmir Gets Scarier,' *The New York Times*, June 29, 1999, p. 5; also see 'Ever More Dangerous in Kashmir,' *The Economist*, June 19, 1999, pp. 32–33.

3. For evidence of Nawaz Sharif's complicity in the Kargil operation see the essay by Bharat Bhushan, 'In the "Enemy Country,"' in *Guns and Yellow Roses*.

4. See text of the Lahore Declaration (in Appendix) signed between Atal Behari Vajpayee and Muhammad Nawaz Sharif on February 21, 1999.

5. See 'Who Really Runs Pakistan?' *The Economist*, June 26, 1999; also see Dinesh Kumar, 'Secret Tapes Bare the Strategy of a State within a State,' *Times of India*, June 12, 1999.

6. For a trenchant Pakistani analysis of this proclivity see Altaf Gauhar, 'Four Wars, One Assumption,' *The Nation* (Islamabad), September 5, 1999.

7. On the difficulties of patrolling this area see the essay by Lieutenant-General (retd.) Moti Dar, 'Blundering Through,' in *Guns and Yellow Roses*.

8. Ranjit Bhushan, 'Kargil, Post Mortem,' *Outlook India*, July 26, 1999, online at http://www.outlookindia.com/full.asp?fodname=19990726§fname=coverstory§sid=1.

9. 'The War in Kargil,' *Frontline* (Chennai), Volume 16, Number 12 (June 5–18, 1999), available at http://www.the-hindu.com/fline/fl1612/16120040.htm.

10. Barry Bearak, 'India Jets Strike Guerilla Force Now in Kashmir,' *The New York Times*, May 27, 1999, p. A1.

11. Bearak, 'India Jets Strike Guerilla Force.' Also see Special Correspondent, 'IAF Strikes Supply Base in Batalik,' *The Hindu* online, June 27, 1999, at http://www.the-hindu.com/stories/01270002.htm.

12. Barry Bearak, '2 Indian Warplanes Lost Over Pakistan's Part of Kashmir,' *The New York Times*, May 28, 1999, p. A3.

13. Arthur Max, 'Pakistan Charges India with Bombing,' Associated Press, May 26, 1999, newswire.

14. This, of course, does not include the air dropping of supplies and equipment to the Indian soldiers encamped on the Siachen Glacier along the Saltoro Range. For a detailed account of the origins, evolution, and current status of the conflict on the Siachen Glacier see Barry Bearak, 'Frozen in Fury on the Roof of the World,' *The New York Times*, May 23, 1999, p. A1.

15. Agence France Presse, 'Delhi's battle bill: $6.8 million a day,' *The Straits Times* (Singapore), June 16, 1999, p. 9.

16. Gaurav C. Sawant, *Dateline Kargil: A Correspondent's Nine-Week Account from the Battleground* (New Delhi: Macmillan, 2000), p. 285.

17. Sumantra Bose, 'Kashmir: Sources of Conflict, Dimensions of Peace,' *Survival*, Autumn 1999, pp.149–71.

18. For early Indian assertion that challenged Pakistan's claim that its security forces were not involved in the Kargil operation see Shujaat Bukhari, 'Clear Proof of Pak Role,' *The Hindu* online, June 6, 1999, http://www.hinduonline.com/today/stories/01060003.

19. Shujaat Bukhari, 'Indian Army Pushed Ahead,' *The Hindu* online, June 7, 1999, http://www.the-hindu.com/stories/01070002.htm. Parenthetically it should be mentioned that the purchase of these Bofors field guns had been the subject of considerable controversy during Rajiv Gandhi's tenure as prime minister.

20. Dinesh Kumar, 'Death Stalks Jawans at Every Step in Kargil,' *The Times of India* online, June 9, 1999, http://www.timesofindia.com/today/09home2.htm.

21. C. Raja Mohan, 'Operations in a Crucial Stage,' *The Hindu* online, June 7, 1999, http://www.the-hindu.com/stories/010700001.htm.

22. The Times of India News Service, 'Undo Kargil Intrusion, PM Tells Pakistan,' *The Economic Times*, June 8, 1999, at http://www.timesofindia.com/story/08home1.htm.

23. Express News Service, 'Talks Yes, but on Kargil,' *Indian Express* online, June 8, 1999, http://www.expressindia.com/ie/daily/19990608/ige08068.html.

24. Stephen Kinzer, 'India and Pakistan to Discuss Flare-up in Kashmir,' *The New York Times*, June 9, 1999, p. A10.

25. Jyoti Malhotra, 'India Shoots Down Pak's "Partial" Offer, Talks End,' *Indian Express* online, June 13, 1999, http://www.expressindia.com/ie/daily/19990613/ige13069.html.

26. Agence France Presse, 'India Retakes Two Key Peaks in Kashmir,' *The Straits Times*, June 16, 1999.

27. Associated Press, 'India Reports Major Highway Recaptured from Rebels,' *The New York Times*, June 21, 1999, p. A7.

28. Farhan Bokhari and May Louise Kazmin, 'US General Presses Pakistan on Kashmir,' *Financial Times*, June 25, 1999.

29. C. Raja Mohan, 'Pak Must Pull Out Troops,' *The Hindu* online, June 28, 1999, http://www.the-hindu.com/stories/001280001.htm.

30. Jane Perlez, 'US Is Expecting Kashmir Pullback by Pakistani Side,' *The New York Times*, July 5, 1999, p. A1.

31. See 'Joint Statement by President Clinton and Prime Minister Sharif of Pakistan,' The White House, Office of the Press Secretary, July 4, 1999.

32. C. Raja Mohan, 'US Opposed to Mediation on Kashmir,' *The Hindu* online, September 27, 1999, http://www.hinduonline.com/today/stories/01280008.htm.

33. Celia W. Dugger, 'Militants Vow to Battle On in Kashmir, Defying Sharif,' *The New York Times*, July 8, 1999, p. A9.

34. Pamela Constable, 'India Captures a Strategic Peak in Kashmir,' *The Washington Post*, July 15, 1999, p. A15.

35. See the analysis in Steven R. Weisman, 'Kashmir: A Story of "Blowback" in Paradise,' *The New York Times*, July 17, 1999, Section 4, p. 8.

36. Jyoti Malhotra, 'Sharif Sends Envoy on "Secret" Mission,' *Indian Express*, June 28, 1999, online at http://www.expressindia.com/ie/daily/19990628/ige28001.html.

37. Kinzer, 'India and Pakistan to Discuss Flare-Up'.

38. The term 'mujahideen' is typically used to describe an Islamic warrior.

39. Barry Bearak, 'Pakistani Makes Case for a Halt to Fighting,' *The New York Times*, July 13, 1999, p. A6.

40. Amit Baruah, 'Our Soldiers Were Involved, Says Pak Columnist,' *The Hindu*, July 24, 1999, online at http://www.the-hindu.com/stories/03240004.htm.

41. Celia W. Dugger, 'Pakistan Backed Force Leaves Indian Kashmir,' *The New York Times*, July 15, 1999, p. A9.

42. Barry Bearak, '20 Hindus Slain in Kashmir, Apparently by Muslim Insurgents,' *The New York Times*, July 21, 1999, p. A3.

43. Celia W. Dugger, 'Kashmir War, Shown on TV, Rallies India's Unity,' *The New York Times*, July 18, 1999.

44. On July 24, the government's Union Cabinet decided to form a

committee to examine the origins of the Kargil crisis and to recommend measures to prevent such incursions in the future. The membership and conclusions of the Kargil Review Committee will be discussed later in the chapter.

45. Ajith Pillai and Nitin A Gokhale, 'On Permanent Watch,' *Outlook* July 18, 1999, online at http://www.outlookindia.com/issue3/affairsr17.htm.

46. For a discussion of the concept of a 'limited probe' see Alexander George and Richard Smoke, *Deterrence in American Foreign Policy* (New York: Columbia University Press, 1974). A limited probe had also been used by Pakistan in 1965, precipitating war with India. See Chapter 2.

47. Murali Krishnan, 'The Forgotten War,' *Outlook*, June 14, 1999, p. 24.

48. Manoj Joshi, *The Lost Rebellion: Kashmir in the 1990s* (New Delhi: Penguin, 1998).

49. Naveen S. Garewal, 'Post-Kargil: Trying Times for India and Pakistan,' *ASIANaffairs*, Number 34, (August 1999), pp. 16–18.

50. The concept of 'compellence' involves getting an aggressor to undo an act. For a discussion of the concept see Thomas Schelling, *Arms and Influence* (New Haven: Yale University Press, 1996).

51. Kapil Kak, 'International Responses,' in Jasjit Singh, ed., *Kargil 1999: Pakistan's Fourth War for Kashmir* (New Delhi: Knowledge World, 1999), pp. 200–201.

52. M.B. Naqvi, 'Looking Beyond Kargil,' *ASIANaffairs*, Number 34 (August 1999), pp. 14–16.

53. For the initial discussion of the 'stability/instability paradox' see Glenn Snyder, 'The Balance of Power and the Balance of Terror,' in Paul Seabury, ed., *The Balance of Power* (San Francisco: Chandler, 1965). For an application of the concept to the South Asian context see Sumit Ganguly, 'Indo-Pakistani Nuclear Issues and the Stability/Instability Paradox,' *Studies in Conflict and Terrorism*, Volume 18, Number 4 (1995), pp. 325–34.

54. Interview with senior US Department of Defence official, Palo Alto, California, December 3, 1999.

55. On this point see Praveen Swami, 'Trouble Ahead in Kashmir,' *Frontline*, Volume 18, Number 6 (March 13–26, 1999), pp. 5–8.

56. B. Raman, 'Was There an Intelligence Failure?' *Frontline*, Volume 16, Number 15 (July 17–30, 1999), online at http://www.the-hindu.com/fline/fl615/16151170.htm.

57. Nitin A. Gokhale and Ajith Pillai, 'The War That Should Never Have Been,' *Outlook*, August 27, 1999, online at http://www.outlookindia.com/issue3/affairsrl1.htm.

58. Nitin A. Gokhale, 'Command Failure,' *Outlook*, August 2, 1999, online at http://www.outlookindia.com/issue3/affairs.htm.

59. In the Simla Agreement, India and Pakistan had, among other things, pledged not to try to resolve the Kashmir dispute using force. The text of the agreement can be found in the Appendix.

60. Praveen Swami, *The Kargil War* (New Delhi: Leftword Books, 2000).

61. Harish Khare, 'Sensitive information "excised" from Kargil panel report,' *The Hindu*, January 7, 2000, online at http://www.the-hindu.com/stories. The government subsequently released its unclassified version of the report, albeit with some important deletions. See *From Surprise to Reckoning: The Kargil Review Committee Report* (New Delhi: Sage Publications, 1999). It chose not to publish the appendices for reasons of national security.

62. Mahendra Ved, 'Kargil Committee Critical of Gaps in Security Set-up,' *The Times of India*, January 7, 2000, online at http://www. timesofindia.com/today/08home1.htm. For a particularly trenchant critique of the report's findings see Praveen Swami, 'A Committee and Some Questions,' *Frontline*, Volume 17, Number 2 (January 22–February 4, 2000), online at http://www.the-hindu.com/fline/fl1702/17020310.htm; and Swami, *The Kargil War*. Swami argues that the report has deliberately withheld information that could be embarrassing to the BJP-led regime. Swami was one of the many individuals that the three-person inquiry committee interviewed.

63. Deccan Herald News Service, 'India to Cross LoC in War: Army Chief,' January 7, 2000, online at http://www.deccanherald.com/deccanherald/jan07/cross.ht.

64. C. Raja Mohan, 'Fernandes Unveils "Limited War" Doctrine,' *The Hindu*, January 25, 2000, online at http://www.the-hindu.com/stories/01250001.htm.

65. Conversations with senior Indian army officer, New Delhi, August 2000.

66. On this point see Sumit Ganguly, 'Pakistan's Never Ending Story: Why the October Coup Was No Surprise,' *Foreign Affairs*, Volume 79, Number 2 (March-April 2000), pp. 2–7.

67. On this subject see the excellent collection of essays *On the Abyss: Pakistan After the Coup* (New Delhi: HarperCollins, 2000), especially the essay by Shahid-ur-Rehman, 'Who Owns Pakistan?'

68. Interview with senior Indian diplomat, Washington, D.C., June 1999.

69. For a discussion of various proposed solutions to the Kashmir problem see Sumit Ganguly, *The Crisis in Kashmir: Portents of War, Hopes of Peace* (Cambridge: Cambridge University Press; Washington, D.C.: Woodrow Wilson Center Press, 1999); also see Alexander Evans, 'Reducing Tension Is Not Enough,' *The Washington Quarterly*, Volume 24, Number 2 (March 2001), pp. 181–94.

Epilogue: A Restive Relationship Enters a New Century

After the Kargil war, the relationship between India and Pakistan settled back into a pattern of mutual recrimination. Outside pressure on the two to resolve their differences over Kashmir continued; some external powers, particularly the United States, argued that the Kargil war had demonstrated that the nuclearization of the subcontinent had not in fact reduced the likelihood of war. Before relations could be repaired following Kargil, however, a military coup overthrew the regime of Nawaz Sharif in Pakistan in October 1999. Gen. Pervez Musharraf, the chief of army staff, declared himself 'chief executive' of the country. As could be expected, relations between India and Pakistan worsened considerably, particularly because Musharraf had been the prime architect of the Kargil operation.

The military coup contributed to Pakistan's further isolation in the global community, as the United States imposed additional sanctions against the military regime. The international community's disapprobation of Pakistan accrued to India's benefit. When US president Bill Clinton visited the subcontinent in March 2000, he spent several days in India but made only a cursory stop of a few hours at the airfield in Islamabad–a pointed rebuke to the military regime. Nevertheless, in the first year after the Pakistani coup, bilateral relations slowly deteriorated. Two events held the potential to change the status quo: the opening of bilateral talks in Agra in July 2001, and the sudden reinvigoration of US interest in subcontinental politics following the September 11, 2001, terrorist attacks on the World Trade Center and the Pentagon, and the ensuing war to oust the Taliban in Afghanistan.

The Journey to Agra

Capitalising on this surge in goodwill, the Indian government decided to try to make progress in its own conundrum in Jammu and Kashmir. On November 19, 2000, at the start of the Muslim holy month of Ramadan, the government of Prime Minister Atal Behari Vajpayee declared a unilateral cease-fire in the state. Initially, the cease-fire was to last until the end of Ramadan, but it was subsequently extended to cover the succeeding seven months. Yet despite this long cease-fire, the levels of violence in Kashmir showed few, if any, signs of ebbing. Vajpayee came under increasing pressure from all domestic quarters—popular, political, and institutional—to terminate the cease-fire.

Indeed, the cease-fire was earning the government no dividends. Particular insurgent groups, most notably the Lashkar-e-Toiba and the Hizb-ul-Mujahideen, had simply disregarded it. Despite the restraint of the army and the paramilitary forces, the insurgents continued their random attacks on both military and civilian targets in the valley. The Vajpayee regime had also seen its efforts to engage the All Parties Hurriyat Conference (APHC) falter despite the appointment of a veteran politician, K.C. Pant, as an interlocutor.[1] Politically, too, the ceasefire was exacting a significant toll, as more-conservative elements within Vajpayee's party and its ancillary organizations argued that the insurgents had construed the cease-fire as a form of weakness. Finally, pressures against this one-sided cease-fire were building within the armed forces.

Yet the prime minister could ill afford to rescind the ceasefire without making some demonstration of a willingness to resolve the Kashmir conundrum.[2] Thus, when the cease-fire was called off on May 23, 2001, Vajpayee, in consultation with his minister of home affairs, L.K. Advani, also decided to invite Gen. Pervez Musharraf, the chief executive of Pakistan (soon to declare himself president), to visit India to discuss possible means to improve bilateral relations.[3] Musharraf readily accepted Vajpayee's invitation, and a summit was planned for July 14–16 in the northern Indian city of Agra, the home of the famed Taj Mahal.

Negotiations at Agra

When Musharraf arrived in Agra, popular and elite expectations on both sides of the border about the summit were low.[4] Prior to the summit, he and his principal foreign policy advisers had made clear that Kashmir would be the 'core issue' that they wanted to discuss at the summit.[5]

Most of Pakistan's attentive public, however, had made it clear that they would not accept the transformation of the Line of Control into an international border.[6] By the same token, Vajpayee and his political allies had asserted that they wanted the summit to focus on Pakistani support for the Kashmiri insurgency. Additionally, they wanted to deal with bilateral issues such as curbing narcotics trafficking, and the disputes over Sir Creek and the Wular Barrage.[7] Key individuals within Vajpayee's party who advocated a tougher stance vis-à-vis Pakistan had publicly ruled out any territorial compromise on the Kashmir question.[8] Additionally, a senior Indian army officer in charge of a critical command had publicly commented that the army was opposed to any troop withdrawal from the Siachen Glacier.[9] His views certainly appeared to echo the sentiments of others in the armed services who expressed limited hopes about any substantive achievements at the summit.[10] Finally, and much to Pakistan's chagrin, New Delhi had made known that the APHC would not be a party to the bilateral talks.[11] Consequently, there was a clear-cut divergence between the two sides on the agenda for the summit.

As could be expected, the political atmosphere immediately prior to the formal meetings in Agra was decidedly mixed. The Indian side was unhappy with Musharraf's decision to invite an APHC delegation to a pre-summit reception hosted by the Pakistani high commissioner in New Delhi. And during a dinner speech at Rashtrapati Bhavan (the official residence of the president of India), hosted by the president of India, K.R. Narayanan, Musharraf stated that the Kashmir dispute could not be militarily resolved.[12]

Despite these initial knots, an atmosphere of cordiality and civility seemed to prevail in the first formal meeting of the Agra summit: the official Indian statement held that the talks had been 'very frank, cordial, and constructive.'[13] Matters quickly started to go wrong, however. The first evening, for reasons that remain the subject of speculation, acrimony, and debate, the Indian minister of information and broadcasting, Sushma Swaraj, held a press briefing for Doordarshan (India's state-run television network), during which she summarized the issues that had been discussed at the talks. In her account she included such matters as India's misgivings about 'cross-border terrorism,' a full accounting of Indian prisoners of war held in Pakistan, and the need to initiate discussions on reducing nuclear tensions on the subcontinent.[14] Missing in her remarks was any mention of the critical Kashmir issue. Whether her failure to mention the Kashmir issue was deliberate or inadvertent, the Pakistani side promptly took exception to it.[15] Later that evening, following her press briefing, the Pakistani delegation issued a statement indicating that Musharraf and Vajpayee had spent most of their one-on-one meeting discussing Kashmir.[16]

The second day of the summit, July 16, started inauspiciously, as Musharraf chose to hold a breakfast press conference for Indian newspaper editors. To the surprise of this assemblage, the entire proceedings were broadcast live by a satellite news network. In this briefing Musharraf took an especially tough line on the Kashmir issue and also made some intemperate remarks about ongoing violence in Kashmir.[17] Under the shadow of this statement and the remarks of the night before, the afternoon talks quickly unraveled. The two sides failed to agree even on the language for a joint communiqué, despite apparently valiant efforts on the part of the negotiators, who had worked late into the previous night. Reportedly, the Indian negotiators received little satisfaction from the Pakistanis on the question of their assistance to the Kashmiri insurgents, while the Indians themselves simultaneously refused to concede that Jammu and Kashmir constituted a 'dispute.'[18]

Later that evening, following a visit with Vajpayee, Musharraf called for another press conference. His request was turned down, however, on the grounds that adequate security precautions could not be taken in the time available.[19] Following this refusal the Pakistani delegation left for Islamabad.

Spreading the Blame

In the aftermath of the summit, the BJP-led government came under considerable criticism both from the opposition in parliament and from within its own ranks.[20] Some hard-line members of the BJP aimed their ire at Foreign Minister Jaswant Singh, in particular, while exonerating Vajpayee.[21] Jaswant Singh defended the government's decision to hold talks with Pakistan, contending that, contrary to the opposition's claims, the Indian side had made adequate preparations and in fact had had an eight-point agenda.[22]

The mood in Pakistan was much more upbeat. Musharraf largely and successfully blamed the failure of the summit on the putative choices of Indian hard-liners. Some commentators attributed the perceived intransigence of certain members of Vajpayee's cabinet to the upcoming state-level elections in Uttar Pradesh. Also, not surprisingly, Pakistani analysts arrived at a markedly different assessment of Musharraf's remarks and performance at the breakfast press conference in Agra. Unlike the largely acerbic Indian assessment, in Pakistan his remarks and his manner were interpreted in a mostly positive light.[23]

Against this backdrop of markedly divergent assessments of the summit, the two sides agreed to hold ministerial-level and foreign secretary–level talks. The failure of the Agra summit, however, had significantly undermined any constituency in India in support of talks with Pakistan. Some desultory discussions in India proposed that Vajpayee meet with Musharraf at the United Nations General Assembly session in September 2001 to try to rejuvenate the peace process. The events of September 11, 2001, however, not only forced the postponement of the General Assembly but also transformed the terms of discussion between the two sides.

The Aftermath of September 11

On September 11, 2001, the United States became the victim of a set of well-planned and highly coordinated terrorist attacks. The perpetrators of the terror, who had hijacked four commercial airliners, managed to strike three out of four intended targets—the two towers of the World Trade Center in New York City, and the Pentagon just outside Washington, D.C.—killing several thousand people, wreaking untold physical and economic damage on the United States and the world economy, and fundamentally transformed the international order.

The attacks, without a doubt, will have significant and far-reaching consequences for American national security and foreign policies, including those directed at South Asia. They also may well transform the dynamics of regional security in South Asia, although their full consequences in this area may not emerge for years. The immediate consequences of the attacks, however, particularly for Pakistan and Afghanistan, were clear and profound. The attacks also subdued the nascent efforts of the new administration of President George W. Bush to improve relations with India.

Prior to September 11, Pakistan had been consigned to the status of a virtual pariah state in the international system and especially in the US foreign policy calculus. Pakistan's decision to test nuclear weapons in the aftermath of the Indian nuclear tests of May 1998, its disastrous violation of the Line of Control in Kargil in April 1999, and Gen. Musharraf's military coup had reaped only international disapprobation and brought on an increasing isolation from the world.[24] That downhill spiral, combined with India's seemingly rising star, seemed to signal the start of a bleak period in Pakistani foreign relations.

But the exigencies of the prosecution of the anti-Taliban war in Afghanistan and the urgency of the hunt for terrorist mastermind Osama bin Laden instantly turned this trend around, as Pakistan became a 'valued ally' in the US fight against terrorism. Two factors contributed to Pakistan's renewed significance in US eyes. American authorities asserted that bin Laden and his Al Qaeda organization were closely involved in the September 11 terrorist attacks. Bin Laden and his Al Qaeda commanders had taken refuge in Afghanistan in 1996 after having been ousted from their previous base in Sudan.[25] Pakistan's shared border with Afghanistan and its extensive links with the Taliban regime made it necessary for the United States to renew and strengthen its diplomatic and military relationship with Islamabad.[26] Any air sorties flown over Afghanistan from aircraft carriers or from the US airbase at Diego Garcia in the Indian Ocean would have to overfly Pakistani territory and therefore required Pakistani support.

Unlike during most of the Cold War and after, when most Indian reactions to US diplomatic difficulties and security threats had been equivocal at best, the attacks on the World Trade Center produced in India a chorus of support for the United States. Indian officials, while lamenting the American failure to adopt a more forthright stance on India's problems with terror, nevertheless, offered to cooperate with the United States to address the new threats.[27] Some Indian commentators called for strong and unequivocal support for the US position.[28] But Indian support was not crucial for the conduct of the war, whereas Pakistan's was. Furthermore, despite India's expressions of solidarity with the United States and the US war effort, Washington could not forthrightly link the September 11 attacks to India's concerns about terror in Kashmir emanating from Pakistan for fear of alienating a state that it urgently needed to prosecute the war effort.[29] Thus in the immediate aftermath of the September 11 attacks, no surge in Indo-US relations was evident.

Pakistani support for the American war effort, however, was at best equivocal—Gen. Musharraf's personal pledge notwithstanding. Many groups and individuals within Pakistan did not support Musharraf's decision to cast his country's lot with the United States. The specific groups opposed to Pakistan's support for the prosecution of a war against Al Qaeda and bin Laden were entirely predictable: among them were the Islamist political wing parties Jamiat-i-Islami and Jamiat-ul-Ulema-e-Islam.[30] Additionally, key members of the ISI actively worked to undermine the attempts at cooperation with the United States.[31] Even some scientists connected with Pakistan's nuclear weapons programme appeared to harbour pro-Taliban sympathies.[32]

Musharraf's decision to aid the United States, public statements aside, stemmed less from his sympathy for the American cause and more from the exigencies confronting his beleaguered regime. Pakistan's foreign debt at the time the crisis ensued stood at $38 billion, and the country's ability to meet upcoming payments was in considerable doubt.[33] Furthermore, despite his having donned civilian garb after declaring himself president in July 2001, Musharraf had not succeeded in bolstering his regime's domestic or international legitimacy. No act of moral courage or altruism, casting his lot with the United States and the rest of the civilized world made virtue out of dire necessity. Musharraf also correctly calculated that if Pakistan did not cooperate with the United States, at the very least the Vajpayee administration in New Delhi, which had been steadily improving its ties with the United States, would seek to marginalize Pakistan; at worst, Pakistan itself could be targeted because of its support for the Taliban and its sponsoring of terrorism in Kashmir, which until then had been swept under the State Department's accusatory carpet.

In fairness, Musharraf's decision to aid the global effort against the Taliban and Al Qaeda was not free of risk. As noted already, he faced considerable domestic opposition to his decision. As a consequence, even after agreeing to support the prosecution of the war effort in Afghanistan, he repeatedly expressed reservations about a protracted war in Afghanistan, for he was acutely cognizant of the tenuousness of his own position within the Pakistani polity.[34]

Courting the United States

It is as yet unclear whether this US dependence on Pakistan will in turn prompt a return of the antagonistic US relationship with India. The Bush administration did initially seek to allay India's misgivings about a renewal of the US-Pakistan military and economic relationship. To this end, the administration dispatched Secretary of State Colin Powell to India immediately after his visit to Pakistan in mid-October 2001. During his visit to Pakistan, Powell had stated that the Kashmir issue was 'central to the relationship' between India and Pakistan,[35] causing considerable consternation in New Delhi, which has consistently held that Pakistan's support for terrorism in Kashmir, and not Kashmir's status, was the key problem in Indo-Pakistani relations. According to Indian sources, the Indian minister for external affairs, Jaswant Singh, in the course of private discussions, made clear his unhappiness to Powell.[36]

Further clouding Powell's visit was an Indian attack on a set of Pakistani military installations along the Line of Control.[37] Some analysts argued that the Indian attack was deliberately orchestrated to convey India's growing frustration with Pakistan's support to the Kashmiri insurgents and was timed to coincide with Powell's visit.[38] Others have suggested that the attacks, while carefully planned to coincide with Powell's visit, also reflected bureaucratic turf battles within the Indian government. According to these sources, these strikes were carried out in an effort to weaken the position of Singh, who reportedly prefers a more conciliatory approach to the handling of the Kashmir issue than does the Indian national security adviser, Brajesh Mishra.[39] Although stories of this battle of wills have often been aired in the Indian press, the veracity of this particular claim cannot be firmly established. However, there is little question that the attacks did convey India's increasing sense of irritation with the Musharraf regime's policy toward Kashmir.

In the continuing effort to maintain the international consensus on the prosecution of the war against the Taliban, the US secretary of defense, Donald Rumsfeld, traveled to Pakistan and India within weeks of Powell's visit. During his stop in New Delhi, Rumsfeld sought to alleviate Indian fears about the newfound US-Pakistan friendship. To the delight of his Indian interlocutors he expressed a willingness to resume military sales to India. The Indian government was especially pleased with the US decision to make available some embargoed General Electric 404 jet engines, which had long been sought by India for the further development and eventual production of its so-called light combat aircraft. Rumsfeld also assured his Indian hosts that US policy toward South Asia, in renewing the relationship with Pakistan, would not overlook India's interests.[40]

In November 2001, both Vajpayee and Musharraf visited the United States to participate in the delayed UN General Assembly. Both individuals met with key US decision-makers and publicly reiterated their respective commitments to the US-led 'war against terror.' Which party gained more from the visits quickly became the subject of much press speculation. Clearly, Musharraf managed to end his international isolation and came across as the more telegenic personality. From a material standpoint, he also succeeded in obtaining promises of American assistance totalling a billion dollars. But he failed to move US policymakers to adopt a more pro-Pakistani stance on Kashmir, nor did he convince them to sell to Islamabad the fleet of F-16 aircraft embargoed by Washington after the end of the Cold War.[41] Neither was Vajpayee's visit an unqualified success. US policymakers failed to even mildly rebuke Pakistan for its support of terror in Kashmir and also counseled India to exercise restraint along the Line of Control. That said, the Indians and the Americans did discuss various other arenas of cooperation, including closer military-to-military ties.[42]

Coming Full Circle

After the destruction of the Taliban and the end of the US war effort, the vexed question of Kashmir persists. Will Pakistan finally abandon its quest to wrest Kashmir from India through the use of force? Will India be willing to settle the dispute by legally ceding the portions of Kashmir under Pakistan and Chinese control? Will Pakistan accept such a dispensation? Finally, will the vast majority of the Kashmiris in Indian-controlled Kashmir settle for a substantial degree of autonomy under the aegis of the Indian constitutional framework? The answers to these questions will depend in large measure on the evolution of US policy toward India and Pakistan. As a result of the events of September 11, the United States is in a unique position to forge a durable peace on the subcontinent. Whether it chooses to do so largely hinges on its willingness to muster the resources to achieve such an end. As a consequence of its deep involvement with Pakistan in prosecuting the war against the Taliban, the United States has acquired unprecedented leverage over Pakistan. The latter's feckless support to various terrorist organizations is now under acute scrutiny as the United States pours resources into Pakistan's depleted exchequer. Consequently, the Bush administration, after having demolished the Taliban and Al Qaeda, could, if it chose to, induce Pakistan to end its support for terror in Kashmir. Radical groups and intransigent individuals within Pakistan will hardly welcome such an American initiative, but given the international mood since September 11 and their association with terror, whether in South Asia or elsewhere, they may have little choice.

India too, will have to make some important concessions and undertake some difficult steps. To win a Pakistani abandonment of terror, the United States will have to press India to provide some accounting for the massive human rights abuses that have transpired during the Kashmiri insurgency. Furthermore, without addressing the human rights issue India cannot hope to win back the sympathies of the aggrieved Kashmiri population. The United States must also prod India to grant the Kashmiris the maximum degree of autonomy possible under its constitutional framework; otherwise the prospects of peace will be dim.

This proposed solution will not meet the maximal goals of India, Pakistan, or some of the more unyielding of the Kashmiri insurgents. However, it offers the most politically viable prospect for the eventual settlement of this perennial conflict. Nonetheless, given the gulf that continues to separate the formal positions of the two sides, the long memories and myths of discord, the existence of powerful and implacable bureaucratic and political constituencies, and the fears of mutual exploitation, there is little likelihood of any breakthrough in bilateral relations in the near future. Any resolution of this conflict, deeply rooted in the self-images of both states and attenuated by each side's selective account of the historical record, will require patience, skill, and long-term commitment—attributes that have thus far been lacking in politicians and decision-makers on both sides of the border. The world will be anxious to see if these attributes will be in adequate supply in the months and years ahead.

Notes

1. Faisal Ahmed and Binoo Joshi, 'Hurriyat Rejects Parleys with Interlocutor,' *India Abroad*, May 4, 2001, p. 15.

2. Barry Bearak, 'For the Newest Nuclear Powers, a Little Chat,' *New York Times*, July 15, 2001, p. 5.

3. Much speculation has circulated in the Indian and Pakistani popular presses that Vajpayee invited Musharraf at the behest of the United States. No evidence, however, has been adduced to support this claim. At best, it can be asserted that the United States urged India and Pakistan to start negotiations to reduce tensions. Aziz Haniffa, 'US Asked India, Pakistan to Talk,' *India Abroad*, July 13, 2001, p. 1. Informed sources argue that the decision to invite Musharraf was made by Vajpayee and Advani after the two had conferred on the situation in Kashmir with the governor of the state, Girish Saxena. Personal communication with senior member of the Congress Party.

4. Tara Shankar Sahay, 'Experts Do Not Expect Much from Meeting,' *India Abroad*, July 6, 2001, p. 6.

5. Ihtasham ul Haque, 'Leaders Extend Support to CE: Kashmir to Be Main Issue at Summit,' *Dawn*, June 28, 2001, at http://www.Dawn.com. Also see Harinder Baweja and Shishir Gupta, 'Kashmir on the Mind,' *India Today*, July 16, 2001, pp. 30–37.

6. Mariana Baabar, 'Battlefield Perspectives,' *Outlook*, June 11, 2001, at http://www.outlookindia.com.

7 . Sheela Bhatt, 'Joint Committee to Thrash Out Thorny Issues,' *India Abroad*, July 6, 2001, p. 1.

8. Sheela Bhatt, '"A Compromise on Kashmir Would Have a Domino Effect on the Rest of India": India's Home Minister L.K. Advani on the India-Pakistan Summit,' *India Abroad*, July 6, 2001, p. 12.

9. Josy Soseph, 'Army Rules Out Troop Withdrawal from Siachen,' *India Abroad*, July 13, 2001, p. 1.

10. Charu Singh, 'Vajpayee-Musharraf Talks a Dialogue of the Deaf, Say Army Officers,' June 1, 2001, at http://www.tehelka.com.

11. Agence-France Press, 'Delhi Rules Out Role for APHC,' *Dawn*, June 29, 2001, at http://www.Dawn.com. Also see India Abroad News Service, 'No Intermediary Role for Hurriyat: Advani,' *India Abroad*, June 1, 2001, p. 23.

12. Sukumar Muralidharan, 'Deadlock in Agra,' *Frontline*, Volume 18, Number 15 (July 21–August 3, 2001), at http://www.hindugroupnet.com. Musharraf reiterated this point on his return to Islamabad after the abortive summit. On his remarks on Pakistani television, see Farhan Bokhari, 'No Military Solution in Kashmir, Says Musharraf,' *Financial Times*, July 21, 2001, p. 4.

13. John Cherian, 'Divergence of Views,' *Frontline*, Volume 18, Number 21 (July 21–August 3, 2001), at http://www.hindugroupnet.com.

14. Sukumar Muralidharan, 'Deadlock at Agra,' *Frontline*, Volume 18, Number 21 (July 21–August 3, 2001), at http://www.hindugroupnet.com.

15. Press Trust of India, 'Musharraf Derailed Summit,' *The Hindu*, July 21, 2001, p. 1.

16. Cherian, 'Divergence of Views.'

17. Prem Shanker Jha, 'The Breakfast Truth,' *Outlook*, July 30, 2001, available at http://www.outlookindia.com.

18. On this point see Siddharth Varadarajan, 'How India and Pakistan Lost Their Way at the Agra Summit,' *Times of India*, July 18, 2001, p. 1; also see David Gardner and Farhan Bokhari, 'India-Pakistan Negotiations Fail to Secure Breakthrough,' *Financial Times*, July 17, 2001, p. 1.

19. Muralidharan, 'Deadlock at Agra.'

20. For a thoughtful assessment of the talks see Salman Haider, 'Requiem for a Summit,' *The Hindu*, July 21, 2001, p. 10.

21. Neena Vyas, 'BJP Blames It on Jaswant Singh,' *The Hindu*, July 21, 2001, p. 1.

22. Deccan Herald News Service, 'Jaswant Warns Pak May Face Anarchy,' *Deccan Herald*, August 7, 2001, at http://www.deccanherald.com.

23. B. Muralidhar Reddy, 'Summit Derailed by Elements Inimical to Peace,' *The Hindu*, July 21, 2001, p. 1. Also see Ayaz Amir, 'What More Could We Have Asked For?' *Dawn*, July 20, 2001, at http://www.Dawn.com.

24. Sumit Ganguly, 'Pakistan's Never-Ending Story,' *Foreign Affairs* 79, Number 2 (March–April 2000), pp. 2–7.

25. For a superb account of bin Laden's involvement in the terror network see Mary Anne Weaver, 'The Real Bin Laden,' *New Yorker*, January 24, 2000, available at http://www.newyorker.com.

26. On the links between Pakistan's Inter-Services Intelligence Directorate (ISI) and the Taliban, see Ahmed Rashid, *Taliban: Militant Islam, Oil, and Fundamentalism in Central Asia* (New Haven: Yale University Press, 2001), and Pankaj Mishra, 'The Making of Afghanistan,' *New York Review of Books* Volume 48, Number 18 (November 15, 2001), pp. 18–21.

27. Joanna Slater and Sadanand Dhume, 'Old Foes Make for Poor Allies,' *Far Eastern Economic Review*, October 4, 2001, pp. 22–24.

28. Brahma Chellaney, 'India Has to Be Firmly on US Side,' *India Abroad*, September 21, 2001, p. 20.

29. Howard LaFranchi, 'Attacks Move Pakistan Up, India Down, on US Agenda,' *Christian Science Monitor*, September 24, 2001, available at http://www.csmonitor.com.

30. Rone Tempest and Megan Stack, 'Pakistan Arrests Backer of Taliban in Crackdown,' *Austin American-Statesman*, November 5, 2001, p. A10.

31. 'Rogue Pakistan Agents Aid Taliban,' *Far Eastern Economic Review*, October 18, 2001, p. 10.

32. John F. Burns, 'Pakistan Releases 3 Scientists Questioned on Ties to Taliban,' *New York Times*, November 3, 2001, p. B5.

33. Joseph Kahn, 'US Planning an Aid Package for Pakistan Worth Billions,' *New York Times*, October 27, 2001, p. B4.

34. John F. Burns, 'Pakistan Chief Says the US Should End Bombing Soon,' *New York Times*, October 27, 2001, p. B1.

35. Times News Network, 'No Place for Terrorists in Civilised World: Powell,' *Times of India*, October 15, 2001, available at: http://www.timesofindia.com.

36. V. Sudarshan, 'Half-a-Bargain Deal,' *Outlook*, October 29, 2001, available at http://www.outlookindia.com.

37. 'Powell Heads Kashmir Peace Talks,' *Guardian*, October 16, 2001, available at http://www.guardian.co.uk.

38. Private correspondence with senior American military officer, October 20, 2001.

39. Interview with prominent South Asian expatriate journalist, November 16, 2001.

40. Celia W. Dugger, 'US and India Map Path to Military Cooperation; More Arms Sales Are Seen,' *New York Times*, November 6, 2001, p. B2.

41. V. Sudarshan, 'Gestures and Ground Reality,' *Outlook*, November 29, 2001, available at http://www.outlookindia.com.

42. Aziz Haniffa, 'US Hot on "Restraint", Cold on "Hot Pursuit,"' *India Abroad*, November 16, 2001, p. 1.

Appendices

Article 370 of the Indian Constitution

(1) Temporary provisions with respect to the State of Jammu and Kashmir.

Notwithstanding anything in this Constitution,-

(a) the provisions of article 238 shall not apply in relation to the State of Jammu and Kashmir;

(b) the power of Parliament to make laws for the said State shall be limited to—

(i) those matters in the Union List and the Concurrent List which, in consultation with the Government of the State, are declared by the President to correspond to matters specified in the Instrument of Accession governing the accession of the State to the Dominion of India as the matter with respect to which the Dominion Legislature may make laws for that State; and

(ii) such other matters in the said Lists as, with the concurrence of the Government of the State, the President may be order specify.

Explanation.- For the purposes of this article, the Government of the State means the person for the time being recognised by the President as the Maharaja of Jammu and Kashmir acting on the advice of the Council of Ministers for the time being in office under the Maharaja's Proclamation dated the fifth day of March, 1948;

(c) the provisions of article 1 and of this article shall apply in relation to that State;

(d) such of the other provisions of this Constitution shall apply in relation to that State subject to such exceptions and modifications as the President may by order specify:

Provided that no such order which relates to the matters specified in the Instrument of Accession of the State referred to in paragraph (i) of sub-clause

(b) shall be issued except in consultation with the Government of the State:

Provided further that no such order which relates to matters other than those referred to in the last preceding proviso shall be issued except with the concurrence of that Government.

(2) If the concurrence of the Government of the State referred to in paragraph (ii) of sub-clause (b) of clause (1) or in the second proviso to sub-clause (d) of that clause be given before the Constituent Assembly for the purpose of framing the Constitution of the State is convened, it shall be placed before such Assembly for such decision as it may take thereon.

(3) Not withstanding anything in the foregoing provisions of this article, the President may, by public notification, declare that this article shall cease to be operative or shall be operative only with such exceptions and modifications and from such date as he may specify:

Provided that the recommendation of the Constituent Assembly of the State referred to in clause (2) shall be necessary before the President issues such a notification.

Source: Constitution of India

Accession of Jammu and Kashmir State to India

Text of Letter Dated October 26, 1947 from Hari Singh, The Maharaja of Jammu & Kashmir to Lord Mountbatten, Governor General of India

Dated: 26 October 1947

My dear Lord Mountbatten,

I have to inform your Excellency that a grave emergency has arisen in my State and request immediate assistance of your Government.

As your Excellency is aware the State of Jammu and Kashmir has not acceded to the Dominion of India or to Pakistan. Geographically my State is contiguous to both the Dominions. It has vital economical and cultural links with both of them. Besides my State has a common boundary with the Soviet Republic and China. In their external relations the Dominions of India and Pakistan cannot ignore this fact.

I wanted to take time to decide to which Dominion I should accede, or whether it is not in the best interests of both the Dominions and my State independent, of course with friendly and cordial relations with both.

I accordingly approached the Dominions of India and Pakistan to enter into Standstill Agreement with my State. The Pakistan Government accepted this Agreement. The Dominion of India desired further discussions with representatives of my Government. I could not arrange this in view of the developments indicated below. In fact the Pakistan Government are operating Post and Telegraph system inside the State.

Though we have got a Standstill Agreement with the Pakistan Government that Government permitted steady and increasing strangulation of supplies like food, salt and petrol to my State.

Afridis, solidiers in plain clothes, and desperadoes with modern weapons have been allowed to infilter into the State at first in Poonch and then in Sialkot and finally in mass area adjoining Hazara District on the Ramkot side. The result has been that the limited number of troops at the disposal of the State had to be dispersed and thus had to face the enemy at the several points simultaneously, that it has become difficult to stop the wanton destruction of life and property and looting. The Mahora powerhouse which supplies the electric current to the whole of Srinagar has been burnt. The number of women who have been kidnapped and raped makes my heart bleed. The wild forces thus let loose on the State are marching on with the aim of capturing Srinagar, the summer Capital of my Government, as first step to over-running the whole State.

The mass infiltration of tribesmen drawn from distant areas of the North-West Frontier coming regularly in motor trucks using Mansehra-Muzaffarabad Road and fully armed with up-to-date weapons cannot possibly be done without the knowledge of the Provisional Government of the North-West Frontier Province and the Government of Pakistan. In spite of repeated requests made by my Government no attempt has been made to check these raiders or stop them from coming into my State. The Pakistan Radio even put out a story that a Provisional Government had been set up in Kashmir. The people of my State both the Muslims and non-Muslims generally have taken no part at all.

With the conditions obtaining at present in my State and the great emergency of the situation as it exists, I have no option but to ask for help from the Indian Dominion. Naturally they cannot send the help asked for by me without my State acceding to the Dominion of India. I have accordingly decided to do so and I attach the Instrument of Accession for acceptance by your Government. The other alternative is to leave my State and my people to free-booters. On this basis no civilized Government can exist or be maintained. This alternative I will never allow to happen as long as I am Ruler of the State and I have life to defend my country.

I am also to inform your Excellency's Government that it is my intention at once to set up an interim Government and ask Sheikh Abdullah to carry the responsibilities in this emergency with my Prime Minister.

If my State has to be saved immediate assistance must be available at Srinagar. Mr Menon is fully aware of the situation and he will explain to you, if further explanation is needed.

In haste and with kind regards.

The Place, Jammu   Your sincerely,
26th October, 1947   Hari Singh

Source: Government of India Publication, October 26, 1947

Text of India's Complaint to the [U.N.] Security Council, 1 January 1948

Letter Dated 1 January, 1948, from the Representative of India to the President of the Security Council (S/628).

The Government of India have instructed me to transmit to you the following telegraphic communication:

'1. Under Article 35 of the Charter of the United Nations, any Member may bring any situation whose continuance is likely to endanger the maintenance of international peace and security to the attention of the Security Council. Such a situation now exists between India and Pakistan owing to the aid which invaders, consisting of nationals of Pakistan and of tribesmen from the territory immediately adjoining Pakistan on the north-west, are drawing from Pakistan for operations against Jammu and Kashmir, a State which has acceded to the Dominion of India and is part of India. The circumstances of accession, the activities of the invaders which led the Government of India to take military action against them, and the assistance which the attackers have received and are still receiving from Pakistan are explained later in this memorandum. The Government of India request the Security Council to call upon Pakistan to put an end immediately to the giving of such assistance, which is an act of aggression against India. If Pakistan does not do so, the Government of India may be compelled, in self-defence, to enter Pakistan territory, in order to take military action against the invaders. The matter is, therefore, one of extreme urgency and calls for immediate action by the Security Council for avoiding a breach of international peace.

'2. From the middle of September 1947, the Government of India had received reports of the infiltration of armed raiders into the western parts of Jammu Province of the Jammu and Kashmir State; Jammu adjoins West Punjab which is a part of the Dominion of Pakistan. These raiders had done a great deal of damage in that area and taken possession of part of the territory of the State. On 24 October, the Government of India heard of a major raid from the Frontier Province of the Dominion of Pakistan into the Valley of Kashmir. Some two thousand or more fully armed and equipped men came in motor transport, crossed over to the territory of the State of Jammu and Kashmir, sacked the town of Muzaffarabad, killing many people, and proceeded along the Jhelum Valley road towards Srinagar, the summer capital of the Jammu and Kashmir State. Intermediate towns and villages were sacked and burnt, and many people killed. These raiders were stopped by Kashmir State troops near Uri, a town some fifty miles from Srinagar, for some time, but the invaders got around them and burnt the power house at Mahora, which supplied electricity to the whole of Kashmir.

'3. The position, on the morning of 26 October, was that these raiders had been held by Kashmir State troops and part of the civil population, who had been armed, at a town called Baramulla. Beyond Baramulla there was no major obstruction up to Srinagar. There was immediate danger of these raiders reaching Srinagar, destroying and massacring large numbers of people, both Hindu and Muslims. The State troops were spread out all over the State and most of them were deployed along the western border of Jammu Province. They had been split up into small isolated groups and were incapable of offering effective resistance to the raiders. Most of the State officials had left the threatened area and the civil administration had ceased to function. All that stood between Srinagar and the fate which had overtaken the places *en route* followed by the raiders was the determination of the inhabitants of Srinagar, of all communities, and practically without arms, to defend themselves. At this time Srinagar had also a large population of Hindu and Sikh refugees who had fled there from West Punjab owing to communal disturbances in that area. There was little doubt that these refugees would be massacred if the raiders reached Srinagar.

'4. Immediately after the raids into the Jammu and Kashmir State commenced, approaches were informally made to the Government of India for the acceptance of the accession of the State to the Indian Dominion. (It might be explained in parenthesis that Jammu and Kashmir form a State whose ruler, prior to the transfer of power by the United Kingdom to the Dominions of India and Pakistan, had been in treaty relations with the British Crown, which controlled its foreign relations and was responsible for its defence. The treaty relations ceased with the transfer of power on 15 August last, and Jammu and Kashmir like other States acquired the right to accede to either Dominion.)

'5. Events moved with great rapidity, and the threat to the Valley of Kashmir became grave. On 26 October, the ruler of the State, His Highness Maharaja Sir Hari Singh, appealed urgently to the Government of India for military help. He also requested that the Jammu and Kashmir State should be allowed to accede to the Indian Dominion. An appeal for help was also simultaneously received by the Government of India from the largest popular organisation in Kashmir, the National Conference, headed by Sheikh Mohammed Abdullah. The Conference further strongly supported the request for the State's accession to the Indian Dominion. The Government of India were thus approached not only officially by the State authorities, but also on behalf of the people of Kashmir, both for military aid and for the accession of the State to India.

'6. The grave threat of the life and property of innocent people in the Kashmir Valley and to the security of the State of Jammu and Kashmir that had developed as a result of the invasion of the Valley demanded immediate decision by the Government of India on both the requests. It was imperative on account of the emergency that the responsibility for the defence of the Jammu and Kashmir State should be taken over by a government capable of discharging it. But, in order to avoid any possible suggestion that India had utilised the State's immediate peril for her own political advantage, the Government of India made it clear that once the soil of the State had been cleared of the invader and normal conditions restored, its people would be free to decide their future by the recognised democratic method of a plebiscite or referendum which, in order to ensure complete impartiality, might be held under international auspices.

'7. The Government of India felt it their duty to respond to the appeal for armed assistance because:

(1) They could not allow a neighbouring and friendly State to be compelled by force to determine either its internal affairs or its external relations;

(2) The accession of the Jammu and Kashmir State to the Dominion of India made India really responsible for the defence of the State.

'8. The intervention of the Government of India resulted in saving Srinagar. The raiders were driven back from Baramulla to Uri and are held there by Indian troops. Nearly 19,000 raiders face the Dominion forces in this area. Since operation in the Valley of Kashmir started, pressure by the raiders against the western and south-western border of the Jammu and Kashmir State has been intensified. Exact figures are not available. It is understood, however, that nearly 15,000 raiders are operating against this part of the State. State troops are besieged in certain areas. Incursions by the raiders into the State territory, involving murder, arson, loot, and the abduction of women, continue. The booty is collected and carried over to the tribal areas to serve as an inducement to the further recruitment of tribesmen to the ranks of the raiders. In addition to those actively participating in the raid, tribesmen and others, estimated at 100,000, have been collected in different places in the districts of West Punjab bordering the Jammu and Kashmir State, and many of them are receiving military training under Pakistani nationals, including officers of the Pakistan Army. They are looked after in Pakistan territory, fed, clothed, armed and otherwise equipped, and transported to the territory of the Jammu and Kashmir State with the help, direct and indirect, of Pakistani officials, both military and civil.

'9. As already stated, the raiders who entered the Kashmir Valley in October came mainly from the tribal areas to the north-west of Pakistan and, in order to reach Kashmir, passed through Pakistan territory. The raids along the south-west border of the State, which had preceded the invasion of the valley proper, had actually been conducted from Pakistan territory, and Pakistan nationals had taken part in them. This process of transmission across Pakistan territory and utilisation of that territory as a base of operations against the Jammu and Kashmir State continues. Recently, military operations against the western and south-western borders of the State have been intensified, and the attackers consist of nationals of Pakistan as well as tribesmen. These invaders are armed with modern weapons, including mortars and medium machine-guns, wear the battle dress of regular soldiers and, in recent engagements, have fought in regular battle formation and are using the tactics of modern warfare. Man-pack wireless sets are in regular use and even mark V mines have been employed. For their transport the invaders have all along used motor vehicles. They are undoubtedly being trained and to some extent led by regular officers of the Pakistan Army. Their rations and other supplies are obtained from Pakistan territory.

'10.These facts point indisputably to the conclusion

'(a) That the invaders are allowed transit across Pakistan territory;

'(b) That they are allowed to use Pakistan territory as a base of operations;

'(c) That they include Pakistan nationals;

'(d) That they draw much of their military equipment, transportation, and supplies (including petrol) from Pakistan; and

'(e) That Pakistan officers are training, guiding, and otherwise actively helping them.

'There is no source other than Pakistan from which they could obtain such quantities of modern military equipment, training or guidance. More than once, the Government of India had asked the Pakistan Government to deny to the invaders facilities which constitute an act of aggression and hostility against India, but without any response. The last occasion on which this request was made was on 22 December, when the Prime Minister of India handed over personally to the Prime Minister of Pakistan a letter in which the various forms of aid given by Pakistan to the invaders were briefly recounted and the Government of Pakistan were asked to put an end to such aid promptly; no reply to this letter has yet been received in spite of a telegraphic reminder sent on 26 December.

'11. It should be clear from the foregoing recital that the Government of Pakistan are unwilling to stop the assistance in material and men which the invaders are receiving from Pakistan territory and from Pakistan nationals, including Pakistan Government personnel, both military and civil. This attitude is not only un-neutral, but constitutes active aggression against India, of which the State of Jammu and Kashmir forms a part.

'12. The Government of India have exerted persuasion and exercised patience to bring about a change in the attitude of Pakistan. But they have failed, and are in consequence confronted with a situation in which their defence of the Jammu and Kashmir State is hampered and their measures to drive the invaders from the territory of the State are greatly impeded by the support which the raiders derive from Pakistan. The invaders are still on the soil of Jammu and Kashmir and the inhabitants of the State are exposed to all the atrocities of which a barbarous foe is capable. The presence, in large number of invaders in those portions of Pakistan territory which adjoin parts of Indian territory other than the Jammu and Kashmir State is a menace to the rest of India. Indefinite continuance of the present operations prolongs the agony of the people of Jammu and Kashmir, is a drain on India's resources and a constant threat to the maintenance of peace between India and Pakistan. The Government of India have no option, therefore, but to take more effective military action in order to rid the Jammu and Kashmir State of the invader.

'13. In order that the objective of expelling the invader from Indian territory and preventing him from launching fresh attacks should be quickly achieved, Indian troops would have to enter Pakistan territory; only thus could the invader be denied the use of bases and cut off from his sources of supplies and reinforcements in Pakistan. Since the aid which the invaders are receiving from Pakistan is an act of aggression against India, the Government of India are entitled, under international law, to send their armed forces across Pakistan territory for dealing effectively with the invaders. However, as such action might involve armed conflict with Pakistan, the Government of India, ever anxious to proceed according to the principles and aims of the Charter of the United Nations, desire to report the situation to the Security Council under Article-35 of the Charter. They feel justified in requesting the Security Council to ask the Government of Pakistan:

(1) To prevent Pakistan Government personnel, military and civil, from participating or assisting in the invasion of the Jammu and Kashmir State;

(2) To call upon other Pakistani nationals to desist from taking any part in the fighting in the Jammu and Kashmir State;

(3) To deny to the invaders: (a) access to any use of its territory for operations against Kashmir, (b) military and other supplies, (c) all other kinds of aid that might tend to prolong the present struggle.

'14. The Government of India would stress the special urgency of the Security Council taking immediate action on their request. They desire to add that military operations in the invaded areas have, in the past few days, been developing so rapidly that they must, in self-defence, reserve to themselves the freedom to take, at any time when it may become necessary, such military action as they may consider the situation requires.

'15. The Government of India deeply regret that a serious crisis should have been reached in their relations with Pakistan. Not only is Pakistan a neighbour but, in spite of the recent separation, India and Pakistan have many ties and many common interests. India desires nothing more earnestly than to live with her neighbour-State on terms of close and lasting friendship. Peace is to the interest of both States; indeed to the interests of the world. The Government of India's approach to the Security Council is inspired by the sincere hope that, through the prompt action of the Council, peace may be preserved.

'16. The text of this reference to the Security Council is being telegraphed to the Government of Pakistan.'

Source: Government of India documents

U.N. Resolution August 13, 1948

The United Nations Commission for India and Pakistan.

Having given careful consideration to the points of view expressed by the representatives of India and Pakistan regarding the situation in the State of Jammu and Kashmir; and

Being of the opinion that the prompt cessation of hostilities and the correction of conditions the continuance of which is likely to endanger international peace and security are essential to implementation of its endeavors to assist the Governments of India and Pakistan in effecting a final settlement of the situation;

Resolves to submit simultaneously to the Governments of India and Pakistan the following proposal:

PART I: CEASE-FIRE ORDER

A. The Governments of India and Pakistan agree that their respective High Commands with issue separately and simultaneously a cease-fire order to apply to all forces under their control and in the State of Jammu and Kashmir as of the earliest practicable date or dates to be mutually agreed upon within four days after these proposals have been accepted by both Governments.

B. The High Commands of the Indian and Pakistani forces agree to refrain from taking any measures that might augment the military potential of the forces under their control in the State of Jammu and Kashmir. (For the purpose of these proposals forces under their control shall be considered to include all forces, organized and unorganized, fighting or participating in hostilities on their respective sides.)

C. The Commanders-in-Chief of the forces of India and Pakistan shall promptly confer regarding any necessary local changes in present dispositions which may facilitate the cease-fire.

D. In its discretion and as the Commission may find practicable, the Commission will appoint military observers who, under the authority of the Commission and with the co-operation of both Commands, will supervise the observance of the cease-fire order.

E. The Government of India and the Government of Pakistan agree to appeal to their respective peoples to assist in creating and maintaining an atmosphere favourable to the promotion of further negotiations.

PART II: TRUCE AGREEMENT

Simultaneously with the acceptance of the proposal for the immediate cessation of hostilities as outlined in Part I, both the Governments accept the following principles as a basis for the formulation of a truce agreement, the details of which shall be worked out in discussion between their representatives and the Commission.

A.

1. As the presence of troops of Pakistan in the territory of the State of Jammu and Kashmir constitutes a material change in the situation since it was represented by the Government of Pakistan before the Security Council, the Government of Pakistan agrees to withdraw its troops from that State.

2. The Government of Pakistan will use its best endeavour to secure the withdrawal from the State of Jammu and Kashmir of tribesmen and Pakistani nationals not normally resident therein who have entered the State for the purpose of fighting.

3. Pending a final solution, the territory evacuated by the Pakistani troops will be administered by the local authorities under the surveillance of the commission.

B.

1. When the commission shall have notified the Government of India that the tirbesmen and Pakistani nationals referred to in Part II, A, 2, hereof have withdrawn, thereby terminating the situation which was represented by the Government of India to the Security Council as having occasioned the presence of Indian forces in the State of Jammu and Kashmir, and further, that the Pakistani forces are being withdrawn from the State of Jammu and Kashmir, the Government of India agrees to begin to withdraw the bulk of its forces from that State in stages to be agreed upon with the Commission.

2. Pending the acceptance of the conditions for a final settlement of the situation in the State of Jammu and Kashmir, the Indian Government will maintain within the lines existing at the moment of the cease-fire the minimum strength of its forces which in agreement with the commission are considered necessary to assist local authorities in the observance of law and order. The Commission will have observers stationed where it deems necessary.

3. The Government of India will undertake to ensure that the Government of the State of Jammu and Kashmir will take all measures within its powers

to make it publicly known that peace, law and order will be safeguard and that all human political rights will be granted.

4. Upon signature, the full text of the truce agreement or a communique containing the principles thereof as agreed upon between the two Governments and the Commission, will be made public.

PART III

The Government of India and the Government of Pakistan reaffirm their wish that the future status of the State of Jammu and Kashmir shall be determined in accordance with the will of the people and to that end, upon acceptance of the truce agreement, both Governments agree to enter into consultations with the Commission to determine fair and equitable conditions whereby such free expression will be assured.

Source: United Nations

Resolution on Assurances Adopted by U.N. Commission for India and Pakistan (UNCIP) 1948

This resolution was in the form of an assurance provided to India before the main U.N. Resolution of August 13, 1948, was to be implemented. The Resolution on Assurance said:

1. Responsibility for the security of J&K rests with Government of India.

2. The sovereignty of the J&K Government over the entire territory of the State shall not be brought under question.

3. There shall be no recognition of the so-called Azad (Free) Kashmir Government.

4. The territory occupied by Pakistan shall not be consolidated to the disadvantage of the State of J&K.

5. The administration of the evacuated areas in the North shall revert to the Government of J&K and its defence to the Government of India, who will, if necessary, maintain garrison for preventing the incursion of tribesmen and for guarding main trade routes.

6. Pakistan shall be excluded from all affairs of J&K in particular in the plebiscite, of one should be held.

7. If a plebiscite is found to be impossible for technical or practical reasons, the Commission will consider other methods of determining fair and equitable conditions for ensuring a free expression of people's will.

8. Plebiscite proposal shall not be binding upon India if Pakistan does not implement Part I and II of the resolution of 13th August, 1948. (The resolution had called upon Pakistan to withdraw troops from occupied Kashmir).

Source: United Nations

Tashkent Declaration, January 10, 1966

The Prime Minister of India and the President of Pakistan, having met at Tashkent and having discussed the existing relations between India and Pakistan hereby declare their firm resolve to restore normal and peaceful relations between their countries of vital importance for the welfare of the 600 million people of India and Pakistan.

(i) The Prime Minister of India and the President of Pakistan agree that both sides will exert all efforts to create good neighbourly relations between India and Pakistan in accordance with the United Nations Charter. They reaffirm their obligation under the Charter not to have recourse to force and to settle their disputes through peaceful means. They considered that the interests of peace in their region and particularly in the Indo-Pakistan subcontinent and indeed, the interests of the peoples of India and Pakistan were not served by the continuance of tension between the two countries. It was against this background that Jammu & Kashmir was discussed, and each of the sides set forth its respective position.

Troops Withdrawal

(ii) The Prime Minister of India and the President of Pakistan have agreed that all armed personnel of the two countries shall be withdrawn not later than 25 February 1966 to the positions they held prior to 5 August 1965, and both sides shall observe the cease-fire terms on the cease-fire line.

(iii) The Prime Minister of India and the President of Pakistan have agreed that relations between India and Pakistan shall be based on the principle of non-interference in the internal affairs of each other.

(iv) The Prime Minister of India and the President of Pakistan have agreed that both sides will discourage any propaganda directed against the other country and will encourage propaganda which promotes the development of friendly relations between the two countries.

(v) The Prime Minister of India and the President of Pakistan have agreed that the High Commissioner of India to Pakistan and the High Commissioner of Pakistan to India will return to their posts and that the normal functioning of diplomatic missions of both countries will be restored. Both Governments shall observe the Vienna Convention of 1961 on Diplomatic Intercourse.

Trade Relations

(vi) The Prime Minister of India and the President of Pakistan have agreed to consider measures towards the restoration of economic and trade relations, communications as well as cultural exchanges between India and Pakistan, and to take measures to implement the existing agreement between India and Pakistan.

(vii) The Prime Minister of India and the President of Pakistan have agreed that they will give instructions to their respective authorities to carry out the repatriation of the prisoners of war.

(viii) The Prime Minister of India and the President of Pakistan have agreed that the two sides will continue the discussions of questions relating to the problems of refugees and eviction of illegal immigrant. They also agreed that both sides will create conditions which will prevent the exodus of people. They further agree to discuss the return of the property and assets taken over by either side in connection with the conflict.

Soviet Leaders Thanked

(ix) The Prime Minister of India and the President of Pakistan have agreed that the two sides will continue meetings both at highest and at other levels of matters of direct concern to both countries. Both sides have recognized the need to up joint Indian-Pakistani bodies which will report to their Governments in order to decide what further steps should be taken.

(x) The Prime Minister of India and the President of Pakistan record their feelings, deep appreciation and gratitude to the leaders of the Soviet Union, the Soviet Government and personally to the Chairman of the Council of Ministers of the USSR for their constructive, friendly and noble part in bringing about the present meeting which has resulted in mutually satisfactory results. They also express to the Government and friendly people of Uzbekistan their sincere thankfulness for their overwhelming reception and generous hospitality.

They invite the Chairman of the Council of Ministers of the USSR to witness this declaration.

Prime Minister of India   President of Pakistan
Lal Bahadur Shastri   **Mohammed Ayub Khan**

Tashkent, January 10, 1966

Source: Government of India

Treaty of Peace, Friendship and Cooperation between the Government of India and the Government of the Union of Soviet Socialist Republics

New Delhi, 9 August 1971

DESIROUS of expanding and consolidating the existing relations of sincere friendship between them,

BELIEVING that the further development of friendship and cooperation meets the basic national interests of both the States as well as the interests of lasting peace in Asia and the world,

DETERMINED to promote the consolidation of universal peace and security and to make steadfast efforts for the relaxation of international tensions and the final elimination of the remnants of colonialism,

UPHOLDING their firm faith in the principles of peaceful coexistence and cooperation between States with different political and social systems,

CONVINCED that in the world today international problems can only be solved by cooperation and not by conflict,

REAFFIRMING their determination to abide by the purposes and principles of the United Nations Charter,

The Republic of India on one side,

AND

The Union of Soviet Socialist Republic on the other side,

HAVE decided to conclude the present Treaty, for which purposes the following Plenipotentiaries have been appointed:

On behalf of the Republic India:
SARDAR SWARAN SINGH,
Minister of External Affairs,

On behalf of the Union of Soviet Socialist Republic:
Mr A.A. GROMYKO,
Minister of Foreign Affairs,

Who, having each presented their Credentials, which are found to be in proper form and due order,

HAVE AGREED AS FOLLOWS:

Article I

The High Contracting Parties solemnly declare that enduring peace and friendship shall prevail between the two countries and their peoples. Each Party shall respect the independence, sovereignty and territorial integrity of the other party and refrain from interfering in the other's internal affairs. The High Contracting Parties shall continue to develop and consolidate the relations of sincere friendship, good neighbourliness and comprehensive cooperation existing between them on the biases of the aforesaid principles as well as those of equality and mutual benefit.

Article II

Guided by the desire to contribute in every possible way to ensure enduring peace and security of their people, the High Contracting Parties declare their determination to continue their efforts to preserve and to strengthen peace in Asia and throughout the world, to hard the arms race and to achieve general and complete disarmament, including both nuclear and conventional, under effective international control.

Article III

Guided by their loyalty to the lofty ideal of equality of all Peoples and Nations, irrespective of race of creed, the High Contracting Parties condemn colonialism and reclaims in all forms and manifestations, and reaffirm their determination to strive for their final and complete elimination.

The High Contracting Parties shall cooperate with other States to achieve these aims and to support the just aspirations of the peoples in their struggle against colonialism and racial domination.

Article IV

The Republic of India respects the peace loving policy of the Union of Soviet Socialist Republics aimed at strengthening friendship and co-operation with all nations.

The Union of Soviet Socialist Republics respects India's policy of non-alignment and reaffirms that this policy constitutes an important factor in the maintenance of universal peace and international security and in the lessening of tensions in the world.

Article V

Deeply interested in ensuring universal peace and security attaching great importance to their mutual cooperation in the international field for achieving those aims, the High Contracting Parties will maintain regular contracts with each other on major international problems affecting the interests of both of States by means of meetings and exchanges of views between their leading statesmen, visits by official delegations and special envoys of the two Governments, and through diplomatic channels.

Article VI

Attaching great importance to economic, scientific and technological co-operation between them, the High Contracting Parties will continue to consolidate and expand mutually advantageous and comprehensive co-operation in these fields as will as expand trade, transport and communications between them on the basis of the principles of equality, mutual benefit and most-favoured-nation treatment, subject to the existing agreements and the special arrangements with contiguous countries as specific in the Indo-Soviet Agreement of December 26, 1970.

Article VII

The High Contracting Parties shall promote further development of ties and contacts between them in the fields of science, art, literature, education, public health, press, radio, television, cinema, tourism and sports.

Article VIII

In accordance with the traditional friendship established between the two countries each of the High Contracting Parties solemnly declares that it shall not enter into or participate in any military alliance directed against the other party.

Each High Contracting Party undertakes to abstain from any aggression the other Party and to prevent the use of its territory for the commission of any act which might inflict military damage on the other High Contracting Party.

Article IX

Each High Contracting Party undertakes to abstain from providing any assistance to any third party that engages in armed conflict with the other Party. In the event of either Party being subjected to and attach or a threat thereof, the High Contracting Parties shall immediately enter into mutual consultations in order to remover such threat and to take appropriate effective measures to ensure peace and the security of their countries.

Article X

Each High Contracting Party solemnly declares that it shall not enter into any obligations, secret or public, with one or more states, which is incompatible with this Treaty. Each High Contracting Party further declares that no obligation exists, nor shall any obligation be entered into, between itself and any other State or States, which might cause military damage to the other Party.

Article XI

The treaty is concluded for the duration of twenty years and will be automatically extended for each successive period of five years unless either High Contracting Party declares its desire to terminate it by giving notice to the other High Contracting Party twelve months prior to the expiration of the Treaty. The Treaty will be subject to ratification and will come into force on the date of the exchange of Instruments of Ratification which will take place in Moscow within one month of the signing of this Treaty.

Article XII

Any difference of interpretation of any Article or Articles of this Treaty that may arise between the High Contracting Parties will be settled bilaterally by peaceful means in a spirit of mutual respect and understanding.

The said Plenipotentiaries have signed the present Treaty in Hindi, Russian and English, all texts being equally authentic and have affixed thereto their seals.

DONE in New Delhi on the ninth day of August in the year one thousand nine hundred and seventy one.

On behalf of the
Republic of India

On behalf of the Union of
Soviet Socialist Republics

SARDAR SWARAN SINGH
Minister of External Affairs.

A.A. GROMYKO
Minister of Foreign Affairs.

Source: Government of India

Simla Agreement, 2 July 1972

The Government of India and the Government of Pakistan are resolved that the two countries put an end to the conflict and confrontation that have hitherto marred their relations and work for the promotion of a friendly and harmonious relationship and the establishment of durable peace in the sub-continent, so that both countries may henceforth devote their resources and energies to the pressing task of advancing the welfare of their peoples.

In order to achieve this objective, the Government of India and the Government of Pakistan have agreed as follows:

(i) That the principles and purposes of the Charter of the United Nations shall govern the relations between the countries;

(ii) That the two countries are resolved to settle their differences by peaceful means through bilateral negotiations or by any other peaceful means mutually agreed upon between them. Pending the final settlement of any of the problems between the two countries, neither side shall unilaterally alter the situation and both shall prevent the organization, assistance or encouragement of any acts detrimental to the maintenance of peaceful and harmonious relations.

(iii) That the pre-requisite for reconciliation, good-neighbourliness and durable peace between them is a commitment by both countries to peaceful co-existence, respect for each other's territorial integrity and sovereignty and non-interference in each other's internal affairs, on the basis of equality and mutual benefit;

(iv) That the basic issues and causes of conflict which have bedevilled the relations between the two countries of the last twenty-five years shall be resolved by peaceful means;

(v) That they shall always respect each other's national unity; territorial integrity; political independence and sovereign equality;

(vi) That in accordance with the Charter of the United Nations, they shall refrain from the threat or use of force against the territorial integrity or political independence of each other;

(II) Both Governments will take all steps within their power to prevent hostile propaganda directed against each other.

Both countries will encourage the dissemination of such information as would promote the development of friendly relations between them;

(III) In order progressively to restore and normalize relations between the two countries step by step, it was agreed that;

(i) Steps shall be taken to resume communications, postal, telegraphic, sea, land including border posts, and air links including overflights;

(ii) Appropriate steps shall be taken to promote travel facilities for the nationals of the other country;

(iii) Trade and co-operation in economic and other agreed fields will be resumed as far as possible.

(iv) Exchange in the fields of science and culture will be promoted.

In this connextion delegations from the two countries will meet from time to time to work out the necessary details.

(IV) In order to initiate the process of the establishment of durable peace, both Governments agree that:

(i) Indian and Pakistani forces shall be withdrawn to their side of the international border;

(ii) In Jammu and Kashmir, the line of control resulting from the cease-fire of December 17, 1971 shall be respected by both sides without prejudice to the recognized position of either side. Neither side shall seek to alter it unilaterally, irrespective of mutual differences and legal interpretations. Both sides further undertake to refrain from the threat of the use of force in violation of this line;

(iii) The withdrawals shall commence upon entry into force of this Agreement and shall be completed within a period of thirty days thereof.

(V) This Agreement will subject to ratification by both countries in accordance with their respective constitutional procedures, and will come into force with effect from the date on which the Instruments of Ratification are exchanged.

(VI) Both Governments agree that their respective Heads will meet again at a mutually convenient time in the future and that, in the meanwhile, the representative of the two sides will meet to discuss further the modalities and arrangements for the establishment of a durable peace and normalization of relations, including the questions of repatriation of prisoners of war and civilian internees, a final settlement of Jammu and Kashmir and the resumption of diplomatic relations.

Indira Gandhi	Zulfiqar Ali Bhutto
Prime Minister	President
Republic of India	Islamic Republic of Pakistan

Source: Government of India, July 2, 1972

The Lahore Declaration

The Prime Ministers of the Republic of India and the Islamic Republic of Pakistan:

Sharing a vision of peace and stability between their countries, and of progress and prosperity for their peoples;

Convinced that durable peace and development of harmonious relations and friendly cooperation will serve the vital interests of the peoples of the two countries, enabling them to devote their energies for a better future;

Recognising that the nuclear dimension of the security environment of the two countries adds to their responsibility for avoidance of conflict between the two countries;

Committed to the principles and purposes of the Charter of the United Nations, and the universally accepted principles of peaceful co-existence;

Reiterating the determination of both countries to implementing the Simla Agreement in letter and spirit;

Committed to the objective of universal nuclear disarmament and non-proliferation;

Convinced of the importance of mutually agreed confidence building measures for improving the security environment.

Recalling their agreement of 23rd September, 1998, that an environment of peace and security is in the supreme national interests of both sides and that the resolution of all outstanding issues, including Jammu and Kashmir, is essential for this purpose;

Have agreed that their respective Governments:

- shall intensify their efforts to resolve all issues, including the issue of Jammu and Kashmir.

- shall refrain from the intervention and interference in each other's internal affairs.

- shall intensify their composite and integrated dialogue process for an early and positive outcome of the agreed bilateral agenda.

- shall take immediate steps for reducing the risk of accidental or unauthorised use of nuclear weapons and discuss concepts and doctrines with a view to elaborating measures for confidence building in the nuclear and conventional fields, aimed at prevention of conflict.

- reaffirm their commitment to the goals and objectives of SAARC and to concert their efforts towards the realisation of the SAARC vision for the year 2000 and beyond with a view to promoting the welfare of the peoples of South Asia and to improve their quality of life through accelerated economic growth, social progress and cultural development.

- reaffirm their condemnation of terrorism in all its forms and manifestations and their determination to combat this menace.

- shall promote and protect all human rights and fundamental freedoms.

Signed at Lahore on the 21st day of February 1999.

Atal Behari Vajpayee　　　　　　　　　**Muhammad Nawaz Sharif**
Prime Minister of the　　　　　　　　Prime Minister of the Islamic
Republic of India　　　　　　　　　　　　　Republic of Pakistan

Source: Government of India

Index